vertiginous
moraine
mines of Potosi
bidonville
anabolism (p. 171)

Tasks

#1 Review p.62 in conj w/ Wonnacott

#2 ?. "regional multipliers" (pp. 67-8)
    a- employment (or economic base) multiplier
    b- input (or matrix) multiplier
    c- income multiplier
 "accelerator"
 "capital stock adjustment"

#3 review Harrod vs Domar: viz. economic growth-in Wonnacott
   ↳ p. 72 ff

#4 "intersectoral coefficients" +
   ↳ review K. Polenske's input-output bibliog-, partic.
   viz. use I/O for public intervention strategies

#5 "value-added" ↑ ibd (p. 116)

#6 def capital vs consumer good

#7 external vs internal economies - def. (p. 199)

#8 Eurobond - Eurodollar mkts - "issues made
   available by leading investment banks" (p. 261)
   ↳ WHAT DOES THIS ALL MEAN VIZ "CAPITAL MKTS"

CAPITAL VERSUS THE REGIONS

Stuart Holland

St. Martin's Press   New York

To Paul Streeten
in admiration
and with
thanks

By the same author

THE REGIONAL PROBLEM

CONTENTS

PREFACE

This book is about capitalism and the regions. In itself, this is more surprising than it should be. Too much regional theory abstracts from the system in which regional problems occur, failing to see the underlying causes of regional imbalance in capitalism itself.

Various factors have led to this state of affairs. One of the most important was the emergence of first-generation regional theory from the self-balance models of resource allocation. Another was the backwater in which regional theory idled between the First and Second World Wars while mainstream economics was focused on the general theory of employment. Since then, Gunnar Myrdal and François Perroux have stressed, through their models, the imbalanced nature of regional distribution. But in the United States in particular, this failed to dislodge the hold of self-balance theory and those various techniques of analysis which depended on self-balance premises. The apparent success of Keynesian employment theory underpinned the assumption that a series of compromises and devices in regional policy (incentives and subsidies to firms) would ensure some kind of regional balance at full employment levels.

This combination of Keynesian and neo-classical theory has increasingly been challenged by the stubbornness of regional problems in the mature capitalist economies. It has become clear that the causes of regional inequality are deeper than the superficial analysis of frictions and imperfections in neo-classical self-balance models would have us believe. It is also plain that indirect state intervention to improve infrastructure or concentrate incentives in growth-pole centres does not reverse the cumulative imbalance in Myrdalian or Perrouxist models of regional growth.

The main reasons for the failure of indirect intervention are analysed in depth in this work. It shows that key features of conventional regional theory are based on either false or limited assumptions which lead to ineffective development policies. It also shows that changes in the modern capitalist firm since the 1950s have introduced new dimensions to regional imbalance which make imperative more direct state inter-vention to redress or alleviate regional problems. This is particularly true of the trend to monopoly and multi-national capital, which has established a new *meso*-economic sector between the conventional macro- and micro-economic ortho-doxies as described in the literature. In the United Kingdom and the United States these meso-economic companies now dominate the upper half of the most regionally mobile sector of the economy – modern manufacturing. Their power to go multi-national rather than multi-regional both undermines indirect intervention through incentives, and decreases the power of the modern capitalist state to harness their resources for the development of problem regions.

The final chapter of the work suggests policies for harnessing the power of meso-economic enterprise as the basis of new regional planning. By drawing on the previous analysis, this shows that new public enterprise in the meso-economic sector is increasingly a necessary condition for reversing cumulative imbalance and establishing new growth centres in problem regions. It is only under such conditions that micro-economic planning at the regional level is likely to prove effective in the future and open the possibility of bringing small-scale plant to areas of persistent unemployment.

The study is the outcome of some ten years work on regional theory and policy in Western Europe and the United States. So many people have helped me in so many places that they will forgive me if I do not mention them all by name. How-ever, I am particularly grateful to The Brookings Institution for its hospitality in Washington, to the SVIMEZ Research Institute in Rome, to DATAR in Paris, and to the Centre for Contemporary European Studies at Sussex University. I am also indebted to Professors Paul Streeten, Paolo Sylos-Labini, Tibor Barna, and Brian Bayliss, who have read the main part of the text and offered most useful suggestions and criticisms. The normal disclaimers of their responsibility for the outcome are very much appropriate.

European School   STUART HOLLAND
University of Sussex

CHAPTER 1

THEORIES OF REGIONAL
SELF-BALANCE

For various reasons, classical economists were not much concerned with the regional distribution of activity. For one thing, it was assumed that capital and labour would migrate to those areas in which they would earn the highest attainable profit or wage. Capitalists therefore would maximise profits by locating where their costs were lowest, and workers would maximise wages by moving to where jobs were to be found. In general, regional questions were relegated to the back of the classical stage. Until the twentieth century most economists were content to leave them there. When they introduced regional location into their analysis it was mainly as a background prop to the scenario of classical or neo-classical theory. The 'where' of activity was subsumed under the 'why' of price and profit theory. Regional questions were neglected.

Both regional theory and mainstream capitalist economics suffered from this neglect. As the Industrial Revolution gained momentum, major disparities of structure and employment were generated between regions. A fuller appreciation of the links between structural and regional inequality could have provoked insights into the inherent imbalance in capitalist development. In fact, as illustrated in Chapter 2, these interrelationships were grasped by Marx, and provided a major part of his analysis of imbalance and disproportion in capitalism. But they were submerged in the neoclassical counter-revolution which swept orthodox economic theory from the end of the nineteenth century. The hold of this theory was powerful partly because of its abstraction from social or regional inequality. In due course the divorce from reality became more complete. The neo-classical theory of location became increasingly unreal as imbalanced capitalist development left a trail of wrecked regions and problem areas which, according to the theory, should never have occurred. Yet, as with societies and cultures faced with a changing situation for which they could not account, neo-classical theory adapted by an extension of the premises which its own founders had not taken as more than a tool of analysis or a theoretical device. Schools of regional analysis arose where technique had tended to become an end in itself, and where the limits of technique had inhibited both theory and analysis.

The Modern Foundation: Weber

This evolution within some branches of regional theory is doubly regrettable inasmuch as the founding father of modern location analysis – Alfred Weber – shared the insight of the original classical economists in appreciating both that economics could represent only one facet of reality, and that techniques should serve only as a means to the end of realistic understanding.[1] Thus although Weber was the first economist to undertake a systematic analysis of location in a neo-classical framework, he also saw and admitted many of the limitations which ultimately rendered much of that framework useless in policy terms.[2] This is shown clearly in the final – and largely neglected – chapters of his principal work, including one appropriately entitled 'The Total Orientation'.[3] Moreover the main part of his theoretical analysis was based on more realistic assumptions than those allowed by some later location theorists who claimed to be neo-Weberian. His initial aim had been to analyse the rationale behind the rapid urbanisation which had accompanied the delayed industrialisation of the German economy, and one of his key premises admitted the uneven geographical distribution of production and consumption. Another key premise admitted that fuel and raw materials were not available at equal cost in all locations. The main assumptions which Weber was careful to stress explicitly as artificial included: (1) that the cost of labour was fixed and its supply unlimited; (2) that transport costs were proportional to distance; (3) the exclusion of institutional factors – in particular capital markets and their influence or the spatial distribution of capital flows; and (4) the exclusion of social, cultural and political factors – including government taxation.

Weber realised that he needed these four artifical assumptions to be able to isolate the role of transport and labour costs in explaining the process of urban agglomeration. He was breaking new ground, and manageability was important. For purposes of exposition he treated the three factors of transport costs, labour costs and 'agglomerating forces' separately in his argument, only later attempting to integrate them in an overall analysis of regional location. He also distinguished carefully between 'regional' and 'locational' factors. Thus transport and labour costs were held to be 'regional' in the sense that 'they direct industries towards places on the surface of the earth which are geographically determined and given, draw industries to definite regions, and thus create a fundamental framework of industrial locations'. Agglomerating and *de*glomerating factors 'contract industry at certain points within such a framework, irrespective of where the framework may be situated geographically'.[4] In other words, Weber's analysis effectively includes a macro and a micro spatial dimension – a distinction which was to be largely lost in later neo-classical theory.

One of the aspects of Weber's argument to which later neo-classical theory became very much attached was the simplification whereby he subsumed certain differences of cost in different locations under transport costs. Thus where raw material or fuel costs are higher in one location than in another, the difference is treated as if one were at a greater distance from the point of consumption than the other. Weber pointed out that *in the case of location of new plant* the site should rationally be located near to raw material and fuel sources if there were a significant loss of weight in the process of production, and near to the final market if the production process significantly added weight to the product. In his own terminology the orientation of new plant would therefore depend upon (1) the 'material index' (the ratio of the weight of localised inputs to the weight of the final product), and (2) the 'locational weight' (the total weight of the product, including localised inputs).[5] The double attraction of this weight-loss and weight-gain analysis in terms of transport and transformation costs was to persist in later location theory long after transport costs had been reduced to relative insignificance by other location factors through technical progress in transportation – in particular the emergence of motor vehicle transport of the kind which was only being pioneered in Weber's time.[6]

Weber was aware that transport costs alone would only be decisive in determining location in extreme cases. More probably, he argued, the labour factor would be dominant, causing most

3

new plant to be located at sites where transport costs were sub-optimal. As he said, 'first we shall find transport orientated ind-ustries somewhat concentrated, and concentrated not very far away from their points of least transportation costs. Second, wherever we encounter an industry which deviates considerably from its transport orientation we shall be safe in assuming, in case of doubt, that it is an industry orientated towards labour'.[7] This overall predominance of labour availability over least trans-port costs foreshadows empirical work done since Weber's time, and shows considerable intuition on his part.[8] However, Weber also foreshadowed some of the best theory to emerge in the 1950s on the reasons for the concentration of activity in certain urban areas – his 'agglomeration factors'. He stressed that the extent to which an industry will concentrate, or agglomerate, de-pended on the extent of the advantages which would result from the close association of several different plant. In technically related production this would amount to achieving internal scale economies through localised external complementarities. Following Marshall he realised that the technical equipment necessary for efficient production had already become so speci-alised that even large firms were not able to make full use of it.[9] Such production therefore tended to be divided between the plant of different firms in such a way that 'the local aggregation of several plants simply carried further the advantages of the large plant'. But he also followed Marshall in being careful to distinguish between principles and practice. In principle the technically interrelated production sequence would function best if the mutually dependent parts were spatially concen-trated. But in practice, he admitted, the plant of auxiliary indus-tries may well be separated from the main plants, and firms could operate at dispersed rather than concentrated locations, not least because firms producing complementary but none the less different products may have different transport orienta-tions. In general, however, once an agglomeration effect had occurred, services locally provided for the whole complex would reinforce its concentration tendencies. In addition there would be advantages for producers in the joint sharing of infrastruc-ture costs, and in the role of agglomerated production areas in providing spatially concentrated markets for the products of at least some of the firms concerned.[10]

4

Weber's concern to specify where he is abstracting from reality is made very plain in his description of the technique on which much later neo-classical theory focused – isodapane analysis, or the technique of describing spatial areas of equal cost. The basic assumption of the technique is simple enough. Any deviation from a minimum-cost point in terms of transport, labour or agglomeration factors will include points at which the costs incurred are equally high. By drawing curves which intersect such equal-cost points for a single location factor, the geographical area including the three minimum-cost points for the three main location factors can be entirely covered. The optimal location for a given industry would be that point at which the three isodapanes overlap. Weber generalised this analysis both graphically and mathematically, including further limiting assumptions in the mathematical treatment.[11] But he also admitted that these further assumptions were highly restrictive, including no less than a uniform density of industry. In making such an admission he emphasised that 'it is important to keep in mind the assumption of a uniform density of industry throughout a given area, an assumption which *will not be valid* for any actual industry or actual country. The formula (of agglomeration) so far as it gives us the number and size of the centres of agglomeration arising from any combination of the various factors has, therefore, *only a theoretical value.*[12]

In his final two chapters Weber breaks through the limitations of such artificial assumptions. In a section entitled 'Reintroducing the Realities' he allowed that factors incapable of analysis by his isodapane technique could counteract agglomeration effects and tend to reinforce the spatial dispersion of activity. Largely ahead of his time, he stressed that technical progress and innovation both were essential to the process of industrialisation, and yet also appeared to be 'entirely independent of environmental conditions such as the level of transportation costs and the density of population'.[13] Technical progress will enable a producer to innovate and substitute new for old parts of the production process. But he may well do so on his existing site, rather than at an optimal least-cost agglomerated location. 'the zig-zag course of production increases when mechanised spinning is torn from mechanised weaving; when the mechanised wood planing and refining factory pushes itself between the

5

nill and the manufacture of various finished products; in short, when everywhere the mechanisation of production creates new stages of production which have *independent* locations.'[14]

In other words, technical progress may reinforce an initially dispersed locational pattern for industries which in ideal cost-optimising terms should be concentrated in a single area. It will do so for a variety of reasons which qualify the force of his three main agglomeration factors. For one thing, it will decrease transportation costs and therefore reduce the attraction of the least-transport cost area. Secondly, it will tend to encourage sectoral concentration, with firms increasingly internalising economies which otherwise would be external to them, and on least-cost transport terms might justify location in a more central area. Moreover, in reality, already located firms are not free to minimise costs by continually undertaking marginal changes in their location. They can only minimise labour costs by moving to such least-cost locations (or at least moving new plant). Thus although a least-cost labour point should constitute a centre of attraction for an industry, Weber stressed that 'the attraction of such a centre is not that of a mere approach. Only migrating to that place would be of use to it.'[15] He castigated contemporary economic theory for its assumption that productive processes were differentiated only by division of labour – as he put it 'the great pillow on which all economists went to sleep'. Yet he fully admitted that his assumption of equal wage costs was 'the great gap in our analysis so far'.[16] In general he emphasised that economic rationality in location was limited not only by the location decisions of the past, or the failure to make rational decisions in the present, but also by that pushing, zig-zag course of technical progress and changing production coefficients, whereby the rational decisions of the past become irrational in a new future.[17] It seems probable that it was for such reasons that he limited his theoretical analysis to a partial rather than a general equilibrium framework. Certainly he intended his study to be only the theoretical introduction to a complementary empirical volume.

The Rise of Regional Metaphysics: Lösch

Weber's influence was universal.[18] Yet those who later declared themselves in his debt chose to construct their own work on the foundation of his purely theoretical and least realistic analysis, rather than fulfil the empirical work which he was not able to complete. This certainly was the case with August Lösch, whose work influenced later self-styled neo-Weberian economists as much or more than that of Weber himself.[19] Lösch criticised Weber for two main limitations: neglect of demand changes in his analysis, and failure to attempt a general rather than a partial equilibrium framework. Neither criticism seems fully justified. In the first place, Weber's assumption of constant demand was intended simply to isolate the principal factors in location, and was relaxed in his last two chapters. Secondly, it is not clear that 'all of Weber's constructions on the supply side collapse' as soon as variability of demand is taken into account.[20] Any firm seeking a minimum-cost location for plant in Weberian terms can only take into account the demand conditions as it knows or can forecast them at the time the analysis is undertaken. Besides, once more, Weber's analysis was intended primarily as a technique of explaining rational behaviour, not as a description of reality. Thirdly, even Weber's purely theoretical explanation of rational location is in fact more realistic than the theory evolved by Lösch. And one of the reasons for this is precisely Weber's restriction of his analysis to a partial equilibrium rather than a general equilibrium framework. A general equilibrium framework demands far more restrictive assumptions than Weber demanded, and their relaxation in order to 're-introduce the realities' undermines the framework more decisively than for the location of firms alone.

For instance, while Weber only needed to assume a uniform density of industry within an area for his mathematical explanation of the working of the least-cost process, Lösch's general analysis defines an economic 'region' as a homogeneous plain with (1) uniform distribution of raw materials; (2) a uniform 'transport surface'; (3) a uniform distribution of population; (4) uniform tastes and preferences; (5) uniform technical knowledge, and (6) uniform production opportunities.[21] Besides, each 'region' follows von Thünen in being completely autarchic

7

or entirely isolated from other regions. In other words all forms of raw materials (mining, water, land) are equally available everywhere, despite the fact that this would demand the simultaneous employment of mines for agriculture, farms for fishing, and so on. The 'uniform transport surface' in practice would mean not only that all geographical space at the same time was either a railway or a road, but that these simultaneously led in all directions. The uniform distribution of population means either no urban areas, or identical urban areas of the same density, but cannot mean some urban areas of greater density and power of attraction than others, as in Weber. Uniform tastes and preferences, technical knowledge and production possibilities for their part mean a far more restrictive perfect competition framework than that admitted by Weber.

These procrustean assumptions enabled Lösch to clear the way for an 'areal' analysis, which he held to be a significant advance on Weber's 'punctiform' approach. For instance, if a producer finds it profitable to produce a surplus over and above his own immediate needs, he will market his produce first in the immediate vicinity of his own production. Since population is evenly distributed and because he has equal transport access in all directions under the assumption of a uniform 'transport surface', he will extend his market simultaneously in all directions. Since competitive conditions are assumed to be perfect, and under the additional assumption that all producers begin this market extension at the same time, each producer expands his market in a circular manner until he meets those of his circularly expanding competitors. Since markets under competitive conditions cannot 'overlap', all markets simultaneously assume a geometric form which covers the total area of the region without overlapping. While a variety of geometric shapes might fit this bill – triangles, squares and pentagons – Lösch's assumption of an initially circular market expansion demands that the shape chosen or established by producers will be that which most nearly approximates to a circle – in fact a hexagon.[22]

Lösch was not the first economist to argue the case for the hexagon. It had already been developed in 1933 by Christaller.[23] But the use to which Lösch put the hexagon market principle both was more extensive than Christaller's, and secured a markedly greater impact abroad – especially in the United States –

8

through the earlier translation of his work into English. For one thing it enabled him to develop a general equilibrium model of location of the kind whose absence he had criticised in Weber, 'valid for independent producers and consumers, for agriculture as well as industry'.[24] The location in a production plain or area of each producer is designated by a set of x, y co-ordinates, and the boundary of each producer's market area is described in equation form.[25] The following are taken as known: the individual demand for a product; its f.o.b. price at a given point as a function of total demand; its average production cost and profit; the rural population per square mile; the urban population; the freight rate; the total number of products, and the size of the entire (isolated) area. The following unknowns are to be found – the factory price of the product; the sales area of its location in square miles; the number of towns which produce it; the co-ordinates of location at the production point; the equations for the boundaries of the market area. Lösch presents a series of equilibrium conditions corresponding to the list of unknowns. They are (1) that the individual producer's location must maximise profits; (2) that the entire geographical space of the given region-plain is occupied; (3) that there should be no abnormal profits, as there would be with imperfections in competition or if some producers were nearer to larger and higher income urban areas; (4) that each producer's market area is small as a consequence of free entry; (5) that at the boundaries of the region-plain it is a matter of indifference to producers to which of two neighbouring locations they belong.

Unsurprisingly these various conditions enable Lösch to secure his 'advance' on Weber and specify a general equilibrium model of location. The number of fulfilling equations equals the number of unknowns; the system is determinate, and the unknowns can be derived. But if all is thus algebraically for the best, it certainly is not in an economic world. In his introduction to Lösch, Stolper wrote that he was 'the first to present a full general equilibrium solution describing in abstract the interrelationship of all locations. To be sure he did not go beyond counting equations and unknowns. But this in itself is a major achievement.'[26] Perhaps, although Isard probably came nearer to the point when he wrote that 'from a functional standpoint – one that is relevant to the incessant struggle within the economy

9

as a whole as well as within its various parts – Lösch's model is anaemic'.[27] The main criticism must be of the extent of his uniformity assumptions. Lösch does not propose an ideal location pattern for a world with uneven distribution of resources, population, technical knowledge, production opportunities, transport facilities, and so on. He produces an ideal economy. The contrast with Weber in this respect is clearest in Lösch's definition of urban areas. While these for Weber represented dynamic centres of attraction, changing in composition and influence over time with the rise and fall of new and old industries, for Lösch both industries and urban areas represent only a superimposition of evenly distributed market areas, similar in composition and influence to the perfectly competitive firms of which they are composed. Thus both industries and urban areas are up-graded firms, without any further qualitative powers of attraction through back-up services not available elsewhere, shared infrastructure costs, or other forms of external economies. Claude Ponsard – who in other respects follows a Löschian approach – emphasises this artificiality in commenting that Lösch 'speaks of areas "rich in towns". This expression seems particularly unfortunate in an expositional system in which towns are defined as super-imposed on space.'[28]

Lösch was to some extent aware of the unreality of his general equilibrium theory, as suggested by a brief chapter entitled 'Economic Regions in Reality', and the fourth and final section of his work entitled 'Examples'. But the status he gives to reality is quite different from Weber's dropping of artificially simplified assumptions which have been adopted in the first place to identify locational factors: given the choice Lösch drops reality. For instance he opens his final section by asserting that 'whoever anxiously submits the result of his thinking to the existent shows little confidence in his own reason. No! Comparison now has to be drawn no longer to test the theory, but to test reality! Now it must be determined whether reality is rational. This, and not verification of theory, is the purpose of the following investigations.'[29] The point is put as emphatically in his first chapter, where he wrote that 'capitulation to reality is as useful as the advice of those who on principle contradict no-one – a comtemptible attitude that is satisfied to accept one's era rather than serving it. No! The real duty of the economist is not to explain our sorry reality, but to improve it.'[30] In other words, no compromise is granted between the subjective status of individual opinions and the objective status of reality. Moreover, the 'improvement' of reality is not the extrapolation from theory of policy formulations which may change it for the better, but to substitute theory for it. Keynes is strongly criticised for failure to follow this example: 'long enough has our science considered indiscriminately everything that *is* even when the problem has not been to explain but to construct, more radically perhaps through a widespread tendency in the United States, and more dangerously through Keynes, whose *General Theory of Employment Interest and Money* is really based on phenomena of decadence [*sic*] in the economy'.[31]

If Weber's influence was universal, that of Lösch has been equally so. While Weber began modern location theory on a road which could have led directly to the use of theory and techniques of analysis to explain reality, Lösch sidetracked it into a theoretical cul-de-sac in which theory became largely an end in itself. In addition Lösch introduced a reversed order of priority for theory and techniques of analysis which has persisted in much location theory since his time, in which the limits of theory were largely imposed by the limitations of the techniques employed to elaborate it. This was very clear in the employment of mathematics not to test reality in an econometric sense, but to sophisticate the regularity and symmetry conditions of the theoretical model. It is because he realises that his framework stands only by virtue of such conditions that Lösch puts up such a fight for them. Thus he admits that when the distribution of factors of production and markets is irregular and discontinuous his uniform region-plain, and simple hexagon market and supply areas would take on different and irregular shapes which would mean that his mathematical analysis proved inapplicable. However, he attributes actual irregularity to 'personal and political' irregularities, not to economic factors.[32] His self-adjusting, frictionless location mechanisms suggest a kind of space which is interplanetary rather than interregional, and he is prepared to admit as much himself: 'the location system, like the solar system, hangs free in space, so to speak, nowhere suspended and held together only by itself'.[33] Therefore, like metaphysical forms, the theoretical equilibrium of the space

11

economy is taken to be more real than actual regional problems.

Migration versus Trade: Ohlin

For a general theory of regional location to emerge which was more related to reality it was important to overcome the restrictions of an analysis limited to perfect competition assumptions and an isolated region. Ohlin attempted both shortly before Lösch first published his own main work.[34] In practice his definition of a 'region' includes different international economies, and his examples frequently include economies which have separate currencies. But his analysis none the less is directly relevant to trade and factor movements between national regions inasmuch as he (1) assumes a high degree of factor mobility – including labour mobility – and (2) considers the markets of his main regions as effectively integrated despite local market variations. He also wishes to overcome the limited assumptions of atomistic perfect competition price theory, and to introduce economies of scale into this theory. In other words he allows for imperfections, indivisibilities and 'frictions' in interregional demand and supply patterns, including transport costs which operate not as the smooth mechanism of location adjustment to be found in Weber or Lösch, but as factors reinforcing the other imperfections and frictions in interregional trade.[35]

In fact it is the admission of such imperfections which enables Ohlin to evolve a theory of interregional trade in the first place. If factor flows between regions are perfect, factor proportions in different regions would be equalised subject only to the constraint of different raw material endowments. Therefore no comparative advantage could be established and little or no interregional trade would arise. But in practice imperfections in factor flows plus different natural resource endowments will mean that 'each region has an advantage in the production of commodities into which enter considerable amounts of factors abundant and cheap in that region'.[36] For instance some individuals will have a greater ability for some tasks than others. In addition, even if ability were universally equal, specialisation of skills would be worthwhile since workmen appreciate that attending to only one task is time and cost saving – in other

12

words it is 'one aspect of the economies of large-scale production'.[37] Like individuals, regions reap certain advantages from specialisation and scale economies quite independently of any differences in their resource endowment, and the advantages of producing a large quantity of a simple commodity rather than a little of all commodities must lead to interregional trade.[38] But Ohlin anyway holds that differences in factor endowments will give rise to interregional trade, and argues that overall it is the proportion of the factors in a region that determines its fitness for specific industries. As an example he gives the contrast in land, labour, capital, and natural resources between Australia and Britain, and comments that 'no further illustration is needed to show how interregional variations in the proportion of factors of production result in different regional adaptations for the same type of production'. It therefore follows that 'one region cannot possibly be superior to others in the production of all commodities in the sense that it is able to produce all of them at lower money costs'.[39]

In general Ohlin concludes that interregional trade and factor movements will have virtuous effects, leading to equalisation of factor and commodity prices in different regions. There will be an equalisation of commodity prices for the normal reasons associated with price equalisation under free-trade conditions. Any producer selling at a higher price than a competitor will lose a market share to him, and therefore be prompted to lower his price to bring it into line. There also will be a self-adjusting equalisation of factor prices in different regions. As he expresses it: 'as factors move from regions where their prices are relatively low to regions where they are dear, their scarcity, and therefore their rewards, in the former are increased, whereas their prices in the latter fall, unless there is at the same time some counteracting tendency'.[40] The kind of counteracting tendency which might arise would be that exercised by 'frictions' in factor mobility and market imperfections. This means that the actual outcome of trade and factor mobility between regions is uncertain. He adds that 'the outcome is even more uncertain when the total income of one region increases compared with the total income in the other'. For one thing, if the total level of income in one region *B* is more than in region *A*, 'the increase in factor movements from *A* to *B* tends to reduce interregional trade'.

13

Basically 'the more productive factors, and thereby consumers, are concentrated in one region, the less is the need for interregional trade, at least if this concentration means at the same time a step towards factor price equalisation'.[41] In other words the greater the extent to which factor flows between regions equalise their relative regional prices, the less the scope for one region to secure a comparative advantage in those factors within it which are relatively abundant and cheap as a basis for interregional trade. For this reason, factor mobility can act as a substitute for trade and dry it up.

Ohlin was mainly interested in this process of interregional factor movements substituting for interregional trade. His main concern in inter*national* trade (jointly with Heckscher) was to extend the traditional classical comparative advantage assumptions in factor-proportions terms, and the essence of the resulting Heckscher–Ohlin theorem is simply that national economies tend to export those commodities requiring more of their plentiful factors.[42] Neither the title nor other parts of Ohlin's work on interregional and international trade indicate to what extent he was interested in regional trade issues other than as an extension of the international trade theory which at the time was of much more preoccupation to most professional economists. But his reference to international economies which were 'integrated' by a high degree of factor mobility within a regional analysis context suggests that he was working down from national to regional economies in terms of the extent to which their greater factor mobility reduced (or could reduce) the factor proportions basis on which he founded his international trade theory. This suggestion is reinforced by the relatively scant consideration which he adduced to support his interregional trade and factor flow argument, concluding briefly at a key point in his argument that 'as a matter of fact, labour and capital have usually gone to regions with scanty supplies of these factors and relatively low aggregate incomes. The migration has considerably increased total income and thus tended to increase interregional trade.'[43]

This working down from international to interregional trade assumptions contrasts with the contemporary analysis of François Brocard, who took the reverse route of working up to international trade and factor movements from the regional and local economy – with different results which were to profoundly

14

influence François Perroux, André Marchal and other post-war French economists.[44] Like Weber's work, Ohlin's analysis is carefully respectful of the facts of the economic world whenever he admits them, and he persistently qualifies his general conclusions with riders to the effect that they will only hold so long as counteracting forces do not secure the reverse result. It also would be historically unjust to criticise him for not appreciating the full force of the imperfections in competition for whose frictions he allows, granted that his work came out in the same year that Joan Robinson and Edward Chamberlin published their own major work on imperfect competition.[45] Their work, like his, was mainly concerned to qualify the existing corpus of perfect competition theory which – in the case of the theory of the firm – had already diverged markedly from even a casual observation of reality. It therefore started from that theory, and remained largely within the theoretical framework which it had posed. In particular, imperfect competition for Ohlin, Robinson and Chamberlin did not suggest that the advantages in expansion accruing to well-managed firms could mean cumulative cost, price and profit advantages which would result in their expanding their market share without any necessary limit. It simply extended the terms of reference of traditional partial equilibrium theory.

Ohlin is less aware of the extent to which partial equilibrium theory of the firm is important for his conclusions than Lösch or some of the later neo-classical regional economists. Nevertheless it is important. For instance, his own argument is based on the assumption that interregional trade arises from a comparative advantage which particular regions will secure from lower prices in those factors in which they have a particular abundance. Yet apart from the 'frictions' in factor movements which may prevent a long-run equalisation of interregional factor prices, other forces more endogenous to the working of the market mechanism may also prevent such an equalisation, and thereby an equalisation of interregional income and employment levels. For if firms are not necessarily restricted in their share of given national markets by limits to product differentiation, or internal diseconomies of scale arising from problems of management divisibility, those located in Ohlin's example of a region in which 'the more productive factors, and thereby consumers, are concent-

15

rated' may cumulatively increase their lead over lower productivity firms in lower income regions. In other words, although Ohlin grasps that scale economies are important, he grasps neither their full importance nor their real implications for the interregional distribution of factors and trade. As Kindleberger has commented on its international application, the Heckscher–Ohlin theorem is too restrictive in assuming similar production functions in different economies.[46] Different production functions in different national regions could mean that firms in the more productive, higher consumption region could expand indefinitely through capital-intensive production techniques permitted through their high regional profits, savings and investment without needing to trade with the less-developed region. Moreover, while they thereby might well attract much or most of the available savings in the less-developed region, they could well need less labour through migration from that region than would have to migrate to equalise interregional capital–labour ratios *even if* capital outflow from the less-developed region were somehow restricted. As it is, one of the more important 'frictions' in interregional factor migration is the 'spatial inelasticity' of labour, or its lower responsiveness to interregional income differentials the further it has to migrate.[47] But by contrast, even in an imperfect world, portfolio capital outflow tends to be highly responsive to interregional differentials – depending as it does under modern communications conditions on either a telephone call, telex, or letter for the transfer of shares from a lower profit company in a less-developed region (L.D.R.) to a higher-profit company in a more-developed region (M.D.R.). Therefore the L.D.R. could consistently lose locally generated savings to the M.D.R. faster than it loses its 'surplus' labour. If the more capital-intensive and larger-scale firms in the M.D.R. consistently chose to locate plant in the L.D.R. to take advantage of its higher labour availability and lower labour costs, this could still lead to an equalisation of interregional factor prices, earnings and income. But, again, while portfolio investment tends to be highly mobile, direct investment in new plant is less so. It frequently replaces existing plant or is located near it in the M.D.R.[48]

In effect, the nature of the 'frictions' for which Ohlin allows can promote increasing divergence between regional factor earnings rather than the equalisation which he assumes. In a historical context, it might be unreasonable to criticise him for not taking such differentials in factor mobility into account in his analysis. The evidence on them has mostly become available after considerable research since the Second World War. His own general concern to qualify the universal application of his conclusions has already been admitted, and his attempt to integrate theory and reality far exceeds, the conscious meta-economics of Lösch. None the less, as with other pioneers in the field such as Weber, his own widening of the terms of reference of interregional analysis has been adopted by later theorists without admission either of the qualifications on which he insisted himself, or empirical evidence which has become available since his work.[49]

One element in Ohlin's interregional analysis for which he probably has not received sufficient credit is the extent to which he did realise *and stress*, that 'frictions' in factor mobility could permit comparative advantage in interregional trade, even if its application in the light of more recent evidence on interregional factor flows and location qualifies the general conclusions which he drew. For instance, although he may be incorrect in maintaining that 'one region cannot possibly be superior to others in the production of all commodities in the sense that it is able to produce all of them at lower money costs', since this could be possible with different factor proportions and scale economies to firms in a more developed region, his analysis does obtain for *potential* rather than actual interregional comparative advantage. For instance, although firms located in a more-developed region in which labour costs in money terms are higher than those obtaining in a less-developed region may still be able to produce at lower money costs than firms in the L.D.R. because of cost savings arising from greater capital intensity and scale economies, this does not mean to say that they would not be able to produce at even lower money costs if they chose to locate plant in the L.D.R. rather than expand continuously in the M.D.R. where they are already located. The extent of their potential cost reduction would depend on the size of the effective wage differential in the two regions concerned. For instance, if labour costs constituted half of total production costs and the wage differential amounted to 20 per cent, they would gain a 10

17

per cent production cost advantage (other things being equal) through location of new plant in the L.D.R. To this extent, plant located and producing in the L.D.R. and operating the same factor proportions as in the M.D.R. would secure a comparative advantage over those remaining in the M.D.R. The difference between potential and actual advantages is, of course, crucial. But the labour-cost advantage which many less-developed regions represent for firms choosing to locate in them remains one of the strongest micro-or macro-economic arguments in favour of the location of plant within them, and from a policy viewpoint should not be overlooked. The dependence of an absolute rather than comparative advantage basis for interregional trade on perfect factor mobility and an interregional equality in factor earnings has been stressed by Streeten, Balassa and McCrone. The fact that this does not occur in practice because of the 'frictions' in labour and direct investment mobility does not qualify their main point that, inasmuch as an L.D.R. proves uncompetitive in trade with an M.D.R., its lack of an independent currency will mean that it cannot define an exchange rate in such a way as to establish lower prices at which it can sell its products to the M.D.R.[50]

The Apotheosis of Technique: Isard

Without Walter Isard there might be nothing recognisable as a post-war 'regional science' school. His contributions to regional theory and analysis have covered several thousand printed pages in three main studies and also numerous articles in the *Journal of Regional Sciences,* of which he has been a founding father and main inspiration.[51] Yet the bulk of this vast output remains within a neo-classical framework which severely limits its use in contributing to the solution of actual regional problems. If anything, its influence has been perverse, obstructing relevant theory, technique and policy.

It has already been mentioned that Isard claims that he has only found it meaningful to undertake location analysis through use of the Weberian approach. But if he had in fact followed such an approach his own work should have led to very different results. What he actually has done is extend the application of those techniques of analysis which Weber himself stressed were

18

based on limited assumptions, and which conflicted with the reality re-introduced in the final and neglected chapters of his book.[52] Moreover, while Isard has utilised such artificially based techniques, the main point of departure in his own work was not Weber but Lösch, whose concern with the solution of theoretical problems which were themselves unreal has had its own persistent influence on Isard's own theory.

This becomes very clear from his first major work, which attempts to dynamise the Löschian framework which Isard himself had criticised as 'anaemic'.[53] It has already been seen that Lösch had rejected Weber's initial inductive approach – which took the irregularity of the spatial distribution of activity as its point of departure – in favour of a deductive approach based on the unrealistic assumptions of a uniform region-plain with a uniform distribution of raw materials; a uniform transport surface (or simultaneous transport access in any direction); a uniform distribution of population; uniform tastes and preferences; uniform technical knowledge, and uniform production opportunities. Isard admits that there is a major inconsistency even in these premises on which the rest of the Löschian superstructure is built, inasmuch as it yields different sizes of concentrations of industrial activity, and thus jobs, at various production centres, yet postulates a uniform distribution of consuming population which clearly is incompatible with such concentration.[54] Yet rather than remedy the premise and start from the concentration and agglomeration phenomenon already admitted by Weber, Isard instead chooses to employ these artificial uniformity assumptions in the Löschian framework as the point of departure for a 'dynamisation' of the Löschian system based on the substitution principle. The application of substitution between alternative locations or production points to such premises allows existing (that is Löschian) location theory to be stated in a form comparable to that of (neo-classical) general pro-theory. The incorporation of locational costs under transport costs (as in Weber) yields a 'spatial transformation function' extending existing production theory so that, 'to a large extent', it can now consider change in a number of parameters, including the relationship between economies of scale and the number and geographic distribution of plant.[55]

In formulating his dynamisation of Lösch, Isard outlines the

19

main elements in the Löschian framework, and first describes a spatial distribution of production with two raw materials and one concentration of labour *without* scale economies (Figure 3(*a*)). The first raw material has the same price at each of two sources, with the same condition for the second raw material (sources M_1 and M_2). The market regions of household consumers (*a* to *d*) are indirectly 'assigned' to the market areas of competing raw material sources via the industrial producers who directly consume the materials. Point 'L' is a cheap labour source. Boundary lines are then defined by substitution points which refer to transport inputs on the finished product, transport inputs on the first and second raw material, and labour outlays. Production takes place only on four pairs of circular arcs, or within the areas contained by them, or at the cheap labour point 'L'.[56] All this is represented graphically, and its economic value is as high (or low) as that of any other pattern drawn according to simple rules with simple consequences.[a] Two assumptions are particularly limiting: (1) the assumption of a fixed price for a single homogeneous product; and (2) the absence of scale economies. Without these assumptions the optimising producer would not have to locate either on the circular arcs or the areas contained within them.

Isard admits such limitations. As he comments:

> producers re-locate at times, take cognizance of each others' reactions, form coalitions, set prices and quotas. All these types of monopolistic and oligopolistic behaviour tend to invalidate the simple clear cut boundary lines depicted. Thus we must constantly bear in mind that (the figure) and similar diagrams pertain to a situation which abstracts from interest conflicts, undercutting and retaliation, advertising strategies, collusive action, market encroachment, and similar phenomena characteristic of firm behaviour.[57]

Granted so wide-reaching an admission, it might be expected that Isard would follow his own advice in introducing scale economies into his areal analysis, and admit how wide a breach they represent for his simple 'areal' picture. But he does not. His further analysis claims to introduce both internal and external scale economies which, following Weber, he stresses as the basis of agglomeration and urban locational economies. But his analysis does not attempt to estimate the way in which such economies invalidate the 'simple clear cut boundary lines' of his earlier diagram. They are simply introduced into its clear-cut areal framework, without admission that they would actually break it up. Thus he takes the same diagram, maintains the same assumptions as before, other than the introduction of economies of scale, and 'eliminates' the smallest of the previous areas considered on the assumption that production scale economies no longer warrant location within it. There now will be five production points (P_1 to P_5) located in three market areas (I_1 to I_3). With multiplication of the number of firms there are new moves within the diagram. Some firms now benefiting from scale economies are able to substitute transport outlays for production outlays, and to move to positions around the raw material sources M_1, M_2, M'_1 and M'_2.[58 b]

No explanation is given of why *this* rather than something else should be the result of the introduction of scale economies into the previous perfect competition situation. Both the framework within which the economies are introduced and the economies themselves are purely definitional: they have meaning only in terms of the particular use to which they are put. There certainly is no analysis of the wider implications of scale economies in oligopolistic or monopolistic competition of the kind which we have been enjoined to bear constantly in mind. The constricted economic meaning of Isard's scale economies can be seen from their artificial use in the areal analysis in which he employs them. For instance, his economies can only mean scale advantages limited in their spatial dimension to the pre-defined market areas. But this must mean the production of a single homogeneous product in all market areas with a uniform production technique (two of the main assumptions taken over from Lösch). If products are differentiated in the Chamberlin sense, the degree of differentiation will mean that producers can sell their products in *other* market areas. In this case they will not be likely to follow the pattern of Isard's dispersed location model, but will follow the pattern of Hotelling's spatial duopoly solution, and locate as near as possible to the centre of *all* the market areas both to minimise transport costs and maximise market access.[59]

21

In addition, if the assumption of a uniform production technique is relaxed in order to secure a closer approximation to reality, one producer may achieve an economy of scale greater than that secured by others, in which case he can sell below their own costs and prices and again break into their market areas, inducing the under-cutting, market encroachment and similar behaviour characteristic of firms as we know them, and to which Isard himself has drawn our attention. The result very probably would be a cumulative increase in the market share of a single firm at the cost of all other firms, and in due course its decision to locate expansion at the least-cost central point site in Weberian terms.

In effect, Isard's scale economies have few parallels elsewhere in the literature (apart from subsequent neo-classical location models derived from him). They are inoperative in any significant sense, since they not only are as undynamic as the Löschian framework but amount in practice to a perfect competition pre-scale economies usage. The only dynamic element within Isard's theory is his introduction of 'urbanisation' economies, which he represents graphically in a further figure.[c] As previously in his analysis, the decision to settle in an urban area entails various substitutions between outlays and revenues. It also, as he says, 'compels us to expand into a multi-commodity framework since urbanisation economies refer to those savings which are realizable when firms producing a variety of commodities agglomerate round a point'. But, as before, Isard does not actually explain *how* such agglomeration occurs, commenting briefly that it 'reflects a complex interplay of historical and institutional forces' and that 'the factors governing the *specific* localities at which different degrees of urbanisation economies become attainable are beyond the pale of our current analytic frameworks'.[60] For an analysis of the general factors operating in urbanisation economies he refers the reader to an earlier chapter, but this happens to be concerned exclusively with agglomeration in a non-industrial or agricultural community.[61] This might appear helpful until it is appreciated that, granted his artificial and Löschian assumptions of an even distribution of population only the assumption of an agricultural economy does not directly contradict the foundation on which his argument is based. Yet this no more overcomes the remaining contradiction between concentration of producers and dispersion of consumers than did Löschian analysis.

If these Isardian arguments were merely the point of departure in his theoretical work, to be extensively qualified later in his argument in a manner comparable with Weber's 'reintroduction of reality', there would be little point in submitting them to such intensive criticism. But in fact they represent the bulk of his concluding chapter, and of his synthesis of the exposition of Weberian and Löschian arguments earlier in the text. As such they represent little advance on Lösch and hardly proceed as far as Weber's progress some fifty years earlier. The same obtains for Isard's analysis of interregional trade, which is less subtle than Ohlin's, and more restrictive in its assumptions. In a very brief chapter devoted to the interrelations of trade and location theory Isard notes a 'falling off with distance' effect in interregional trade in the United States, and in international trade in Europe.[62] He attributes this uniquely to higher transport costs with increased distance and proceeds with a purely theoretical inter*national* trade model in which there are opportunity costs from trading with a further rather than a nearer region. Since shipping services are among the 'exports' which he considers in his trade model, it is relevant to observe that Ohlin was nearer the mark in realising that transport costs are not the only factor influencing international location patterns, and that Australia could effectively be considered an economic region of Britain despite the fact that it was at the other end of the world. In other words, apart from historical, cultural and political influences, Ohlin's factor-proportions case at least could be added to transport orientation in providing an explanation of particular locations of activity. Isard does not admit this, and claims that the transport-cost orientation case permits no less than an explanation of 'the industrial structure of each country, the composition of trade, exchange values, and the magnitude and characteristics of other significant elements associated with the simultaneous determination of location of economic activities and commodity flows'.[63] But, as before, he does not actually show how this would occur. Also, while his final chapter includes one diagram of interregional trade, the argument on which it is based refers to the inter*national* trade model which he has previously elaborated. Moreover, in dynamising the interregional example, he chooses to translate it into an international example through the introduction of national boundaries and long-run factor immobility.[64]

Throughout Isard's early work there are examples drawn from reality which encourage the impression that the theory is realistically based. For instance, he has constructed a diagram which indicates scale diseconomies with increasing urban size, which is consistent with available data on such diseconomies.[d] In fact his own much quoted figure is purely hypothetical, based on assumed diseconomies for an agricultural rather than an industrial economy. It is this which helps him retain the main fabric of central place theory of the Christaller–Lösch type where the emphasis is on the distribution of homogeneous goods rather than on the changing structure of an industrial urban area and the region or regions from which its factors of production are drawn and in which its changing pattern of goods and services are bought and sold. Following the Löschian precedent, Isard uses empirical data to serve his theory rather than basing his theory on the data. When faced with the choice of modifying his theory to account for reality, Isard modifies reality, introducing extensive uniformity and regularity assumptions of a kind which are not characteristic of actual regions.

In his latest encyclopaedic work Isard gives a frank enough comment on the limited usefulness of his early analysis which indirectly shows that he intended it to be of practical use in regional policy rather than a theoretical exercise. As he says,

> its theory was not operational. It did not spell out the techniques that could be put to work on basic questions such as (1) industry location problems; (2) unemployment and income problems of regions of industrialised nations; (3) growth problems of the developed areas of the world; (4) marketing and distribution problems of firms; and particularly (5) the urban problems of society which were then beginning to take on their horrendous character.[65]

He claims that it was to remedy such deficiencies that he undertook his second work, which presents 'the set of *tested* tools and techniques'.[66] Without doubt some of these techniques are of the first importance for analysis of actual regional problems, inclu-

24

ding population projection, migration estimation, regional income and social accounting, interregional commodity and money flow analysis, and regional cycle and multiplier analysis.[67] But, in themselves such techniques can only serve to describe such problems, not explain them. They are useful in policy terms only as a supplement or an empirical base for a theory of regional behaviour, and cannot properly be used as a substitute for it. And it was principally the lack of such a theoretical framework which could explain regional problems which handicapped Isard's early work – a handicap which is not remedied by the elaboration of techniques alone. Moreover, there is a major difference between techniques which can usefully describe reality as it is, and others which depend for their use on extensively artificial assumptions about reality.

Such artificially based techniques include both the dynamisation of input–output analysis and linear programming, with which key sections of Isard's *Methods of Regional Analysis* are concerned.[68] Isard himself admits the limitations of both input-output analysis and linear programming in regional analysis granted that they cannot take account of (1) the external economies which are of such importance in the Weberian agglomeration process; (2) relative price changes and their influence on input substitution; (3) the effects of technical progress and innovation in changing input coefficients. He observes that 'when we leave the isolated regional economy and consider an interregional system, the objections to the use of constant coefficients mount'. In this context he allows that 'when these and other limitations to interregional input-output are listed together with the restrictions imposed by inadequate data, we may question whether there is any merit at all in the use of this analysis for projection'. However, he adds that 'upon further reflection, it becomes apparent to many that there is room for the input-output technique in the regional scientist's kit of tools providing this technique is used in a flexible manner and complemented with other techniques of analysis.'[69]

What this flexible manner involves is much the same as the assuming away of the actual impact of scale economies on location patterns in his early work. Thus he maintains that the effects of scale economies and price changes can to a certain extent be anticipated and taken into account in the projection. If this is to be realistic, it would in fact involve a test case in which enquiry is made from firms of the extent to which they anticipate price changes or scale effects over the given projection time period. Such enquiry would be limited by definition, inasmuch as no firm can estimate the impact of its own price and scale effects on other firms without perfect knowledge of the perfect competition type, but Isard anyway does not attempt it. Having made the verbal allowance that scale and price effects could be anticipated, and should be so if the techniques are to relate to real circumstances, his own work – and that undertaken in collaboration – limits itself to the methodology of input–output analysis and linear programming without attempting to take such effects into account. With regard to the fact that input–output analysis cannot take unforeseen technological change into account, he comments that 'neither can any other existing social science technique. Of necessity any projection must be imperfect in such a dynamic society as ours. At the same time projections, however imperfect, must be made. When combined with *intuition* and *hunch*, input–output projections yield results at least *as good* as those based on intuition and hunch alone.'[70]

It would be hard to secure a clearer picture of the 'scientific' basis of the Isardian regional-science school. It is scientific not in the sense of a physical science, nor even of a social science which attempts to organise and abstract from empirical evidence, but in the sense of intuition and hunch combined with unrealistic and inapplicable analytical techniques. And if we abstract the techniques themselves from the considerable bulk of Isard's total output, the intuition and the hunch which remain are a small return in opportunity-cost terms for the very considerable expenditure of intellectual effort and resources, amounting mainly to the suggestion of ways in which an imperfectly competitive world of changing factor proportions and prices *could be* considered to work in the same way as the perfect competition model. Yet the reason why Isard and other economists within the regional science school allow themselves to be restricted by that model is precisely because it is essential for their techniques. A perfectly competitive regional economy shows the regularity, uniformity and symmetry which allows these techniques easily to be applied and sophisticated. But, technical sophistication is mere sophistry if its premise is unsound. In neglecting this, the

regional science school also disregards the radical chang
analysis and policy necessary to transform the five basic p
lems which Isard admitted had not been covered in his ear
work, that is to say, industry location, unemployment and income, growth, marketing and distribution, and urban
problems.[71]

In effect Isard's early work lacked the techniques necessary
for a theory capable of explaining the reality of regional and
urban problems. The techniques outlined in his second main
study constrained rather than extended his already restricted
and 'non-operational' perfect competition framework. In the
introduction to his third main study he has admitted that the
techniques employed in *Methods of Regional Analysis* were, in
fact, inadequate. But he considers them inadequate not because
they are based on premises which are unreal, but because there
were not enough of them. As he expressed it; 'there was a gross
imbalance among the different social sciences in their contribution to the set. The fields of sociology, geography, political science, anthropology and planning were under-represented, and
some of these were barely represented.' He adds that 'each of
these fields is equally as important as economics for understanding and effectively attacking community, urban, regional and
spatial problems'.[72] Isard fails to admit that there are important
differences between his equilibrium models of an idealised capitalist system and disequilibrium models in which regional problems are caused by capitalism itself. His earlier approach never
followed through the implications for his own spatial and
regional theory of the real effects of scale, price changes,
innovation, different tastes and incomes, difference in the
mobility of different factors of production, and so on. But it was
this rather than the lack of other social sciences which made it of
such little use in understanding and attacking community,
urban, regional and spatial problems. In other words, it is not
the *number* of approaches, but the *nature* of any approach which
is important in such an understanding. And maintaining the
standard perfect-competition rationality and maximising assumptions between atomistic competitors (whether persons,
firms or regions) can remain as unhelpful in achieving such
understanding when combined with other social sciences as it
did in the first place.

27

This is particularly the case when the other social sciences with which perfect competition economics is combined are themselves either directly derived from or similar to perfect competition. And this is precisely the kind of social science on which Isard and his collaborators have chosen to draw in their latest major work. It arises from the assumption that all men are utility maximisers in economic and non-economic activities, and that their maximisation is undertaken in a mechanistic incremental manner, with proportionately increasing or diminishing returns from different action paths. They have not only constant tastes and preferences in various social, political, economic and regional conflict situations, but also complete knowledge of other individuals' goal objectives. These various conflicts are undertaken in a 'one-state environment', or in other words on a complete *ceteris paribus* assumption.[73] It is because of these unrealistic assumptions about human behaviour and decision-making that Isard and his collaborators are able to fulfil their main aim as expressed in the sub-title of the book – conflict analysis of the game theory type. It is the application of game theory to abstractly defined 'regions' which occupies the bulk of the study. The political factor in regional development policies is in many cases as important or more important than the policies themselves. But to introduce political decision-making into a general theory of regional economics by assuming that politicians are 'mechanistic maximisers' (Isard's term) is as unhelpful as assuming that there is no political problem at all.[74] The practical problem of measuring political attitudes so that they can be numerically ranked in a game theory context is not faced. It is *assumed* that they can be ranked, much as it is assumed that useful values can be given in interregional trade matrices for which no trade figures exist.

In effect Isard's latest work is a general theory, but different from what he assumed. It is regional metaphysics rather than regional economics. Its practical relevance is negligible. The opportunity cost of proceeding further on Isardian lines and assuming that improvements in our information or techniques will enable us to dress the model with operational facts is mistaken because of the assumptions in the model itself. These include precisely those unreal limitations of the early Isard work which must be dropped before an approach to understanding

actual regional problems can be begun. (That is, uniform distribution of the consuming population, uniform transport sur-
faces, firms and sectors which are homogeneous in structure
and performance, and regions which are differentiated by size
or distance rather than structural composition.) One new
distinction is made between types of firms, but this is between
firms which are perfectly competitive (called 'non-co-op') and
those which are perfectly non-competitive (called 'co-op'). In
other words firms are assumed to be either perfectly competitive
or perfectly collusive without consideration of the intervening
range of more probable oligopolistic behaviour and tactics which
Isard himself enjoined us to bear constantly in mind more than
ten years earlier in his *Location and Space Economy*.[75] An additional major neglect for a book allegedly concerned with general
theory is the failure to take into account the impact of factor migration in regional change, when the asymmetry and imperfec-
tion in such migration constitutes one of the cardinal elements in
actual regional problems. Isard simply identifies factor migration in a later chapter of his work as one of several areas which
he recommends for future research, without appreciating that it
is to a substantial extent the migration of agricultural under-
employed workers to core areas of urban under-employment
which has caused the 'horrendous' urban problem in the United
States which he identified in his introduction as one of the main
areas which his analysis would tackle.[76]

The Cul-de-Sac of 'Regional Science'

Most of the limitations of Isard's work are shared by other post-
war neo-classical economists who have tried to advance on his
own arguments – especially members of the so-called Regional
Science Association of which he has been the guiding light. They
fail to appreciate that their reasoning is almost entirely circular,
and that in genuinely scientific terms it is a cul-de-sac leading
nowhere. To make any progress they must reverse their
method, adopt a more divergent approach, and abandon their
most cherished self-balance or equilibrium assumptions.

For instance, Lefeber has criticised Isard for taking the concept of a 'uniform transport surface' from Lösch, without distinguishing output variables at the location of production and mar-

ket variables denoting final goods delivered at the locations in which they are consumed. As he remarks the two do not coincide unless the production and consumption locations coincide, in which case there are no transport costs at all. In his own work Lefeber suggests a means of overcoming this limitation in Isard's analysis, but to do so resorts to the setting of the entire analysis in a purely competitive framework 'in the sense that no individual firm or owner of resources can affect the market in which he is dealing'. He points out that this is essential if the theory is to explain an optimum location since introducing the possibility that firms can affect the market through partly controlling price (and thus the behaviour of other firms) gives 'immediate deviations from the ideal optimum'.[77]

Böventer introduces monopolistic competition assumptions to his analysis in order to advance on the Lefeber approach, and to this extent his analysis is less restrictive than either Lefeber's or Isard's. In so doing he focuses on the extent to which Chamberlin-type product differentiation will reinforce the spatial concentration and agglomeration process in a manner already described (since firms would not disperse their locations to take neat shares of a given 'regional' market for themselves to the exclusion of competitors, but would concentrate at the Weberian least-transport-cost location). But just as Lefeber is constrained to assume that markets are perfectly competitive in order to isolate the effects of transport costs on different production and consumption locations, so Böventer limits the extent of Chamberlin-type monopolistic competition in order to preserve precision in his conclusions. In other words the qualification of the perfectly competitive framework is modified only by the immediate impact of product differentiation on location. The further impact which inter-firm price and marketing tactics of an oligopolistic kind might exert on the revised location pattern are neglected because this would not permit a unique location pattern. In reality 'there are numerous optima, and the *optimum optimorum* is itself a function of the *historical* process'. And when the historical process – that is to say actual regions – are introduced into the analysis, Böventer admits that the 'Walrasian system loses the important qualities of elegance and clarity which distinguish it'.[78]

Tinbergen has attempted to overcome the neglect of differ-

30

ences in industrial structure in neo-classical analysis in two complementary articles.[79] His model is based upon the assumption of four different sectors, one of which is agriculture. Only agriculture of the total four is distributed throughout the total area of the region, and it alone is restricted by the distribution of natural resources. But these are 'supposed distributed homogeneously throughout the territory', so that there is no intraregional differentiation between types of agricultural production.[80] Only one of the three remaining sectors 'exports' to other market areas. In addition it is assumed that all goods produced are final rather than intermediate. In other words, Tinbergen's analysis is restricted to the distribution of products, to the neglect of inter-industry demand or industrial and agricultural demand on location patterns. There is no analysis of scale economies and their possible revision of the market areas of the firms and industries involved. Nor does he analyse the implications of technical progress and innovation in altering the product and market structure of the firms and industries. The sectors which are specified are homogeneous and uniform in not only structure and composition, but also, therefore, in behaviour. The results are considerably less helpful than the analysis of the impact of innovation in Weber's concluding chapters.

Bos has criticised both Lefeber and Böventer for limiting their analysis to static equilibrium situations without consideration of the locational impact of scale economies, different industrial composition within regions, and the possibility of an evolving rather than a given demand pattern. His own work claims to introduce (1) discontinuous and heterogeneous dispersion of demand; (2) economies of scale, and (3) intermediate as well as final industrial goods. But to introduce his discontinuous and heterogeneous demand conditions he posits a market area which is perfectly circular in shape, and which on his own account 'is divided systematically into small sub-areas of about equal size'. He assumes that transportation costs for all products from the periphery to the centre of the circular market area are equal. In this way the discontinuity in the dispersion of demand is entirely systematic and regular, lacking precisely the irregularity which makes it of such pressing interest in actual regional problems. In addition, the 'heterogeneity of demand' is defined in such a way as to abolish most of its heterogeneous characteris-

31

tics, which are defined as 'dependent on the location'. His scale economies similarly have their scale effects defined away by the assumption of precisely the *same* economies of scale for each firm in each industry. As a result the Bos market region corresponds to the perfect competition region of Löschian analysis, and the end of this evolution is in fact a direct return to strict hexagonal market area forms, as in Lösch.[81]

The return to the hexagon is one of the most regular features of later neo-classical location theory. Yet while still employed in what is nominally a 'regional' context, that context itself has increasingly become an 'urban region'.[82] The reasons for this metamorphosis are evident enough. The smaller the area considered, the less the extent to which inconvenient exogenous factors break up the symmetry of the hexagon. The assumption of least-cost transportation points at the centre of hexagonal market areas has a certain relevance to new town planning. But no more. Few new towns are located in geographically uniform region plains in which the planners need not take account of either existing transport axes, or the linking of the market area of the new town with other *non*-contiguous market areas. Moreover, fewer new towns are composed either of population with equal incomes, tastes and purchasing patterns, or of firms selling homogeneous products within the same hexagon-bounded market areas. If the radial street and road pattern of the hexagon shape has continuing attraction for new town planners it arises from the basic centralisation of road systems in a downtown area, and not from the supplementary features assumed for the hexagon principle by Lösch and others. In other words, its virtues are purely spatial and geographic rather than economic. It is not even economic for producers or distributors in a least-cost transport sense unless they are all located at the central downtown point – or precisely the area which, in the case of the United States, most producers currently wish to avoid for a variety of economic and non-economic reasons.[c] Besides, a strictly radial hexagon shape is increasingly being rejected by town planners precisely because of its uniformity and symmetry characteristics, and the extent to which it reduces the possibility of giving particular identity to local areas through encompassing natural geographical irregularities.

Two examples help illustrate the barrenness of this approach and the theory and policy cul-de-sac to which it leads. For instance, Leslie Curry has asked whether central place theory has reached a dead end, and claimed that it has not because

> an ideal and still to be developed central place theory would integrate the facts of location and operation of stores, of behaviour of consumers, of flow of traffic, of the route networks, of the flow of funds and all the myriad observations of the relevant parts of the urban economy. Two or more sets of events not having any conceivable dependence can nevertheless be thought of as obeying the same 'laws'. As a simple example, all spatial interaction whether social, economic, or physical must incur a fractional effect of distance. Much more complex processes may have analogues in different phenomenological fields with a common or similar mathematical formalizing. The possibility of the intellectual economy afforded by such theory is its justification. Clearly, at the formal level it is advantageous to have the language divorced as far as possible from any phenomenological content. The possibility of having this type of theory available in geography is appealing, burdened as we are with such a wide range of phenomena.

In practice Curry makes most of the limiting assumptions in Löschian analysis, including 'homogeneous' space; 'economizing' by rational individuals who maximise their location decisions in terms of least-cost locations, and a 'closed space', which in practice means an urban economy which is entirely autarchic in character, buying from and selling to itself rather than to other urban areas or regions, with no immigration or emigration. For these reasons his analysis fails to account for the differences between urban slums and suburban middle-class residences, for urban or regional trade patterns and their influence on urban expansion or contraction, or the capacity of an urban area to adapt its physical and economic structure to labour inflow.[83]

On the whole Curry's analysis contributes little to the abstract and anaemic Löschian framework. This is less the case with another recent example of central place theory undertaken by Gunnar Olsson. But Olsson's contribution is also Löschian in the sense of choosing to adopt physical science based explanations of urban structure and change rather than abstract theoretical implications from evidence based on actual urban areas. Like Curry he assumes conditions which will permit the rational self-adjustment of the urban structure to evolving producer and consumer needs. In his own case this is the 'equal advantage' principle, in which the advantage to be equalised is expressed through the housing and transportation costs of locating at any given distance from the city centre. The argument assumes an urban land-rent structure which decreases symmetrically from the high cost urban centre to lower cost peripheral areas. The site chosen by any particular purchaser or leasee will reflect his equilibrium between lower rents on more peripheral locations, and the time and cost savings from locating nearer to the urban centre. The whole framework is limited by implicit assumptions such as 'homogeneous' urban structure, with uniform transport costs; equal incomes and tastes among location choosers, and so on. This is necessary in order for rent (which subsumes consumer housing costs in particular locations) to be expressed as a function of distance from the city centre. When dynamised, the analysis is based on entropy theory, which 'specifies the direction in which a closed system will move in order to reach equilibrium', such as the direction in which energy will move from hotter to cooler bodies. In other words, the argument assumes self-adjustment in the urban structure in relation to particular changes, such as increase in population. Among other things its rent-distance function neglects the unequal bargaining position of the urban immigrant in relation to the rack-rent landlord, while its self-adjusting 'entropy' mechanism neglects that the main movement of the middle-income middle class to 'cooler' suburban areas may not reduce the temperature of downtown urban ghettoes.[84]

NOTES

[a] See Figure 3(a), p.290.
[b] See Figure 3(b), p.290.

[c] Figure 4(*a*), p.291. The author cannot explain the meaning of the various symbols in the figure since Isard neglects to do so.

[d] Cf. Figure 4(*b*), p.291.

[e] For an analysis of urban in relation to regional imbalance see later this text, Chapter 5.

CHAPTER 2

THEORIES OF REGIONAL
IMBALANCE

Capitalist Industry and the Regions: Marx

Bibliographies of recent studies on the regional problem are not notable for their reference to Marx. There may be a variety of reasons for this. One undoubtedly is the extent to which many 'regional economists' take their theoretical terms of reference (like their professional training) from mainly neo-classical sources. Another may be the extent to which Marx's classic works stay in the library of the great unread (much, one suspects, like some of Keynes's own masterpieces, which are so damning in their indictment of the self-adjustment assumptions transferred from classical to neo-classical theory). Thirdly, Marxist economists themselves have been mainly concerned with aspects of Marx's economics other than spatial or regional resource allocation in a national economy. The spatial and regional dimension is there, but mainly in terms of its international application and the theory of imperialism.

Since Marx has not managed an entry to the stage of the regional debate it might seem superfluous to refer to the regional dimension of his own analysis. But in fact there is a wealth of virtually unmined regional source material in Marx whose relevance to regional problems in contemporary capitalist economies is compelling. Many of the factors which have later been taken up in regional imbalance theory of the Myrdal and Perroux type have been anticipated by Marx. Yet Marx also correlated features of the growth mechanism in capitalist economies with regional imbalance in ways which have not been pursued in depth by the modern imbalance school. In general the 'modernity' of his analysis is striking.

One of the key factors which Marx grasped was the extent to which the spatial concentration of production in particular areas was not caused primarily by raw material deposits or the need to reduce transport costs but by the sectoral concentration of production.[1] The concentration of the means of production into larger units, which occurred with the application of machinery and extensive scale production, created a Modern Industry which displaced the previously more dispersed handicraft manufacturers. According to Marx, 'capitalist production only really begins when the labour process is carried on on an extensive scale and yields, relatively, large quantities of products'.[2] A key characteristic is a change in the status of workers in relation to the new means of production, where the organisation of interrelated machines means that 'one machine is constantly kept employed by another (and) a fixed relation is established between their numbers, their size and their speed'.[3] This mass production machinery and the creation of automated machine-making machines reduces the skill of the handicraft manufacturer to the status of a single task (and sometimes to a supervisory operation). Whereas previously the handicraft worker's machinery was his own instrument, he now becomes the instrument of the machine. He also changes his own mastership of the means of production for a new capitalist master who owns his machinery.[4]

The best-known aspect of Marx's analysis of the introduction of large-scale machinery production in a capitalist system is its role in displacing labour. The main context of such displacement is within modern capitalist industry itself, where the cost-reducing powers of machinery pressure the capitalist to replace workers on machinery of one generation by that of the next. Such employment of machinery first draws the worker into the factory (possibly with his wife and children) and then displaces him as the capitalist finds it necessary to lower costs through the substitution of constant capital (plant and machinery, and so on) for variable capital (labour). Marx does not assume that this causes a crisis of underconsumption under any circumstances, since 'the immediate effect is to increase production in the other industries that furnish the first with the means of production'. As a result 'although machinery necessarily throws men out of work in those industries into which it is introduced, yet it may, not withstanding this, bring about an increase of employment in other industries'. Modern capitalist industry also creates employment inasmuch as it opens up new world markets for both raw materials and finished products, and promotes demand for labour in creating new infrastructure (canals, docks,

37

tunnels, bridges, and so on). Marx also allows that 'entirely new branches of production, creating new fields of labour, are also formed, as the direct result either of machinery or of the general industrial changes brought about by it'.[5]

Marx argues through, in some detail, what in contemporary terms might be called the 'demand pull' for labour in these branches of Modern Industry. Capitalist production 'can by no means content itself with the quantity of disposable labour-power which the natural increase of population yields. It requires for itself an industrial reserve army independent of these natural limits.' Wages may rise where production becomes more extensive (where the variable capital increases). 'If, e.g. in consequence of favourable circumstances, accumulation in a particular sphere of production becomes especially active, and profits in it, being greater than the average profits, attract additional capital, of course the demand for labour rises and wages also rise.' Labour is pulled into these particular spheres of production when the working day has been lengthened to the maximum physically possible (without State legislation) or to the maximum legally possibly (where State legislation on working hours is enforced); then the reserve army of the urban area is drawn into the factory (the female reserve army and children, unless legislation against child employment is enforced). But the labour demand of urban manufacturers is then supplied by the emigration of surplus agricultural labour: 'Part of the agricultural population is therefore constantly on the point of passing over into an urban or manufacturing proletariat, and on the look out for circumstances favourable to this transformation.' (Manufacture is used here in the sense of all non-agricultural industries).[6]

Marx gives this rural–urban labour transfer a crucial place in his general explanation of economic history. He clearly sees it as the spatial foundation of the process of division of labour on which advance in the productivity of means of production is based. 'The foundation of every division of labour that is well developed, and brought about by an exchange of commodities, is the separation of town and country. It may be said that the whole economic history of society is summed up in the movement of this antithesis.'[7] The process is stimulated to higher levels by manufacturing, which agglomerates specialised activities in particular areas: 'The territorial division of labour, which confines special branches of production to special districts of a country, acquires a fresh stimulus from the manufacturing system, which exploits every special advantage'.[8] He also appreciates that the urban agglomeration brings scale-economy benefits, and describes them in terms which emphasise internal rather than external scale-economy effects:

> Just as a certain number of simultaneously employed labourers are the material pre-requisites for division of labour in manufacture, so are the number and density of the population, which here correspond to the agglomeration in one workshop, a necessary condition for the division of labour in society.[9]

He emphasises that such density of agglomeration is relative to the *quality* of communications rather than simply to a generalised and abstract schedule of quantitative transport costs:

> This density is more or less relative. A relatively thinly populated country, with well-developed means of communication, has a denser population than a more numerously populated country with badly developed means of communication: and in this sense the Northern States of the American Union, for instance, are more thickly populated than India.[10]

However, unlike neo-classical regional theorists who later emphasised a claimed self-adjustment between demand for labour in urban industry and labour supply from rural agriculture, Marx stressed (1) that rural labour outflow was accelerated involuntarily by a migration-push process, and (2) that urban inflow neither led to assured long-term employment nor to a self-adjusting urban structure with equilibriated welfare effects for the immigrants.

In analysing involuntary rural out-migration Marx underlined the extent to which a rural surplus population was produced by the progressive introduction of capitalist farming techniques, where the need for scale economies in production demanded the elimination of smallholders and the progressive enclosure of common lands. This is one aspect of the regional di-

mension of Marx's analysis which has been extensively covered
by economic and social historians. But, granted neo-classical
theory's neglect of scale economies in agriculture as an
emigration-push factor, apart from its failure to make any clear
distinction of the difference between large-scale capitalist farmers and tenant smallholders, it is worth recapitulating some of
the main elements in Marx's analysis. As he argues, the process
of expropriation and displacement of agricultural labour began
long before the rise of large-scale Modern Industry. But it was
based on the pressure for large units to reduce costs and raise
profits. 'This contest at first takes place more between the large
and small landed proprietors than between capital and wage labour.' Later 'the labourers are first driven from the land, and
then come the sheep. Land grabbing on a great scale, such as
was perpetrated in England, is the first step in creating a field
for the establishment of agriculture on a great scale.'[11]

But with the rise of Modern Industry and 'the swift, unbroken
extension of the markets, *viz. the towns'* the situation changes for
the worse, especially when the domestic capitalist farmer must
compete with least-price world imports of food, as was the case
in Britain after the repeal of the Corn Laws.[12] Large landowners
not only needed more clear land for large-scale cultivation but
also more machinery (constant capital) relative to labour (variable capital). They therefore needed not only to displace agricultural workers now made redundant by mechanisation but
also to clear resident non-working population when this lay in
their power through foreclosure of leases, eviction, and similar
measures.[13] In other words the demand-pull of the food needs
of the expanding urban labour force and cost competition from
international trade compelled an emigration push from the
land. The scale of this involuntary exodus from the land was
massive when its restraining threshold was lowered by particular
calamities such as the Irish famine.[14]

But the major 'threshold' factor was the massively expanded
demand for labour in large-scale mechanised urban industry, to
which reference has already been made. This demand for labour might be compared with the demand-pull migration analysis
of neo-classical models of interregional adjustment.[15] But the
comparison is superficial in the sense that Marx stresses that neither the push of displaced labour from agriculture nor the pull

of labour into urban Modern Industry automatically assures full rural or urban employment, or 'interregional' income equalisation. For one thing, agricultural workers do not move from relatively low-paid rural employment to higher-paid urban employment with a temporary frictional cost of moving. He cites extensive evidence from Public Health Reports to show that rural living standards were suppressed in many cases to near or actual subsistence levels before displaced agricultural workers left for the towns. He also 'regionalises' this evidence in the sense of giving detailed data on twelve separate English counties.[16] Moreover, the urban immigrants are not guaranteed employment once they arrive. There are various reasons for this in addition to the displacement of labour by machinery and the tendency for the employment of labour in entirely new industries to be neutralised by technological unemployment. One of them is the effect of immigration on labour demand and labour costs in industries where profits, demand for labour and wages are rising. As Marx states;

> the higher wages draw a larger part of the working population into the more favoured sphere (of production) until it is glutted with labour power, and wages at length fall again to their average level or below it, if the pressure is too great. Then, not only does the immigration of labourers into the branch of industry cease; it gives place to their emigration.[17]

In general, the industrial reserve army

> during the periods of stagnation and average prosperity, weighs down the active labour-army; during the periods of over-production and paroxysm, it holds its pretensions in check. Relative surplus population is therefore the pivot upon which the law of demand and supply of labour works.[18]

Marx distinguishes five categories of this relative surplus population, each of which finds a parallel in analysis of the regional problem in capitalist economies a century after he wrote. They include:

(1) a 'floating' urban surplus population, comparable with

41

some definitions of 'frictional unemployment' but essentially involuntary:

> In the centres of modern industry ... the labourers are sometimes repelled, sometimes attracted again in greater masses, the number of those employed increasing on the whole, although in a constantly decreasing proportion to the scale of production ... Part of them emigrates, following in fact capital that has emigrated;[19]

(2) 'latent' labour, which compares directly with the contemporary concept of disguised unemployment, with the important exception that Marx employs the concept in the context of emigration push rather than demand pull:

> As soon as capitalist production takes possession of agriculture, and, in proportion to the extent to which it does so, the demand for agricultural labour falls absolutely, while the accumulation of the capital employed in agriculture advances, without this repulsion being, as in non-agricultural industries, compensated by a greater attraction;[20]

(3) 'stagnant' labour in irregular service employment, mainly in urban areas, and 'characterised by maximum of working time, and minimum of wages'.[21] In general Marx undoubtedly miscalculated the potential explosion of services employment, and under-estimated the potential discovery and exploitation of 'entirely new industries', despite the fact that in the period before he completed the first volume of *Capital* most technical progress was embodied in *process* rather than *product* innovations, raising the rate of technological unemployment more than income and employment multipliers from new industrial sectors, and thereby corroborating his analysis. But reference to the working conditions of the substantially immigrant labour in menial service trades such as waitering and transport broadly corroborates his distinction of a separate labour category in modern capitalist economies.

(4) a 'pauper' labour class, which Marx separates principally into (i) those able to work and (ii) those unable to work. Of the former he comments that their quantity 'increases with every

42

crisis and diminishes with every revival of trade'. In the second he includes 'people who have passed the normal age of the labourer; the victims of industry, whose number increases with the increase of dangerous machinery, of mines, chemical works, etc.'[22] While it might be considered that the extension of State welfare and accident compensation has mitigated the condition of such labour in modern capitalist economies, his distinction of a 'pauper' class is still relevant to (i) the high proportion of the unemployed of over middle age in problem regions whom incoming firms reject in favour of younger and more 'adaptable' workers, and whose income from State unemployment compensation over the long term is a fraction of what they could gain in employment, as well as (ii) the smaller but none the less regionally concentrated victims of health hazards and industrial accidents in relatively risk-prone sectors such as mining (where injured workers and silicosis victims in many cases are relegated to low-paid surface work).

(5) Marx also defines a special group of workers 'whose origin is agricultural, but whose occupation is in great part industrial' which he vividly calls both the 'light infantry of capital' and 'nomad labour'. This is the migrant labour force which follows major infrastructural projects from region to region as they are completed or improved and the contractors move elsewhere: 'Nomad labour is used for various operations of building and draining, brick-making, lime burning, railway making etc.... thrown by (capital), according to its needs, now to this point, now to that'.[23] Such 'nomad labour' has a real parallel in most capitalist economies where agriculture still has a sizeable proportion of the working population in the sense that agricultural labour is 'shoehorned' off the ground by infrastructural projects in the neighbourhood, and then drifts temporarily into unskilled employment, following the path of the projects. The negative consequences are the failure to guarantee permanent longer-term employment in the areas after acclimatising the workers to high (in some cases very high) income levels. Many such workers opt out of infrastructural employment as the projects move too far from home, and then join the urban unemployment pool (or under-employed and underpaid menial services) before migrating (frequently with considerable reluctance) to more-developed regions.[a]

In analysing the impact of immigration on urban areas, Marx realised (i) that the inner urban slum syndrome was directly related to the overcrowding of existing housing facilities by immigrant labour; (ii) that slum conditions could not be solved by 'cosmetic' public works programmes on general social infrastructure but tended to be aggravated by them; (iii) that urban structures in capitalist systems based on free factor migration were inherently unstable, so that present improvements entail no guarantee of future real welfare increases, and (iv) that such problems tend to be intensified and aggravated the higher the rate of capitalist growth.

Thus he wrote that 'Every unprejudiced observer sees that the greater the centralisation of the means of production, the greater is the corresponding heaping together of the labourers within a given space; that therefore the swifter the capitalistic accumulation, the more miserable are the dwellings of the work people.' Again making good use of Public Health Reports for the period (1866) he cited an inspector's evidence:

> on two points: first, that there are about twenty large colonies in London of about 10,000 persons each, whose miserable condition exceeds almost anything he has seen elsewhere in England, and is almost entirely the result of their bad house accommodation; second, that the crowded and dilapidated condition of the houses of these colonies is much worse than was the case twenty years ago.[24]

On the effect of social infrastructure as an indirect means of urban improvement Marx wrote that 'Improvements of towns, accompanying the increase in wealth, by the demolition of badly built quarters, the erection of palaces for banks, warehouses, etc., the widening of streets for business traffic, for the carriage of luxury, and for the introduction of tramways, etc., drive away the poor into even worse and more crowded hiding places.'[25]

This 'shunt' effect, or moving of the badly housed to worse housing conditions is aggravated by speculation from the raised relative scarcity of even low-quality housing: 'everyone knows that the dearness of dwellings is in inverse ratio to their excellence, and that the mines of misery are exploited by house speculators with more profit or less cost than ever were the mines of Potosi'.[26] The congestion costs from raised land and accommodation scarcity in central urban areas concern not only the 'pauper' labour class but also the labouring class in general, plus 'small shopkeepers and other elements of the lower middle class ... as "improvements" and with them the demolition of old streets and houses advance, as factories and the afflux of human beings grow in the metropolis, and finally as house rents grow with ground rents'. He cites further Public Health Report evidence to the effect that 'Rents have become so heavy that few labouring men can afford more than one room', and observes that the inflationary effect of speculation is accentuated by the impact of raised values in large-scale establishments on smaller sites:

> there is almost no house property in London that is not overburdened with a number of middlemen. For the price of land in London is always very high in comparison with its yearly revenue, and therefore every buyer speculates on getting rid of it again at a jury price (the expropriation valuation fixed by jurymen) or on pocketing an extraordinary increase of value arising from the neighbourhood of some large establishment.[27]

The speculation in rents, house prices and land values does not lead to an automatic long-run equilibrium in which urban demand matches supply at a higher price. For one thing speculation may involve a holding back of property under scarcity conditions. Marx cites the fact that in Bradford in 1861 nearly two thousand houses were uninhabited while 'the frightful cellar habitations and rooms registered on the (Public Health Inspector's) list ... were for the most part inhabited by well-paid labourers. They declared that they would willingly pay for better dwellings if they were to be had'. According to Marx one of the reasons why they were not to be had was the degree of uncertainty facing even progressive municipalities in matching supply of new housing to demand under unpredictable immigration and emigration conditions:

> As a result of the ebbing and flowing of capital and labour, the state of the dwellings of an industrial town may today be

45

bearable, tomorrow hideous. Or the aedileship of the town may have pulled itself together for the removal of the most shocking abuses. Tomorrow, like a swarm of locusts, come crowding in masses of ragged Irishmen or decayed English agricultural labourers. They are stowed away in cellars and lofts, or the hitherto respectable labourer's dwelling is transformed into a lodging house whose *personnel* changes as quickly as the billets in the 30 Years' War. Example: Bradford (Yorkshire).[28]

It might well be argued that the rise of the Modern Capitalist State, with a major increase in central and local government expenditure on housing and local authority welfare provision had transformed this picture in the later twentieth century. Also, it now appears that net immigration into the major urban areas in Britain from other cities and regions has declined to relatively small proportions, with some of the main areas such as London actually losing working population. But in fact this neither 'disproves' the accuracy of Marx's mid-nineteenth-century diagnosis nor the relevance of many of his observations to current regional and urban problems. For one thing he was careful to qualify the generality of his analysis of the spatial effects of capital accumulation: 'The more extensive, finally, the lazarus layers of the working class and the industrial reserve army, the greater is official pauperism. This is the absolute general law of capitalist accumulation. Like all other laws it is modified in its working by many circumstances.'[29]

In general his observations reflect many of the problems with which urban authorities throughout the capitalist world are still confronted. His evidence on the inner London slum 'colonies' compares directly with the 'ghetto' slum syndrome in North America and North Italy, and the 'bidonville' shanty-town conditions of workers in the Paris agglomeration and the major urban areas in most capitalist countries in the Third World. His observation on the 'shunt' effects of 'the erection of palaces for banks...(and) the widening of streets for business traffic' directly parallels the building of prestige offices rather than domestic housing in central urban areas, and the ravages of indiscriminate urban motorway building on both the housing it directly displaces and the adjacent housing which it indirectly depreciates. The inverse ratio of income to quality from exploitation of slum housing is corroborated by contemporary evidence from the United States, where overcrowding means a higher rent per head for low use-value in the rentable area. He also appreciated the scale and complexity of what now are called 'congestion costs' long before they made a cautious entrance on the stage of twentieth-century urban theory. Taken with his previously cited obervations on rural–urban imbalance and the role of migrant labour and relative surplus population as the 'lever' of capital accumulation, this might well be considered a record of the first historical order independently of any views which are formed on his use of the labour theory of value or the declining rate of profit and a generalised crisis in the capitalist system.

It is striking that, a hundred years after Marx published volume I of *Capital*, the inner London areas which he identified as 'colonies' appear stuck in the same vicious circle despite extensive intervention by both local and central government. For instance, the South-east Joint Planning Team found in the late 1960s that social deprivation and the vicious circle of poverty, poor housing, poor education, poor jobs and low motivation from one generation to the next were found in their most acute form in six inner boroughs located just south and east of the centre of the metropolitan area.[30] This century-long perspective should encourage considerable scepticism of the kind of intervention now being adopted to cope with the problems of inner urban areas in both Western Europe and the United States. Local solutions will not work unless related to the wider spatial distribution of resources in the economy. And in the twentieth century, despite new policies, the capitalist firm remains largely free to determine the location of investment, jobs and incomes. Indirect incentives, disincentives and indicative planning of new towns will not fundamentally change this underlying cause of regional–urban imbalance.[b]

Cumulative Imbalance: Myrdal

With François Perroux, Myrdal is known as the main exponent of the case that the free working of the market mechanism promotes an imbalance in regional resource use. Their work closely parallels that of Marx, although there is no indication that either

Myrdal or Perroux have been aware of this. Myrdal completed his main work on regional theory shortly after Perroux's entry to the field, but developed his methodology of circular and cumulative causation some years earlier in sociological analysis of the racial problem in the United States.[31] He argued that 'the play of forces in the market normally tends to increase rather than decrease the inequalities between regions'. It does so because economic growth by definition must begin only in some rather than in all areas in geographical space. As it continues, not only trade but also labour and capital will be attracted to those areas in which it initially began. When the growth concerned is industrial, this will mean that profits generated in agriculture will be invested in those firms engaged in industrial expansion, rather than re-invested in agriculture, benefiting investors from the higher return on industrial than agricultural investment. This attraction will tend to be cumulative, and reinforced by increasing internal and external economies in the faster growing area, with the external economies concerned 'interpreted in the widest possible sense to include a working population trained in various crafts, easy communications, the feeling of growth and elbow room and the spirit of new enterprise'. Myrdal emphasises that this process will have certain positive 'spread' effects, whereby the expansionary momentum of the growth area is spread centrifugally on other areas. However, it also will have 'backwash' effects inasmuch as the growing centres attract factors of production away from other areas and regions, leaving them 'more or less in a backwater'.[32] The 'backwash' effect is important to Myrdal's argument, and to that later in the present text, since it means that the benefits to more-developed regions will be at the expense of development in factor donor regions and areas. The process is cumulative not in the sense that all market forces influencing the spatial distribution of factors of production work in the same direction, but that an initial push or pull of factors to one region or area rather than another will then tend to move factors increasingly towards them and away from others. As he puts it, 'this is so because the variables are so interlocked in circular causation that a change in one induces the others to change in such a way that these secondary changes support the first change, with similar tertiary effects upon the first variable affected, and so on'.[33] The result is a 'virtuous' upwards growth spiral for the factor receiving areas and a 'vicious' downwards growth spiral for the factor donor areas. Nurkse has stressed a similar 'vicious circle' theory in the related field of development economics:

> A country is poor because it is poor. This may seem a trite proposition, but it does express the circular relationships that afflict the demand and supply side of the problem of capital formation in economically backward areas ... the concept implies a circular constellation of forces tending to act and react upon one another in such a way to keep a poor country in a state of poverty. For example, a poor man may not have enough to eat; being undernourished his health may be weak, his working capacity low, which means that he is poor, which in turn means that he will not have enough to eat, and so on.[34]

Spatial Polarisation: Perroux

Perroux also has emphasised that the spatial distribution of economic activity does not fluctuate around a long-term equilibrium norm, but tends to promote the concentration of growth in some areas at the expense of others. As he says, 'the plain fact is that growth does not happen everywhere at the same time; it shows itself in certain points or growth poles, with different intensities.' By analogy with the concept of attraction to a magnetic pole, he employs the concept of 'polarisation' to describe this attraction of factors of production and trade to certain areas. As with Myrdal's 'spread' effect, this process will be constructive for the areas concerned inasmuch as the inflow of factors and the attraction of trade reinforces their initial growth. But it also is destructive in a sense comparable with Myrdal's 'backwash' effect inasmuch as other areas will lose factors and trade to the faster growing growth centres. Like Myrdal, Perroux stressed the role of internal and external economies in promoting the growth of centres or poles which had established an initial growth lead. He developed his argument to include the role which growth firms and growth sectors played in further promoting the polarisation process. His main policy conclusion was that governments should establish counter-poles to those which had been established in faster growing regions through

ie free working of the market, and in due course hope to
harness polarisation in favour of less-developed regions.[35]

Perroux's work has more directly influenced European
regional theory than Myrdal's, perhaps because 'polarisation' includes both the main elements of Myrdal's 'spread' and 'backwash' analysis and incorporates it in a striking, readily intellig-
ible term. Certainly a spate of 'growth-pole' literature followed
the publication of Perroux's original article in 1955. A year later
Milhau wrote that 'economic activity never develops in a uniform manner over the whole area of a given territory. It is never
a matter of phenomena spreading in spherical waves in an isoth-
ropic ether, but of growth beginning in certain epicentres and
moving more or less quickly in certain directions, sometimes increased and sometimes decreased by the nature of the area.'[36]
Two years after Perroux's initial article, Hirschman wrote that
'on probability grounds alone, economic growth is unlikely to
start everywhere at the same speed within an economy', and repeated the point later in terms which, virtually, amounted to a
translation of Perroux: 'we may take it for granted that economic progress does not appear everywhere at the same time, and
that once it has appeared powerful forces make for a spatial concentration of economic growth around the initial starting
point.'[37]

The Limits of the Growth-Pole Concept

This tendency to reiterate rather than extend Perroux's initial
analysis has led to the claim that the main elements of polarisation theory amount to no more than 'enunciations', and in some
cases the claim is not without foundation.[38] For instance Professor Boudeville has produced a considerable body of work in
recent years which is more notable for its unquestioning
acceptance of the Perrouxist approach than for a serious
attempt to extend, modify or reformulate it.[39] Yet such qualification of what has now emerged as a growth-pole orthodoxy is
particularly pressing in view of the extent to which its
application in regional policy has so far proved disappointing.
This has certainly been the case in the Italian experience,
where the designation of growth areas and nuclei intended

50

to function as growth poles for the South has not resulted in a self-sustaining process of growth generation within the region.[40]

A variety of factors appear to have influenced this over-estimation of the efficacy of growth poles as an instrument of regional development. Paelinck has stressed that it should be regarded only as 'a *conditional* theory of regional growth, valuable chiefly to the extent that it clearly indicates conditions under which accelerated regional development can occur'.[41] As Niles Hansen comments, such a conditional approach implies that the relevance of the theory to concrete cases will vary with the particular regions in question, and the particular fulfilling conditions which they present for polarised growth.[42] Without doubt this is true enough. A policy of improving infrastructure and services within an already industrialised area in the early stages of declining employment will be likely to provide quicker results in re-establishing that area as an attractive location for incoming direct investment than will the same policy in a chronically depressed or under-developed region.

But there are additional factors in the over-estimation of the policy potential of the growth-pole concept which depend on more than its intelligent adaptation to the particular areas in which it is to be employed. One of the most important is the implicit assumption that management will optimise locational benefits and therefore respond in a fully rational, cost-saving manner to the incentives to locate in an area which is designated as a 'growth pole'. In practice, management no more maximises such a potential than it maximises short-term profits at the cost of other factors in the long-term growth of the firm. Another vital factor appears to have been the over-estimation of the role of external economies in the location process, and a failure to admit the extent to which medium-to large-sized firms of the kind which have the highest growth promotion potential for less-developed regions either internalise production economies, or are assured of major external production economies through regularised long-term contracts with other producers on whom they frequently have an oligopsonistic hold. Thirdly, the falling proportion of transport in relation to total production costs has dramatically widened the market area which can be served by an individual firm from a single initial location, reducing its need to 'get into' the market of a less-developed region by the location

51

there of subsidiary plant. Fourthly, according to the only extensive international comparison of industrial location, only about one-fifth of total net investment in industrialised economies takes the form of investment in entirely new plant, so that only a minor proportion of total investment normally is available for location in new initiatives in problem regions.[43]

These are some of the most important factors undermining the potential of the growth-pole concept as an instrument for stemming the interregional polarisation or cumulative disequilibrium process. But others arise from an over-emphasis on the objective of establishing self-sustaining growth poles at the cost of a more dispersed location policy. Much of the literature endorsing the growth-pole orthodoxy has assumed the role of external economies to be directly related in some way with the size of the growth pole or urban area, and therefore has suggested a critical minimum size below which the assumed self-sustaining growth process of the growth pole cannot take place. In the first place this relies to an unjustifiable extent on external economies of a kind which are later argued to be either illusory or only relevant to some firms in particular activities. In the second place, since the minimum urban area suggested frequently is quite large – in the order of 300,000 persons – it implies the abandonment of smaller yet still large urban areas as centres for future industrial location rather than centres for future labour outflow.[44] But the same theory for the most part has not coped with the other end of the polarisation process – the metropolis whose labour inflow may outstrip its employment-creation opportunities because of the large sites needed for new plant of a kind which are not available in downtown areas. In other words, it can adapt itself to medium-sized areas in which growth anyway is taking place, but cannot handle the problem of urban congestion in a growth pole which has gone 'critical'.[45]

Finally, the growth-pole analysis which follows the Paelinck–Hansen line of focusing attention on particular problem areas in order to gain the intrinsically desirable objective of a specific and practical regional policy may suffer from failure to relate the location aspect of growth-pole policy with the wider aspects of interregional disequilibrium. For instance, the question of which industries to locate in a particular growth 'complex' cannot usefully be determined without an evaluation of the interrelationship between the designated growth pole and other growth areas (or other firms supplying or buying from the firms in the growth pole concerned). And this itself will suffer if it neglects the wider general context of inter-firm oligopolistic competition, granted that firms operate essentially in markets which are to a lesser or greater extent the field of inter-firm price, marketing, innovation and other tactics. A *ceteris paribus* assumption which takes it for granted that firms will thrive simply because they are favoured through government incentives in growth areas is not likely to be soundly based unless these firms are themselves able to cope with national and multi-national oligopolies as well as the competitive local or regional firms. For similar reasons, concentration on only one or two growth areas within a major problem region such as the South of Italy, the South-west of France or the North-west of Britain may result in the firms within the new growth pole purchasing from and selling to firms outside problem regions precisely because they cannot secure inputs or markets in the right volume, quality and price in the problem region itself because insufficient attention has been paid in government policy to the wider question of ensuring an adequate range of industries within the region.[c]

In other words, growth-pole policy not only may limit the feasible effectiveness of regional policy through neglect of the possibility of a more dispersed location of plant, but also may fail to promote self-generating growth in the wider area of the region concerned through excessive concentration on purely locational factors, and insufficient attention to the intra-sectoral and inter-sectoral structure of production and competition at both the regional and national level. In addition, the low proportion of net industrial investment in the form of entirely new plant and the low degree of location cost consciousness among firms outside problem regions may mean that imperative rather than indicative or exhortatory policies are necessary to ensure that a designated growth area grows even as fast as the rest of the regional or national economy (which would only maintain previous disparities rather than reduce them).

In effect, Perroux has made an unquestionable contribution to regional economic theory. But the scale of change necessary to ensure that growth poles actually were established in less-developed regions in such a way as to offset cumulative im-

53

balance escaped him. On the other hand, the trend to monopoly and multi-national capital in the period in which he pioneered his theory was less marked than the evidence which has become available since the late 1960s. There was also less evidence at that time that only new public ownership and control of leading firms could actually ensure the base from which planned growth centres or complexes could be developed.

Perspectives on Imbalance Theory

Much of this text is an extension of imbalance or disequilibrium theory, and an attempt to demonstrate that the trend to regional inequality is intrinsic to capitalist economic growth. In this sense, the analysis is an extended consideration of both the scope and limits of the theory of regional imbalance. Essentially it corroborates main elements of Marx's analysis of capital versus the regions as well as some of the post-war work of Myrdal and Perroux. It also attempts to advance on these pioneering analyses by a closer consideration of the role of the State in identifying and trying to offset problems arising from regional imbalance in the use of resources.

Imbalance theory has greater scope than the theory of regional self-balance in explaining why regional problems occur. There are various reasons. One is the artificial assumptions demanded for most self-balance models of regional resource allocation. These abstract from internal and external economies of scale, neglect asymmetry in the response of labour and capital to interregional differences in potential earnings, and so on. In other words, regional self-balance theory starts with a blindfold to the main features of the regional world, and introverts into an idealised, unrealistic analysis. It can be more complete than imbalance analysis, but only at the cost of being more unreal.

Imbalance theory abstracts from what actually happens in capitalist economies. It admits the importance of both internal and external scale economies, plus the asymmetry or inequality in interregional movement of capital and labour. Its strength lies in the extent to which it identifies regional problems as the spatial dimension of tendencies to inequality in the general working of the capitalist market. It fulfils at least part of the hope expressed by Meyer in a major survey of regional theory that

54

'regional economics may increasingly be indistinguishable from the rest of economics'.[46] On the other hand, the theory can only gain force if it maintains distinctions between self-balance and imbalance theory in 'the rest of economics'. The neo-classical theory of spatial equilibrium is matched in the rest of economics by both macro- and micro-economic theories of equilibrium. This argument has sought to show that such theories are false in major respects, and are supported neither by Keynes's own analysis, nor observable features of the growth of the modern capitalist firm. A better understanding of regional imbalance therefore can only be gained by identifying key trends to imbalance at the macro-, micro- and intermediate meso-economic levels.

What of the limits to imbalance theory? One is basic and should be borne in mind in considering the analysis of forces working for imbalance in capitalist economies. This is the role of the State in offsetting observable trends to disequilibrium in the spatial distribution of resources or the trend to monopoly in inter-firm competition. Myrdal saw 'the Welfare State' as intervening through development policies to offset the cumulative disequilibrium process which he analysed. Perroux focused his recommendation for State intervention in growth-pole policy. Marx died before the rise of the modern capitalist State, which undertakes the roles of umpire, regulator and planner of resources distribution. He also died before union bargaining strength and relative labour shortages in particular regions and countries increased the real wages paid to organised labour and offset the tendency to falling profit through under-consumption.

Both the role of the modern capitalist State and rising regional incomes through trade union bargaining power have acted to offset those imbalances between regions which otherwise would have occurred through the long-run working of the market. Between them the role of the State probably has been more important, although the extension of union bargaining has tended to mean an interregional equalisation of incomes paid in similar firms and industries. Much State action which offsets inequalities promoted by the market has little to do directly with regional policy as such. The offering of social welfare benefits in all regions in a country, and central government assistance to local authorities in the wide area of social infrastructure (housing, health, education, roads and transport) has tended to increase

55

with economic development and political maturity. The scale of central State expenditure in these areas tends to exceed regional aid and assistance to firms and industries by a wide margin. It is the submerged but massive part of the iceberg of State intervention in favour of problem regions.[d]

This emerges in the differences between regional disparities in product per head and income per head in the welfare-state economies of Western Europe. Disparities in product per head can be as much as 100 per cent, while disparities in income per head tend to be smaller, and in some cases, such as Britain, much smaller. In the United States the combination of federal welfare payments to population in problem regions, plus the national extension of union bargaining on minimum wages, have helped to promote a gradual convergence in income per head between States. In practice, this convergence of regional income per head is also occurring in Western Europe and the more-developed, non-European economies. This has been noted by Williamson in a wide-ranging international comparison of regional incomes.[47]

Granted such a trend to date, why should we worry about any underlying trend to imbalance through the free working of modern capitalism, or bother to up-date and extend the imbalance theory of Marx, Myrdal or Perroux? There are several reasons. It has been stressed that the most important concerns change in the structure of modern capitalist competition, and the impact which this registers on the income equalisation role open to the welfare state. Evidence in Britain and other Western European economies shows an acceleration of two trends in modern capitalism: (1) the rise of meso-economic power in national economies and (2) the spread of multi-national operations by big-league firms. For various reasons these trends are decreasing the effectiveness of regional policies adopted since the war in modern capitalist countries. The trend to monopoly is accompanied by super-normal profits over the long run for leading companies. In combination with their use of cheap labour in the Third World countries, and the syphoning of profits to tax-havens abroad, this means global profit gains far in excess of the regional incentives or disincentives offered by governments in the 1970s. The multi-national trend itself is causing problems on a new scale in regional policy. Basically, the greater

56

attractiveness of labour in the Third World (frequently in countries 'suspending' normal union activities) means that much investment which hitherto would have gone to the problem regions of a national economy now goes abroad and hence outside the home country's control.

This trend to multi-national rather than multi-regional companies justifies one of the assumptions of the self-balance theorists. Capital now is moving from high-wage to low-wage areas on a major scale. But this does not mean the smooth adjustment of interregional differences in employment in national economies. It tends to intensify the imbalance between metropolitan regions in developed economies, and the less-developed regions which multi-nationals neglect. Capital is not moving in the incremental shuffle beloved of perfect-competition theorists, but strides the world in seven-league boots, over-stepping problem regions in both developed and less-developed countries. This is a phenomenon which so far has been partly disguised by the prevalence of branch plants of multi-national companies in some of the main problem regions in Britain and Belgium. For instance, in Scotland, multi-nationals have undertaken a considerable degree of expansion in some areas of the lower Clyde and the Glasgow–Edinburgh belt. But in many cases this has resulted from the takeover of national firms as part of a strategy of national market penetration. Some of these firms had developed in areas such as the central Scotland belt at a period when it represented a growth area for the British economy. It is partly their decline in such regions which gave rise to multi-national takeovers in the first place.

Expressed differently, there are new dimensions to regional inequality in a capitalist system which can only be traced by following the location pattern of the new capitalist leaders in the meso-economic sector. This pattern changes over time in different economies, with the different stages of development of capitalism itself. To identify it, governments must inform themselves more closely on the behaviour of big-league firms, and the global pattern of their operation. Without this they will not be in a position to harness their dynamism to the needs of problem regions and areas, whether by State Capitalism or other means.

But in addition to these changes in the national and multi-national location of leading firms, there is clear evidence that

57

Marx's prediction of a long-term substitution of capital for labour in manufacturing is taking place in the mature capitalist economies. This emerges in the evidence on the falling rate of expansion of jobs in manufacturing industry, despite the continued expansion of entirely new manufacturing sectors which Marx himself under-estimated in predicting the swelling of the labour reserve army through the rising organic composition of capital, or relative capital-intensity in production. It is a commonplace among economists that the decline of employment in agriculture is being offset by a marked expansion of jobs in services. But from a regional policy viewpoint, this only partly helps offset the other forces which now are working to aggravate the regional problem. Not all services are equally mobile between regions, and the bulk of them are not mobile at all. They are in distribution and other activities which by definition are location-bound, so that they cannot be shifted into problem regions.

All of these changes affect the capacity of the modern capitalist State to offset the tendency to interregional imbalance by fiscal transfers and expenditure on infrastructure. Basically, such transfers have tended to prove relatively effective in the post-war period because (1) differences in the competitive potential of similarly structured regions were less wide than the gaps which now are emerging; (2) higher rates of job expansion in manufacturing meant that more jobs could be harnessed in problem regions by given policy measures; and (3) the greater proportion of national output accounted for by nationally bound firms (non-multi-nationals) meant that they were more responsive to fiscal and other policies designed to focus expansion in problem regions.

The evidence now emerging and analysed through this text indicates (1) that such policies are becoming more difficult because of the trend of big-league firms to multi-national rather than multi-regional locations; (2) the relative shrinkage of jobs in the manufacturing sector, which still remains a crucial base for balanced job mix in problem regions, and will necessitate more relocation of existing manufacturing rather than simply the regional location of new manufacturing investment; (3) the emerging crisis for many inner urban areas in metropolitan centres, where the initial middle-class core has 'gone critical' and has become caught in the immigrant inflow and slum syndrome;

58

(4) the increasing trend for nation-states to share the main features of nation-regions with multi-nationalism of capital movements, labour migration and trade, most sharply focused in the case of international economic integration; and (5) the evident trend for major areas in the E.E.C. to share the main features of national problem regions inasmuch as multi-national capital misses their peripheral areas in its migration to the Third World.

In simple terms this means that the imbalance between job and income structure between regions in mature capitalist economies is increasing rather than decreasing. If modern capitalist governments are to accept continuing responsibility for regional employment and welfare rather than face regional disintegration, it will mean one of two main outcomes: either more people are paid for not working in job-loss regions, or more jobs are brought to those regions. In either case modern capitalism as we know it is bound to be considerably changed. There not only is the fact that many people in L.D.R.s prefer paid work to less well-paid unemployment, but also there is resistance to massive unemployment benefit from those in M.D.R.s who see themselves as paying for them. In a federal structure such as the United States this could give rise to increasing strains at a time when some of the highest welfare benefits in the world do not make downtown New York a safe place after dark. It could also intensify pressures against further interregional migration to decrease pressure on labour inflow areas, with the distinctly unliberal overtones of racial discrimination in both the United States and the main immigrant areas of Western Europe (which now tend to be served by non-European labour inflow).

NOTES

[a] Cf. further, Chapter 6.

[b] The nearest to real restraint of such freedom so far attempted for private enterprise have been the British location controls, whose scope and limits are considered in later chapters.

[c] The Preston–Leyland Chorley new-town venture undertaken by the Labour

Government in the North-west in the late 1960s appears to have suffered precisely from too limited a focus on one potential growth-pole area.

[d] In the E.E.C., by far the biggest equalisation of interregional incomes resulting from Community policy is found in the Common Agricultural Policy not in regional development policy.

[e] This accounts for the different regional product performance in terms of rates of growth for regions which otherwise show a similar inter-sectoral structure. See further, Chapters 5 and 6.

CHAPTER 3

IMBALANCED GROWTH
AND TRADE

The Scope and Limits of Keynesian Models

Regional theory now includes an extensive variety of Keynesian models. Most of them post-date the emphasis already given to demand in Myrdal or Perroux while it has already been seen that pre-Keynesian theory (for example, Marx and Ohlin) had stressed the role of factor demand in the process of regional resource allocation. In some cases Keynesian models have helped towards an understanding of regional growth and trade mechanisms, especially when tested against available evidence rather than elaborated in complete abstraction. But as some of their own exponents admit, many of these models are limited by relatively simplistic assumptions, and in several cases are subject to internal contradictions which severely limit their use in explaining problems in regional imbalance. More importantly, most of them are based on a Keynesian–neo-classical synthesis of a kind which Keynes's own theory hardly supports. For instance, they stress equilibrium conditions under which regional self-balance or equilibrium *could* occur rather than analyse why imbalance and disequilibrium more frequently *does* occur. To spell out the contrast, they try to explain conditions under which the free working of the market could result in regional full-employment equilibrium, whereas Keynes's own concern was mainly to show why, at the national level, it did not. The result, of course, can be of the first importance for regional policy. Keynesian–neo-classical models are mainly concerned with explaining mechanisms which automatically work towards equilibrium, and therefore emphasise conditions under which government intervention either is unnecessary or can promote an equilibrium trend through minor policy adjustments. Since they share the perfect-competition assumptions of primary neo-classical theory they also tend to conclude that the policy adjustments concerned need not extend beyond a regionalisation of national monetary and fiscal policy.

Expressed differently, many Keynesian models suggest that regionally differentiated interest and tax rates (including interest and tax concessions or grants) will exercise a 'pull' effect on low income and employment regions paralleling the demand-pull effect of national monetary and fiscal policy. They thereby neglect (i) the extent to which such Keynesian policies have proved inadequate to move initially low-growth national economies such as Britain to a sustained high growth path rather than through a stop–go bump and grind; (ii) the very considerable absolute percentage growth rates necessary to equilibrate income levels in backward regions with leading regions; (iii) the structural obstacles which may prevent the management of even assisted problem-region firms from achieving income and employment growth rates above the national average (including the entry and expansion barriers from national and multi-national oligopoly); (iv) the arguments of Marx, Myrdal and Perroux that regional inequality is reinforced by high national growth in the absence of more extensive regional intervention than fiscal and monetary policies; (v) the instability or imbalance implications of Keynesian models themselves, as applied in a growth context by pioneers such as Harrod; (vi) the cumulative instability of Harrod models when their national factor immobility assumptions are relaxed and interregional factor mobility admitted; and (vii) the role of demand and profit expectations by management in undertaking current investment expenditure (i.e. the Harrod 'warranted' growth rate) as against the potential full employment growth capacity of the economy (the Harrod 'natural rate').

Another major limitation of Keynesian regional theory is the extent to which it has stressed capacity models of economic growth of the Domar type, rather than models which in fact are more Keynesian in the true sense in including a theory of management behaviour under different business-cycle and growth conditions, that is to say Harrod growth models. The two approaches basically reflect the Keynesian-neo-classical and Keynesian approaches which have been confused by the association of Harrod–Domar models as one and the same thing (in practice a defeat of Harrod's emphasis by Domar's). As with the emphasis on ascertaining equilibrium growth conditions of a kind which are of no real use to the regional policy-maker, the emphasis on neo-classical capacity models of the Domar type reflects a neglect of one of the key factors which can make a national or regional economic system unstable in its growth path – the business judgement of the entrepreneur or management board.

A further limitation of the use to which many Keynesian models are put in regional theory is the *ceteris paribus* assumption frequently made for *different* models. These often are used in isolation to show how balanced regional growth conditions could be achieved, without admitting the extent to which a combination of Keynesian concepts gives an explosive or disequilibrium growth trend. Besides which, unrealistic values often have to be given to their parameters to avoid giving disequilibrium results. For instance, as Richardson has pointed out, regional business cycle theory explains how an original expansion of activity through an exogenous increase in exports may give rise to continuous fluctuations, but fails to take account of the effects of interregional trade, 'the existence of which propagates cycles from one region to another'. Foreign trade multiplier theory applied in a regional context can explain the transmission of fluctuations but does not show how they arise in the first place. Richardson finds that two-region business-cycle models of the multiplier–accelerator type give damped fluctuations of an equilibriating kind

only when the parameters in the equations have unrealistically low values. If we assign realistic values to them we almost invariably obtain explosive growth patterns. [He adds that] the addition of inter-regional trade coefficients makes the multiplier–accelerator model even less satisfactory as a stylised model of real world cycles than when the model is applied to the national economy ... if we are to give the structural coefficients values that have a measure of realism, then we can only get regular or damped fluctuations by introducing buffers into the model. Full employment of labour. regional productive capacity constraints, or regional bottlenecks in the supply of investment funds are examples of the buffers that might be brought into the system. Alternatively, a more comprehensive multiplier–accelerator model could be deployed allowing for activities by the central government.[1]

63

It is worth spelling out just what this means. Put more directly, the prevention of cumulative regional imbalance through the application of multiplier–accelerator models depends either on State intervention to prevent the market mechanism promoting such imbalance, or on (1) full employment of labour, in which case there is no interregional employment disparity; (2) productive capacity constraints, that is to say diminishing returns to scale or lower-scale economies with additional capacity in the M.D.R. than in the L.D.R., and (3) limits to the M.D.R.'s access to investible funds, or no interregional or international capital flows. Expressed more bluntly, equilibrium solutions assume no regional problem in the first place.

Richardson stresses that similarly restrictive conditions must be specified if Harrod–Domar models are to secure interregional balance or equilibrium conditions. Leaving aside for the moment the differences between Harrod and Domar models, it is worth specifying just how restrictive these conditions are. They include (1) only one good or commodity, which can be used either for consumption or as a production input; (2) 'homogeneous' labour (labour of uniform cost and skill in different regions); (3) no scale economies (and therefore no tendency through increasing returns to regional oligopoly or monopoly); (4) no technical progress (no inter-regional bias in the distribution of innovations and therefore no industries growing faster than others); (5) a constant propensity to save (no savings flows from low to high growth regions); (6) fixed coefficients in production (equal ratios of capital to labour, and therefore equal capital–output ratios given no regional differentials in scale economies or technical progress); and (7) a constant rate of population growth (i.e. no higher rate of population increase in lower income regions).

Some of these restrictive assumptions can be relaxed while preserving interregional equilibrium conditions. For instance, if regional capital–output ratios differ, a region may have a higher propensity to save offset by a higher capital–output ratio without damaging equilibrium. But this again implies a degree of regional homogeneity which assumes away problems arising from disparities. As Richardson says, it 'does not free the restrictive conditions of equilibrium to any great extent. Any hope that the crucial constraints will have the same values in all regions will depend, in the first place, on how homogeneous the regions of the system are.'[2] Moreover, higher capital–output ratios in practice do not simply absorb higher savings. They have a variety of consequences under dynamic conditions, including the raising of productivity through embodied technical progress, raising self-financing, distributed profits, or both, and thereby disequilibriating interregional savings flows. A further relaxation of the restrictive conditions is that any tendency for regional savings to exceed regional investment may preserve interregional equilibrium provided the gap between savings and investment is exactly closed by running an export surplus equal to the gap. Similarly, excess regional labour may be eliminated by out-migration or a deficiency in labour supply met by immigration from other regions in the system. Both these 'relaxations' assume *ceteris paribus* conditions in what, in regional terms, is a highly unequal dynamic system. The import deficit region will have to finance its import payments to preserve the equilibrium situation. Temporarily it may do so by selling assets and securities. But over the longer run – assuming no government transfer payments or government sanctioning of regionally differentiated interest rates – it will have to finance the imports by increasing exports. This involves the whole book of structural adjustment problems, including inter-sectoral composition and intra-sectoral competition, which the 'relaxation' leaves out of account.[a] In the same way the argument that excess regional labour may be eliminated by outmigration assumes away both (i) the 'spatial inelasticity' of labour, or its increased resistance to migration the greater the distance to be moved, and (ii) the raising of the growth potential of the immigration region through labour inflow.[b]

An additional 'relaxation' of equilibrium assumptions is the supposition that where initial regional incomes are unequal, regional propensities to save also are likely to be unequal and lower in the poorer region. In this case interregional equilibrium depends on capital flowing from the higher to the lower income region. But as Richardson comments,

> unless investment opportunities are abundant in low income regions (because of higher risk and the greater cost of investible funds they need to be *more* abundant) and are near exhaustion in the high income regions, then capital will not

flow in the required direction. Indeed it may tend to flow in the opposite direction since investment opportunities (certainly when viewed subjectively) may be greater in the high income region. In this case capital flows will be disequilibriating, accelerating the rate of growth in the richer region and slowing it down in the poorer one.[3]

This is clearly correct, although it is not so clear that Richardson is right in maintaining (1) that 'on *a priori* grounds, we should expect labour flows to be more likely to be equilibriating than capital flows' or (2) that 'whether or not capital flows are equilibriating or disequilibriating is a matter for empirical verification'.[4] The outcome of the *a priori* analysis depends on whether one remains within the restricted assumptions of the neo-classical framework. For instance, under the artificial assumptions of no scale economies, no technical progress, no problems of structural adjustment, and so on, an *a priori* interregional equilibrium solution can be established. But in practice some of the main problems of regional imbalance arise because of the failure of capitalist economies to conform to this 'lost world' of a perfectly competitive and continually self-adjusting model.

Evidence and Evaluation

Similarly, the outcome of 'empirical verification' depends on the assumption that the evidence verified reflects the free working of the market mechanism rather than State intervention to offset disequilibriating factor flows. This is one of the basic limitations underlying the conclusions which emerge from Brown's encyclopaedic testing of Keynesian models and concepts against post-war British evidence.[5] In the concluding chapter of his study Brown is careful in trying to isolate the effects of government intervention on British regions. But elsewhere in his text there is an ambiguity about just what is being tested against the available evidence. For instance, in analysing the direction of 'manufacturing capital' for 1961 Brown estimates South-east England (almost certainly excluding East Anglia), the East Midlands, and Yorkshire and Humberside were 'the big net providers of funds' and that the South-west, Wales, Northern Ireland, Scotland and, on a smaller scale, the North of England were 'the absorbers', with the West Midlands and the North-west breaking 'more or less even'. In other words the picture describes capital moving from the more-developed to the less-developed British regions. As Brown states, the flows 'really indicate movements of entrepreneurship in manufacturing industry rather than movements of the factor of production capital in either a proper or a comprehensive sense'.[6] It is clear that Brown and his collaborators in the analysis are aware that this does not test the free working of the market mechanism, with entrepreneurs offsetting other factors promoting regional imbalance through taking plant and jobs to the less-developed regions. Later in the same chapter he admits that 'the inter-regional flow of jobs, however interpreted, ... is undeniably affected strongly by policy' – in the British case a policy of locational controls requiring permits (Industrial Development Certificates) for expansion of plant and jobs in the more-developed regions. He also admits that the relatively frequent changes in policy in Britain in the 1960s make even the estimation of policy effects difficult, and that they 'cannot be tested *a priori*'.[7]

This is not meant to suggest that Brown's analysis is consciously misleading. It is impressively laced with qualifications, besides filling a notable gap in our previous knowledge. But it is worth drawing attention to the care which should be exercised by those raiding the store of information he has provided if they choose to use that information to support particular hypotheses on the free working of the market mechanism.

Making this allowance, Brown's empirical results on the size of the various regional multipliers and their interrelation with capital stock adjustment and technical progress are important. His general conclusion is that regional multipliers tend to be relatively low – not very far above unity – and not verq different in different regions.[8] The multipliers considered include (1) the employment (or economic-base) multiplier; (2) the input (or matrix) multiplier; and (3) the income multiplier. Brown stresses that considerable differences emerge from the short and long-run estimates for both the employment and income multipliers. For instance, in form the Keynesian income multiplier is identical with the economic-base multiplier. The former, calculated *ex ante* for the short run from changes in money flows, has relatively low values of between $1 \cdot 15$ and $1 \cdot 25$, but the latter, calculated *ex post* from changes in employment over periods of thirty and forty years show values between $1 \cdot 7$ and $1 \cdot 8$. One reason for the disparity is the different assumptions made for government expenditure on goods and services geared to raise gross domestic product over the longer run. Size of region is also important. The numerical value of the long-run income multiplier rises to just under $1 \cdot 9$ for a large region and just under $1 \cdot 6$ for a small region.[9] The input multiplier is difficult to calculate from input–output data, and also varies considerably between regions, depending on their degree of intra-regional linkage. For labour inputs it ranges from 6 per cent for oil refining to 60 per cent for coal mining. For primary inputs in an intra-regional industry such as the motor vehicle complex of the West Midlands it will be high, though it may be low elsewhere (for instance only about 20 per cent in the Central Lancashire Leyland complex).[10] Brown concluded that for most industries in the British case the highest value likely to be found was somewhere round $1 \cdot 5$.[11]

One of the main reasons why short-run regional multipliers are low is because import leakages are high in a regional or 'open' economy. Brown also comments that 'no multiplier by itself can lead to a divergent process of growth or decay. To achieve this we have to invoke some other mechanism. The mechanism that immediately comes to mind is capital-stock adjustment. It is well known that when this is combined with the multiplier impressive possibilities of instability are opened up.' The mechanism works basically through the accelerator (in cases where a rise in income accelerates itself through the stimulation which is given to investment). Or, in the inverse case, through what might appropriately be called the decelerator (where a fall in income decelerates itself through the depression of investment). Brown stresses that the capital-stock-adjustment principle (like the multiplier) is strongest in a closed economy, where productive capacity is geared wholly to domestic demand, and weak in a highly open regional economy. He also claims that manufacturing and primary industry investment in most regions is geared to production for extra-regional markets. In fact this claim will depend very much on the size of region considered and the scale and structure of interregional disparities. It will be more true, for example, of British Standard Regions than of

68

'dualistic' economies such as North and South Italy, or less-developed countries such as Brazil, where the industrialised regions may satisfy their extra-regional imports from abroad rather than other national regions. Also, Brown stresses that manufacturing and primary industry investment is far from being the major part of total capital formation, and that the greater part of the remainder (investment in housing, distribution, social services and public utilities) is much more geared to local demand. But this explicitly introduces government intervention into the outcome of the empirical testing (in the British case local authority housing financed through central government grants, and centrally financed social services and public utilities). The result is not evidence of the interregional instability effects which could be expected through the free working of the market mechanism without such intervention.[12]

It is important to bear this in mind in considering any general relevance of the results Brown derives from his estimates of British interregional income differentials from multiplier and capital-stock-adjustment mechanisms over the long run. It is also worth observing that Brown's estimates are based on the application of British national incremental capital–output ratios to different regional growth rates of population. This means (1) the assumption of a homogeneous adaptive capacity to income changes by firms and industries in different regions, which in many cases is likely to be not only untrue but an underlying cause of regional instability in the first place. It also means (2) the assumption that government intervention through taxation and public expenditure transfers is sufficiently large for regional income growth to be effectively in direct proportion to population growth. Again, despite major government transfers, this is not wholly the case in the British economy, and is certainly not the case in less interventionist economies. Brown divides the British economy into what constitutes roughly its more-developed half (the South-east, East Anglia and the Midlands) and the rest, and presumes that the differences in internal demand pressure generated by the superior growth rates of the more developed regions over fifteen or twenty post-war years has been of the order of 1 to 1·5 per cent of the relevant regional incomes. He adds that 'when it comes to testing these presumptions we suffer from a sad lack of data', and in the testing

69

itself he relies on (1) capital formation as a proxy for *per capita* expenditures and (2) the previously mentioned use of population trends as a proxy for regional income trends. What emerges, in his own words, 'is perhaps two rather weak generalisations'. These could be summarised as (1) differences in mean capital–output ratios (because of differences in the composition of investment) and differences in the age (or modernity) of the capital stock 'are sufficient to upset any presumption that faster growth of population or income goes with higher *per capita* gross capital formation'; (2) some indication that within regions 'an acceleration of the rate of growth of population, in so far as it induces a higher rate of capital formation, does so only after a fairly long, and distributed, time lag'.[13]

Regional Labour and Capitalist Accumulation

To advance on the qualified generalisations of the Brown and Richardson type, regional growth theory must take into account the wider tendencies to imbalance in the distribution of capital and labour in national and international economies. There are two main needs to do such a job. First it is necessary to see any macro-economic analysis as an abstraction from the resource distribution which in the last analysis depends on the behaviour of leading firms and industries.

One of the ways of achieving such an advance is admission of the different effect on different companies of Keynesian macro-policy measures, such as the regional devaluation which a labour subsidy in problem areas is supposed to engender. Leading multi-national companies publicly admit that such a devaluation has little or no impact on their location, production or trade behaviour because the scale of their multi-national gains far outstrips the gains of feasible subsidies. But another means of advance is admission of the impact of macro-economic factors on firms in different regions, and especially differences in regional growth and trade made possible by labour and capital migration. Between these, labour migration now plays the more important role, and very much on the lines anticipated by Marx in analysing the role of the reserve army of labour (which he appreciated was concentrated in particular outflow areas, serving demand for labour in inflow areas).

70

However, Keynesian macro theory does not have to go back to Marx to permit a clearer insight into the macro problem of regional imbalance, or the influence of macro factors on firms. This can be done by going back to Harrod's pioneering application of Keynesian concepts to the theory of economic growth, and then wedding Harrod instability theory to the regional imbalance promoted by labour migration.

As Harrod himself says, his own growth model is a marriage of the acceleration principle and the multiplier theory, and is a development of his own previous trade-cycle analysis.[14] He stresses that it should not be judged solely by reference to the validity or convenience of its particular equations, and that it involves a method of thinking and an approach to certain problems of divergence from equilibrium under dynamic conditions. That equilibrium condition is described as $G_w C_r = s$, where C_r is the required capital coefficient or capital–output ratio, and G_w is the warranted growth rate, or that rate which, if it occurs, 'will leave all parties satisfied that they have produced neither more nor less than the right amount (or) will put them in a frame of mind to give such orders as will maintain the same rate of growth'. In practice, Harrod argues, any divergence from such an equilibrium growth path – either contraction or expansion – will tend to be cumulative, centrifugal and self-reinforcing. He makes a cross reference in this context to Keynes's *Treatise on Money*, where Keynes said that if investment exceeded saving, the system would be stimulated to expand, and vice versa. Putting this in the context of *ex ante* investment exceeding saving, and expressing it in his own terminology, he supposes that actual growth (G) exceeds the warranted growth rate (G_w). The result will be that C, the actual increase in capital goods per unit increment of output, will fall below C_r, or that increase which is desired. There will be an undue shortage of equipment, which will be made up by increasing investment, so that the system is stimulated to further expansion. In other words, the actual growth rate (G), instead of returning to the original warranted rate (G_w), will move further away from it in an upwards direction, with a greater stimulus to further expansion the greater the divergence between G and G_w. Inversely, if G falls below G_w, there will be a redundance of capital goods, and a depressing influence on the demand for investment, which will

71

cause a further divergence and a still stronger depressing influence, and so on.[15]

As Harrod himself puts it, 'a departure from equilibrium, instead of being self-righting will be self-aggravating'.[16] In other words, once an initial upwards stimulus to the growth of the system occurs, the reaction of entrepreneurs to the expansion of income (accelerator) will cause them to invest over and above that rate which they had anticipated would satisfy the expansion of demand for their products. The multiplier effect of their investment will generate further demand reinforcing the increased excess of demand over and above their second-round anticipation. Expressed differently, once an unexpected expansion occurs, intrepreneurial or management reaction will ensure that it increases, since the failure to increase investment in line with the demand increase would mean forgone profits. Inversely, in the event of an unexpected contraction, their cut back in second- and third-round investment in order to avoid being left with spare capacity on their hands will ensure a further downwards movement in demand and investment.

In principle, the result of such a cumulative expansion or contraction of the system would mean either that the economy 'hit the ceiling' or inversely 'hit the floor'. The ceiling concerned, in Harrod's own terminology, is the 'natural' growth rate (G_n), which he defines as 'the maximum rate of growth allowed by the increase in population, accumulation of capital, technological improvement and the work–leisure preference schedule, supposing that there always is full employment in some sense'. The warranted growth rate might happen to coincide with the natural rate, in which case it would be the warranted rate 'proper to the economy', but the system cannot advance more rapidly than the warranted rate allows.[17] In a review of *Towards a Dynamic Economics* Hicks extended this analysis in a trade-cycle context, and argued that the upper limit to expansion would in practice amount to a Full Employment Ceiling (subsequently in our terminology F.E.C.), while the lower limit to contraction would be represented by a 'long range investment' trend which was not affected by accelerator type reactions to the current level of income.[18] In practical terms this can be given significance by allowing for differences in the time period of investment decision-making (for example, major investment in certain types

72

of equipment during an initial equilibrium growth phase preventing a major contraction of the economy through its own multiplier effects in the event of an accelerator type reaction causing a cut back in shorter-term investment). The distinction between short- and long-term investment is too simple if the model is intended to explain the vast range of differences in particular types of investment, and take account of variations in the level of initial stocks, depletions, and so on. None the less it makes particular sense in a development context in which government expenditure on major infrastructural programmes may prevent a further fall in demand and investment of a kind which has been induced in the Harrod contraction manner in the private sector.[c]

Hick's upper equilibrium line represents the limit to which income can grow in an expanding economy through both 'natural' growth and the reduction in unemployed resources. After it is reached only 'natural' growth is possible. In the short term 'having reached its full employment limit, the system must begin to turn round again and output to go down, at least relatively to the trend'. This of course is the trade-cycle downturn, which is assumed to operate under 'normal' international trade conditions through (1) the raising of the cost of labour to a level at which management is constrained to cut back on the rate of growth of output, and (2) the loss of international competitiveness through an inflation of domestic relative to international prices, an increase in imports from abroad and (under flexible downwards factor-return assumptions) a fall in both domestic wages and prices. It is the wage-cost element within Hicks's upper equilibrium line or range which has been extended by Phillips since the early post-war trade-cycle models, and has given rise to a new orthodoxy concerning the level of unemployment at which the system must be run in order to avoid such wage inflationary pressures and payments imbalance.[19]

Phillips's assumptions have rightly been challenged on the grounds that they abstract from institutional, social and political factors which may prove predominant in determining the rate of growth of money-wage claims under particular unemployment levels before the 'full-employment' level. In addition, the Hicks trade-cycle model is only one amongst a subsequent variety of models, and necessarily limited by its pioneering over-simplification. But inasmuch as the Hicks upper equilibrium line and the Phillips full-employment ceilings do indicate the inflationary and growth-restraining problems which may face an economy under full-employment conditions, they provide useful terms of reference for indicating the manner in which interregional factor flows can modify both the nature of the trade-cycle downturn and the trade-adjustment process in a regional rather than a national economy. When combined with the Harrod 'warranted' and 'natural' growth rate concepts they extend the context of Marxian and Myrdalian cumulative interregional disequilibrium analysis.

For instance, it is evident enough that the Hicksian full-employment ceiling depends on the assumption that labour availability is limited in the short term by the level of unemployment and in the longer run by the natural rate of increase of the labour force. In the case of interregional labour migration, however, it is not limited in this way. If one of two regions in the economy reaches a full-employment ceiling before the other, the inflationary and growth-restraining effects of reaching such a ceiling may be offset by migration from the other region. This mechanism is illustrated diagramatically in Figs 5 and 6 (pp. 292–3). Fig. 5 represents the growth paths of a more-developed region (M.D.R.) and a less-developed region (L.D.R.). It is assumed for purposes of argument that regional unemployment in the M.D.R. at the beginning of phase 1 is lower than that obtaining in the L.D.R., but that both regions have the same full-employment ceiling (respectively A^1 and B^2) and grow initially at the same rate. Under these assumptions the M.D.R. reaches its full-employment ceiling earlier than the L.D.R. If the regions concerned were isolated economies without interregional factor flows, point A^1 would represent the peak of the growth cycle for the M.D.R. and result in a cyclical downturn of activity, to B^3. However, for a variety of reasons, freedom of factor movement between the two regions enables the M.D.R. to raise its full-employment ceiling and to sustain an upward growth path over and above what would be its Harrodian 'natural' rate if it were an isolated national economy.

In the first place, although initially equal growth rates in the two regions might entail an assumption that the return to investment or m.e.c. schedule in the two regions was identical, the approach of the M.D.R. to its regional full-employment ceiling would be likely to result in an incentive to management to employ relatively more capital-intensive (and thus higher productivity) investment than that obtaining either before or at the same time in the L.D.R. For this reason the interest rate on indigenous regional savings would be likely to rise. It also would be likely to be raised if the region concerned were an autonomous authority with control or influence over local interest rates (in order to prevent an inflationary surge bursting through the full-employment ceiling). At the same time, increasing tightness in the regional labour market with the approach to a full-employment ceiling in the M.D.R. would be likely to raise money wages in the region in relation to the L.D.R. For both reasons, migration of capital and labour from the L.D.R. to the M.D.R. would be promoted over and above any previous migration rate or level.

The result of such factor migration for the M.D.R. would be (1) a raising of its previous full-employment ceiling (R.F.E.C.) equal to the volume of labour inflow from the L.D.R., plus (2) a raising of regional investment in excess of regional savings equal to the volume of savings inflow from the L.D.R. In Harrod terms, this raises the 'natural' growth rate of the economy of the more-developed region and permits it to continue on an upwards growth path in phase 2 (A^1 to B^1). The result in terms of the Harrod 'warranted' growth rate would be a continued confidence that the previous growth rate could be sustained in the second phase, with the line A^1 to B^1 representing the equilibrium growth path proper to the economy of the M.D.R., and therefore a coincidence between the warranted and natural growth rates. This contrasts with the implication of the Harrod and Hicks models that without factor migration the warranted growth rate of the M.D.R. would decline as a result of the regional economy hitting an unmoveable full-employment ceiling, resulting in a downturn in both the warranted and natural rates from A^1 to B^3. The probability of such an outcome would depend on the rate of productivity gains from capital substitution for labour in the period of approach to a full-employment ceiling. If the approach were very gradual and the gains very large it is possible that such gains could delay the downturn for some time and might delay it indefinitely. But in practice this would be likely to be the case only when the rate of innovation and labour-saving productivity gains were exceptionally large in relation to the period before the approach to full employment. A downturn in the no-factor migration case is the more probable the shorter the time period of the first phase.

The trouble for the two-region economy as a whole from such a sustained upwards rate of growth of the M.D.R. is the impact of factor migration on the growth path of the L.D.R. Essentially the M.D.R.'s gain is the L.D.R.'s loss during the second phase of the growth model. Granted a higher initial unemployment level in the L.D.R., it may gain in the short run through labour migration to the M.D.R. But this labour migration would only represent a net gain if interregional capital migration could be controlled, since capital outflow to the M.D.R. depletes the L.D.R.'s savings and thus its potential investment relative to the remaining population. Also, in practice, labour tends to be less responsive to interregional differences in earnings than is capital, so that the L.D.R.'s savings will tend to be depleted faster than it loses labour and reduces its level of unemployment.[d] In terms of the Harrod growth and Hicks trade-cycle models, a cut back in the actual rate of investment in the L.D.R. would initiate a cumulative downwards spiral in the warranted growth rate reinforcing the loss in the 'natural' growth rate of the L.D.R. through savings outflow. In Fig. 5, this declining growth path is represented by the line A^2 to B^4. According to the Hicks model for a national economy, this would in due course be reversed by multiplier effects from long-term investment which has not responded to changes in the current level of income. If interregional income transfers are held appropriate by the national government, and if they also are secured through investment in long-term expenditure programmes such as infrastructural improvement, it could be that such expenditure could maintain a lower equilibrium line (L.E.L.) for the L.D.R., and prompt an upturn in the falling actual growth path to C^4 rather than C^5 in the third phase of the model. But in the event of such expenditure depending entirely on regional savings (either private or public), the Hicksian lower equilibrium line in the L.D.R. would in due course be depressed by the fall in the shorter-term warranted and natural growth paths in the region. Expressing it differently, if regional long-term expenditure is a direct or indirect function of the short-term growth rate, it will suffer a lagged decline reflecting (1) the completion period for long-term private and public investment projects, (2) the fall in taxation receipts within the region from lower income, and (3) the consequent fall in indigenous public savings for regional expenditure (from A^3 to B^5 in Fig. 5). The result for the L.D.R. would be a further decline in the warranted and natural growth rates in the third phase of the growth cycle (from B^4 to C^5 in Fig. 5).

It has already been allowed that a variety of factors could offset such a cumulative decline process. One of the most important could be the growth-sustaining effects of exports from the L.D.R. if it has a competitive export sector. Another is the possibility of interest-rate differentials between the two regions stemming capital outflow from the L.D.R. and perhaps promoting capital inflow. In addition, although the M.D.R. would benefit from both labour and capital inflow from the L.D.R. during the second phase of the cycle, the fall in regional income in the L.D.R. during that phase could be likely to mean that the portfolio investment outflow from the L.D.R. to the M.D.R. fell off during the second phase, with the M.D.R. gaining mainly or exclusively from labour outflow during phase 3 of the cycle. In principle, this could result in a fall back in the rate of its own investment, and precipitate a cumulative decline in its own natural and warranted growth rate. Moreover, granted the evidence that labour migrates much more slowly than portfolio investment, it could well be that the rate of labour emigration from the L.D.R. to the M.D.R. was insufficient to prevent cost-push inflation in the M.D.R. with a consequent fall in its warranted growth rate. Further, if the M.D.R. both grew so fast as to entail a high rate of investment in entirely new (and thus potentially footloose) plant, and if it simultaneously began to feel the pressure of cost-push wage inflation, its management could in principle locate a proportion of the new plant in the L.D.R. in order to take advantage of the lower wage costs which could be assumed to follow from an increase in the level of regional unemployment in the L.D.R.

None the less such a Keynesian model corroborates Marx's analysis of the role of the reserve army of labour in an L.D.R. as a lever of capital accumulation on a M.D.R. It has already been

observed that one of the most marked features of direct investment in even entirely new plant is its high spatial inelasticity – or
response to interregional differentials in wage costs.[e] Secondly,
as the following section elaborates, the interregional trade-
adjustment process may aggravate rather than reduce interregional disparities in investment and growth. Thirdly, unless specific interest-rate concessions are adopted in favour of the L.D.R.,
it is possible that the movement of either national or regional interest rates will not benefit the L.D.R. in such a way as to promote a capital inflow which would necessarily offset an initial
cumulative decline in its warranted and natural growth rates.
For instance, as Ingram has stressed in the U.S. case, the rate of
interest will differ only marginally between regions for those
securities which are sold in national financial markets.[20] This is
one of the costs for an L.D.R. of effective integration in a national capital market. Even if a degree of regional autonomy is
allowed for the regions concerned, which permits them to set
their own regional interest rates, it is likely that the authorities in
the M.D.R. will raise rates as the M.D.R. initially approaches its
full-employment ceiling in the first phase of the expansionary
cycle. While this might affect the warranted growth rate of the
M.D.R. through depressing management confidence in the continuation of the actual growth rate, it would depend upon the
degree of sensitivity of capital accumulation and investment to
marginal interest-rate changes. If the firms concerned are oligopolistic in character, with a high rate of self-financing through
internally generated funds, and if also they are already benefiting from a significant investment inflow from the L.D.R. (via
national-bank lending or from international capital markets),
their net capital needs for continued expansion may not be significantly affected by such interest-rate changes.[f]

Particular emphasis has been placed in the previous analysis
on the role of labour supply in permitting 'super-normal' growth in an M.D.R. through raising its indigenous full-
employment ceiling (or that full-employment level which would
have obtained in the absence of interregional labour migration).
This appears to have been corroborated in practice in post-war
Italian growth, whereby the North-west region in which the bulk
of the nation's modern industry was located avoided a cyclical
downturn between 1951 and 1961, and grew at a sustained rate

heralded at the time as miraculous. In particular, the role of labour immigration from the South appears to have been instrumental in preventing cost-push inflation in the key growth-initiating sector of manufacturing, where the annual rate of increase of productivity significantly outstripped the annual increase in money wages through the period from 1953 to 1961.[21] As with any particular case, political, institutional, social and psychological factors played an important role in this sustained expansion. The North-west of the country started the post-war recovery period from a level of industrial structure and *per capita* income strikingly in advance of the under-industrialised and predominantly agricultural South. The initial stimulus to an accelerated expansion came from the widespread pressure of northern management to reconstruct pre-war production and profit levels rather than from an approach to a regional full-employment ceiling of the kind hypothesised in the previous model. This was backed by the injection of Marshall Aid, an oligopolistic structure of production which permitted high self-financing, a liberation of initiative from the period of fascist corporatism, and a progressive liberalisation of the economy which permitted well-based northern firms to exploit labour costs which were low in relation to their principal international competitors. In addition, union bargaining power in Italy in the 1950s was low not only because of high unemployment levels, but also because of a fractionalised union structure, with the main engineering unions split on party political lines. It was partly the 'opening to the Left' of Italian politics in the early 1960s, as well as the approach of the national economy to nominally frictional unemployment levels, which permitted increased union pressure in these years, with the result that manufacturers conceded wage increases in excess of productivity increases, and passed them on in increased prices, promoting the first major national balance-of-payments deficit since the war.

In other words, a variety of particular factors must be taken into account in describing the Italian case. None the less the role of interregional migration in permitting so long and sustained an investment boom in Northern Italian industry in the 1950s cannot be discounted, and certainly appears consistent with the mechanics of the interregional growth model which has been outlined. In essentials, it can be maintained that it was the migration of South Italian labour which raised the regional full-employment ceiling of the North-west in such a way as to permit not only a sustained warranted growth rate within the region (and, through direct spread effects, to much of the rest of the North) but also an increase in the 'natural' growth rate of the region over and above what it would have been in the absence of such immigration. As analysis elsewhere on the Italian case indicates, *per capita* income between the South and North of Italy converged rather than diverged in the 1950 to 1967 period, yet did so principally through the expenditure on infrastructure and other public investment undertaken by the national government. In this sense there could be said to have been a converging Hicksian lower equilibrium investment path through the period, rather than the divergent and increasingly downward sloping line (A^3 to C^6) of the model. Yet this is not inconsistent with the hypothesis that such a lower equilibrium path would have increasingly declined in the absence of such public expenditure, granted that the region's share of industrial value-added in private enterprise dominated sectors declined relatively to the North during the period concerned.[22]

- In general the model distinguishes between increased labour supply through immigration which is growth-sustaining, and the primary growth initiation process from increased investment. To this extent it parallels the Kindleberger labour supply growth hypothesis.[23] Kindleberger not only applies his model to post-war Italy, but also the principal other Western European economies, allowing for exceptions in the case of France and Austria. In fact it seems clear enough that he overstates his case, and that the multiplicity of growth-sustaining factors in the main Western European economies since the war has been wider in range and effect than he allows.[24] Moreover, while allowing for the interregional nature of the labour flows involved in his growth-sustaining hypothesis, he chooses to emphasise inter-*sectoral* migration from agriculture to industry, following the Lewis and Ranis and Fei models.[25] To this extent he fails to elaborate inter-reaction models of the type outlined earlier in this chapter, and in part neglects the significance of actual interregional migration in the economies he considers. This has tended to be from provincial urban areas of significant unemployment in the less-developed regions towards faster growing employ-

80

ment areas elsewhere, with the decline in agricultural employment occurring mainly through natural wastage and the unwillingness of the rural young to enter farm employment. None the less, if one allows the consideration of post-war East and West Germany, before the building of the Berlin wall in 1961, as regions of the same economy, his argument that the net addition of not less than 7 million East Germans to the West German labour force by the end of the 1950s permitted the super-growth of the West German economy in that decade appears incontrovertible, and impressive-enough evidence of the way in which labour inflow can permit a long-term investment boom through a continued upwards movement of the full-employment ceiling of the more-developed region.

Trade-Led Growth and Decline

The previous analysis abstracted from interregional trade, but allowed that trade effects might offset the progressive cumulative divergence process between hypothetical regions. In Chapter 1 it was admitted that the Ohlin factor-proportions case carried considerable weight in terms of potential rather than actual competitive advantage for a region which had an abundance of (therefore) cheap labour in relation to a more-developed region. But it was stressed that Ohlin's analysis was restricted (1) by assuming similar production functions in different regions, thereby failing to make allowance for the effects of scale economies in benefiting an M.D.R., and (2) failing to allow for the principal characteristic of 'frictions' in factor mobility – in particular the significant spatial inelasticity of new direct investment, which can be a principal reason why portfolio inflow into an M.D.R. is not offset by direct investment outflow to an L.D.R.

A less-developed region might benefit from increased exports to a faster-growing M.D.R. and offset or reverse its fall back in income and employment from the lower export prices which lower wages would permit. In principle, this could allow a stemming of the cumulative decline of the region's warranted and natural growth rates before any upturn effect from a Hicksian lower equilibrium line. But as Professor Whitman has argued, this export-countervailance case is based on limited as-

81

sumptions which are unlikely to apply over the longer run, and for reasons largely related to scale-economy effects.[26]

Professor Whitman has expressed her argument in terms of a Keynesian (or neo-Keynesian) model reproduced in Fig. 7, which represents two regions which we shall call North and South respectively.[8] The North is defined as a region experiencing rapid growth and inflationary pressure in its export sector. The immediate effect of an increase in the demand for its exports is equivalent to a surplus on its 'current account'. The m.e.c. schedule in the export sector will rise, causing capital to flow into the region from the other region of the closed economy (South). At the same time a multiplier effect will be registered on regional income, increasing real wages and/or decreasing unemployment. Increased employment opportunities will in turn promote increased labour inflow into the region. The reverse process will occur in the South, or the region experiencing a decline in exports. The m.e.c. schedule will fall, funds for and investment in the export sector will decline, with a consequent fall in the multiplier effect from the export sector on regional income, leading to a decrease in employment in the region (or an increase in unemployment), and accelerated labour outflow. In the case of initially export-led growth, Professor Whitman allows that the first round of investment in the export sector may convert the North's surplus in the short term into a deficit through increased imports from the South. However, she maintains that in the longer term the region benefiting from the initial export surplus will be placed in a stronger competitive position because of second-round investment effects in both the export sector and (through the accelerator) on other sectors, reinforcing its initial expansionary advantage. She also points out that capital flows into the region are likely to alter the capital–labour ratio and thus raise labour productivity, allowing cost and price reductions in exports which thereby further increase the relative competitiveness of the North in relation to the South.[27]

Thus, in the longer run, there will be a 'capacity effect' on the structure of production and competitiveness of the region benefiting from an autonomous increase in exports. It is such an effect which neo-classical analysis, including that of Ohlin, does not take into account. Professor Whitman emphasises that the sequence of her argument is simplified for exposition purposes, and should not be taken too literallly. In practice the various effects will sometimes follow each other and sometimes occur simultaneously. These qualifications clearly should be allowed. As with the previous application of Harrod–Hicks models, the clear-cut distinction between first and second-round effects is an analytical simplification. The gestation period for investment in different firms and different sectors will itself differ, with first- and second-round export periods overlapping for different firms. None the less, in practice this might reinforce the advantage in favour of the faster growing region, with the leading second-round firms stimulating further output from supplier firms in the North rather than the South. Besides, the argument is reinforced by relaxing Professor Whitman's assumption of a two-region economy, and allowing for imports to the North and South from other regions or other international economies. In practice this could mean that the North secured its second-round imports not from the South but from abroad. In this way the South could lose both its factors of production and fail to secure second-round exports to the North. In other words, its main export would be labour and capital rather than goods.[h]

Professor Whitman's analysis is further strengthened by extending the initial impetus in favour of one region beyond the case of an autonomous increase in exports. She herself allows that the effects on regional income and the current-account balance would be similar if the initial investment expansion in one region were to take the form of import substitution, allowing for the fact that the effects on interregional capital flows probably would be weaker in that investors (whether interregional or international) are generally more sensitive to changes in investment opportunities in the export sector than import substitution. Besides, the introduction of technical progress and innovation considerably extends her case. For instance, some firms in the North may innovate new products or production techniques which permit significant cost and price reductions for given products. This may either be the result of regional technical progress or through the import of innovations from other economies on a licence basis.[i] If this were not matched by the less-developed South it would be likely to lead to an increase in exports from North to South. It is likely that the impact of the new products or techniques would stimulate some imitative invest-

83

ment in the South, but the region's capacity to introduce such counter-innovations (or specialise in complementary and consequential innovations for exports to the North) would depend upon the response capacity of its firms in the sectors concerned. The longer the period of cumulative divergence in regional growth rates the lower this would be likely to be. Any advantage in this respect to the firms in the M.D.R. would reinforce the Whitman 'capacity effect' in terms of m.e.c. shifts and multiplier increases.

Professor Whitman stresses that the implications of her analysis are at variance with the implications of Keynesian analysis of trade adjustment in the absence of labour flows, inasmuch as these take account of the effects of capital flows on income, but not on employment. As she points out, in the 'traditional' Keynesian international analysis it is likely that a current-account surplus will lead to inflation of either the cost-push or demand-pull types in not only the export sector but also other sectors, which will induce an import round and payments deficit. This process will be reinforced to the extent that previous exports are diverted during the inflationary period of more profitable domestic demand. By contrast, the inflow of both capital and labour to a region with an initial export surplus both provides an anti-inflationary effect from increased labour availability, and a capacity-creating effect through increased availability of capital. In this way it is possible for a region with expanding exports to continue indefinitely in surplus. Inversely, a region with decreasing exports can continue indefinitely in deficit and therefore be condemned to indefinite deflation.[28]

The Whitman analysis thus provides a Keynesian elaboration of the Myrdal–Perroux cumulative disequilibrium or polarisation effects. A similar extension of the Myrdal–Perroux case has been undertaken by Borts and Stein, who place greater emphasis on the interrelationship of labour migration and capital accumulation in the factor-receiving region.[29] Like Professor Whitman they assume that there is an initial rise in a region's exports which is caused by increased import demand in other regions. They also point out that in 'traditional' Keynesian trade-adjustment analysis of international economies it would be assumed that the economy with the higher demand for its exports undergoes a domestic price inflation, an increase in its money stock, and a rise in imports. However, factor migration again alters the traditional international picture. The growth of exports and export prices leads to an increase in the region's capital stock both from internal sources and from capital inflow, and consequently to an increase in its rate of growth. This increase in the capital stock itself tends to increase with the capital–labour ratio and productivity and wages in the factor-receiving region, thereby attracting labour inflow. But this process does not lead to any stable growth pattern whereby all regions ultimately grow at the same rate, since investment can exceed savings permanently in the factor-receiving region through inflow from other regions. This means that there may be a permanent and increasing divergence between regional growth rates.[30]

Borts and Stein allow various disturbances which in practice could either modify or extend the divergence process which they have described, including (1) autonomous shifts of labour between regions; (2) autonomous inter-sectoral shifts of labour in regions, and (3) technological change. The autonomous shift of labour between regions might be for reasons of climate. This is of considerable relevance in the United States, where 'peripheral' regions such as the Pacific Coast and Florida have constituted major recreation and retirement areas. In such a case income is injected into the local economies without the vacation or retirement population adding directly to the local labour force.[j] Inter-sectoral shifts of labour within a faster-growing region will occur when labour moves from lower to higher productivity and income sectors. (In practice such a case could result in either the specialisation of the regional economy in the higher productivity activities, or in the substitution of immigrant for indigenous labour in the lower productivity and income sectors.[k] In either case this would reinforce the cumulative-divergence hypothesis inasmuch as the L.D.R. was left with specialisation in lower productivity lines.) The analysis of technological change in the export sector undertaken by Borts and Stein effectively corroborates the cumulative export-led growth case argued by Professor Whitman.

The Limits of 'Export-Base' Theory

The Whitman analysis has stressed that cumulative disequilibrium is likely to be irreversible if left to the free working of the market mechanism without government intervention. Borts and Stein's position is less clear, as analysed later elsewhere.[1] But in practice it is as unlikely that the cumulative-divergence mechanisms which they have described (or those outlined in the previous section) will operate in an uninterrupted manner as it is unlikely that direct investment flows to an L.D.R. will automatically offset portfolio and labour outflows to an M.D.R. experiencing a higher macro-economic growth rate. On the other hand, the higher degree of realism in the cumulative-divergence models than in neo-classical cumulative convergence theory provides more workable parameters for the development of government policies of a kind which can ensure that any offsetting of the divergence process is not left entirely to chance factors.

The Whitman and the Borts–Stein analyses certainly improve upon either the simpler versions of 'export-base' theory of regional growth, or upon Keynesian interregional models which fail to distinguish between general mechanisms and particular offsetting factors including government policy. The 'export base' theory in fact was developed mainly in an urban area rather than in a wider regional context,[31] but is most closely associated with Douglass North.[32] North claimed that (1) the concept of a region should be defined in terms of its development around a common export base; (2) that 'the success of the export base has been the determining factor in the rate of growth of regions'; (3) that the export base of a region has a 'primary role in determining the level of absolute and *per capita* income in a region, and therefore in determining the amount of residentiary, secondary and tertiary activity that will develop'. He also claims that the export base has significantly influenced the character of subsidiary industry, the distribution of population and urbanisation patterns, the character of the labour force, and the social and political character of the region. He concludes that a region need not necessarily develop a manufacturing base in order to achieve sustained export growth.

In making these claims North was essentially challenging a structural-change model of regional growth, rather than an export-led decline hypothesis of the Whitman type. The model concerned was the stages-of-growth explanation of regional change proposed by Hoover and Fisher, which suggested that most (though not all) regions begin their economic history with the stage of a self-sufficient subsistence economy in which only basic needs are met, and there is little internal or external trade.[33] The growth of trade makes it possible for such a primitive region to grow by specialising in lines of production for which it is particularly suited, which might in fact be agriculture.[m] But a continued increase in population makes it increasingly difficult to keep *per capita* income increasing through agricultural development, granted the income inelasticity of demand for food in relation to other products or services, the limited capacity of agriculture for intensive production, and so on. Under these conditions, Hoover and Fisher suggested, 'it remains true that if a region is to continue to increase both its total and *per capita* real income it must eventually *industrialise*'. Their own further analysis concentrates on the difficulties of transition from an agricultural and subsistence economy to an industrial one. They anticipated the Myrdal and Perroux emphasis on 'vicious-circle' arguments by observing that a non-industrial region may reach a limit to its growth and that in this case 'it is likely to retrogress or decay. Metaphorically speaking, if it misses the bus when still in full stride, and exhaustion sets in, the bus becomes still harder to catch. Stagnation and decay too may be cumulative.'[34]

Hoover and Fisher allow that a non-manufacturing region may succeed in securing a high and growing level of *per capita* income through specialisation, for instance in large-scale mining and mineral-reduction or the exploitation of oil, but emphasise that in this case it will be dependent upon the importation of capital from elsewhere. They also stress the dangers of over-specialisation, especially in cases in which the primary exploitation of the raw materials is undertaken where they are mined, but the bulk-reducing stages including processing and subsequent use occur outside the region.[35]

In challenging the Hoover–Fisher case, North cites the Pacific North-west region of the United States, which has successfully grown through specialisation in forestry and timber exports. He also claims that the stages-of-growth case may make sense for the European economy, in which the main problem of development has been changing a subsistence and initially manorial system to one capable of capitalist growth, but does not apply to the regional development of the United States, in which he claims that growth began through specialisation and trade for the integrated U.S. market, with agricultural producers selling thousands of miles away, rather than for local subsistence needs. It was on the 'base' of these exports (agricultural, industrial and service) that the regions developed, experimenting initially on a trial-and-error basis to discover those goods in which they had a competitive interregional advantage. Thus, he claims that the early town centres in the United States were located not only to service the agriculture of the local area but also to implement the export of the region's 'staples'.

The North argument is useful in distinguishing the growth problems of under-developed and undeveloped economies. In the former case, the difficulties of transition from agricultural to other forms of production may result in both a relative and an absolute decline of income as (1) the terms of trade of the interregional economy move against agriculture, and (2) the rate of growth of agricultural population outstrips the rate of growth of productivity. In the latter case, the development of potentially rich and previously unexploited agricultural areas by the inflow of skilled and enterprising immigrants is facilitated by initially high land–labour ratios of a kind which do not obtain with older agricultural areas which have failed to make the transition to non-agricultural production and suffer from fractionalised land-holding. In addition, in the development of agriculture in a previously undeveloped economy in which some regions have special advantages over others in the production of agricultural products, capital inflow to the agricultural areas concerned is likely if rapid industrialisation is taking place in the non-agricultural regions – such as the North-eastern seaboard of the United States during the nineteenth century. But these are special conditions for successful agricultural growth of productivity and *per capita* income, and in themselves do not constitute a general theory of regional growth through agricultural and later non-agricultural exports of a kind which completely refutes the Hoover–Fisher case. Moreover, there is no assurance that the free working of the market mechanism even in a fast-growing, hitherto undeveloped economy will ensure either (1) the inflow of sufficient capital to undeveloped agricultural areas to permit their successful exploitation in the first place, or (2) a smooth and cumulative transition of their regional economies through a change in their export base from agricultural to non-agricultural activities sufficient to permit equal interregional rates of growth of income, or even their convergence.

The former point is well illustrated by the historical case of the United States, where – contrary perhaps to popular impression – the infrastructure essential for the development of the Mid and Far West was provided in the first place by government rather than private risk capital. It was only after the 'take off' of the agricultural export economies of these regions that the pressure for government rather than private finance was reversed.[36] The crisis of the Mid-Western farming states and of the 'staple' exporting South after the boom years of the mid-nineteenth century also shows that the Hoover–Fisher emphasis on the dangers of over-specialisation and problems of adjustment was not ill-placed. The federal programme of the New Deal was not only aimed at recovery from the cyclical depression following the Wall Street collapse of 1929, but was aimed at getting the farmer 'out of the mud' in which the era of *laissez-faire* had stranded him.[37] In this sense, the longer term regional evolution of the United States corroborates the cumulative-divergence and decline models of the Harrod–Hicks, Whitman type, rather than the cumulative adjustment of the export base as hypothesised by North.[38] Moreover, as Werner Hochwald has pointed out, the South began as a classic export economy, excelling in the export staples of tobacco, rice, sugar and cotton on the basis of a slave-labour economy which should have permitted the generation of sufficient regional savings for successful transition to a more diversified industrial economy. Yet at the time of the Civil War, sufficient regional savings for successful transition to a more diversified industrial economy. Yet at the time of the Civil War, New Orleans was the only southern city ranking among the first fifteen in the United States, and the development of local or 'residentiary' industries and services stimulated by the export base were conspicuously fewer than elsewhere.[39] In addition the cumulative decline of the South was so marked for so long that even a massive concentration of federal aid plus federal defence expenditure in the region since the war has been insufficient to

89

permit the key southern states to do more than hold their own with a *per capita* income level less than two-thirds that of the mideast from 1948 to 1968.[40]

It has been argued that the North export-base theory of growth is misleading inasmuch as it assumes that regions will be able to adapt their export structure to that of the rest of the economy, and thus diversify their export and residentiary (or non-export) base in a self-sustaining process. It is particularly misleading in that it assumes that 'ultimately, we may expect with long run factor mobility more equalisation of *per capita* income and a wider dispersion of production'.[41] This neglects the asymmetry observed in factor flows, with capital and labour outflow tending to be one way, and not balanced by counter inflows of direct investment in search of lower cost and more available labour in the L.D.R.[42] The L.D.R. may never achieve a breakthrough from agriculture to higher income and productivity non-agricultural activities on a sufficient scale to ensure a convergence of regional income levels *without significant government intervention.*[n]

The export-base approach also is misleading in its identification of exports as the *sole* basis of regional income change. As Charles Tiebout has commented;

> in an exchange economy one person considered in a spatial context may be entirely dependent on his ability to export his services. Probably this is true of a neighbourhood area, except for the corner grocer. For the Community as a whole, the income originating in non-exports increases. In the United States exports account for only a small part of national income. Obviously, for the world as a whole there are no exports. Thus the quantitative importance of exports as an explanatory factor in regional income determination depends, in part, on the size of the region under study.[43]

But it is not only the size of the foreign trade sector which is important in regional income determination.[o] For instance, an M.D.R. may attain such a superior level of development through factor inflow from the L.D.R. that its productive structure becomes qualitatively different from that of the L.D.R. The type of goods and services which it either needs or can afford will change with changes in the level and rate of growth of income,

90

even allowing for a maintained social distribution of income within the region.[p] Embodied technical progress and innovation will reinforce the Whitman 'capacity effect' to a point at which those goods which nominally enter into the same national-accounts classification constitute effectively different products for different regional markets. As a result, in a two-region economy isolated from international trade, the M.D.R. would tend to develop increasingly autarchic tendencies, with the qualitative disparity in the nature of traded goods reinforcing the quantitative reduction in interregional trade. Moreover, in an economy exposed to international trade subject only to tariff and foreign-exchange constraints, the M.D.R. would be more likely to trade with more-developed regions in other countries than with the L.D.R. in its own country.

In practice, it is more likely that parts of the L.D.R. will remain integrated with the M.D.R., and constitute poles of attraction for trade and factor movement within the L.D.R. itself. In this way there will be a variety of spread and backwash effects within as well as between regions, whose identification demands a higher degree of disaggregation than that undertaken in the present macro-analysis context.[q]

The fact that a major region cannot count on export-led growth as a basis for continuing and cumulative expansion is even more marked in the South of Italy case than in that of the Deep South of the United States. The cases differ in important respects. The agricultural economy of the South of Italy in the mid-nineteenth century was archaic, fragmented, and heavily over-populated. Massive out-migration of labour in the late-nineteenth and early-twentieth centuries did not suffice to reduce under-employment to a point at which productivity gains could stimulate an export-led growth process in agricultural products.[44] It is generally agreed that the problems of the South were aggravated rather than reduced by its integration with the more-developed North (and in particular the North-west) following the political integration of the country in 1861. Saraceno has drawn attention to the negative effects of both tariff abolition and improved communications through railway construction, which 'overthrew the local markets on which the precarious life of southern producers was based'.[45] The problem of an inadequate infrastructure in the South to support industrial-

91

isation was admitted by the government from 1861, and it embarked on a succession of limited public-works programmes in particular areas. But it did not appreciate that the growth of regional agricultural productivity or industrial employment and product could not proceed in the same manner as before tariff reduction and the improvement of interregional transport because of northern competition for southern markets, particularly in manufacturing industry.

Fortunately, no doubt, for the resident population of the South of Italy, the intensified development expenditure in the region's favour in the post-war period means that figures on the region's trade and investment which have become available since the war do not provide a test of the pure working of the market mechanism in interregional resource allocation. However, it is notable that during the period 1951–61 when government assistance programmes were concentrated almost exclusively in infrastructural expenditure, with only a minor proportion allocated to incentives for industrial development, regional fixed investment was persistently lower than regional net imports. In other words, despite the emigration of 1·7 million people from the region, the South failed to achieve any investment from its own regional savings. The tide turned in 1962, and in 1968 regional fixed investment totalled 19·5 per cent of regional resources against 15·1 per cent constituted by net imports.[46] In other words, a trend had been established towards a degree of regional investment financed from regional savings. On the other hand, net imports still amounted to three-quarters of the fixed investment within the region, which had not in any sense achieved self-sufficiency in its capital formation. Moreover, as shown later in this text, the main improvement in the region's share in national capital formation was provided not through some automatic self-adjustment through the free working of the market, but through the implementation of government legislation introduced in 1957 which obliged Italian public enterprise agencies (then located almost exclusively outside the South) to locate 60 per cent of their investment in new plant and 40 per cent of their total investment within the region. Expressed differently, there is no evidence that the South would have been able to register much increase in its own investment without State control over the location of public enterprise as well as massive infrastructural expenditure in the region.[r]

A clear indication of the degree of concentration of national investment in the initially more-developed regions is available from their proportion of Italian value-added and employment in the main growth-promoting sectors in 1951 and 1967. This shows that the South's share of national employment in manufacturing *declined* from 19.5 per cent to 18.1 per cent of the national total over the 1951–67 period (against a share of national population of 36 per cent), while its share of national value-added in manufacturing rose from only 12·6 per cent to 13·4 per cent. Productivity in terms of value-added per employee rose in southern manufacturing over the period, but from only 53·5 per cent to 63·2 per cent of the value added per employee in manufacturing in the more-developed North-west. Moreover, it was mainly the higher than national average productivity of the new plant located by the public enterprise agencies I.R.I. and E.N.I. in steel and petro-chemicals which contributed to this partial closing of the manufacturing productivity gap between the South and the North-west.[s] Overall, both manufacturing employment and product remained concentrated in the North-west (26·5 per cent of national population) and a few areas of the central North-eastern part of the country (37.5 per cent of national population). In 1967 these regions included, respectively, some 45 per cent and 37 per cent of total national employment in manufacturing, and 53 per cent and 34 per cent of national manufacturing value-added. The concentration in favour of the most-developed North-west becomes most plain by a breakdown of the more modern manufacturing sectors, including metallurgy, engineering, chemicals and chemical products, paper, rubber, and textiles. Whereas the South in 1967 included only some 9 per cent of national value-added in these sectors, the North-west (with a substantially smaller share of national population) included nearly two-thirds.[t]

These figures are only illustrative. They indicate the degree of backwardness of a major region such as the South of Italy rather than wholly explain it. Their usefulness depends in part on assumptions concerning the role of sectoral structure in regional growth whose relevance has so far been only outlined rather than analysed in any depth.[u] None the less, a clear indication of

93

the force of the cumulative imbalance already analysed in Keynesian growth and trade-cycle terms is suggested by the net decline of the South's share of national manufacturing employment and its almost insignificant improvement in terms of the share of national manufacturing value-added. The polarisation of activity in the main growth area of the North-west is indicated by the proportion of international trade accounted for by the three cities of the so-called 'golden triangle' of the North-west region. In 1969 these three cities (Milan, Turin and Genoa) and their provinces accounted for more than *half* of Italian exports and imports, with a resident urban population equal to only 6 per cent of the national total. By contrast, Rome and the main cities of the South (Naples, Palermo and Bari) together accounted for 8 per cent of total national population in 1969, 10 per cent of national imports, and only 6 per cent of national exports.[47]

Regional Structure and Optimum Currencies

General policy implications from the foregoing analysis are drawn later in this work. But there is one policy question in regional growth and trade which merits specific attention, especially in view of the European Community's current programme for abolition of independent currencies and the creation of a common currency by 1980. It may well be that such a step is not taken on schedule, and possible that it will not be taken at all. But if taken it would mean the abolition of a key factor which at present distinguishes nation states from national regions. It is particularly questionable granted the stubbornness of structural disparities between regions in national economies, and the economic case – on macro-economic grounds – for a major region in the E.E.C. such as the South of Italy to reverse present Community policy and go it alone with a unilateral declaration of monetary independence.

The main gain from an independent currency is the capacity to alter the exchange rate and, especially, to devalue. Devaluation should increase the price-competitiveness of exports, subject to the discounting of exchange-rate changes by multinational firms in subsidiary trade. But the structural composition of both production and foreign trade is important, as is the relative size of the foreign-trade sector. To take the size point,

94

the larger the total foreign-trade sector, the smaller the total effective elasticity of demand for imports. McKinnon has put this clearly by taking the case of Monaco, where virtually all consumption goods are imported, and where the effective elasticity of demand for all imports, given a price change induced by a devaluation, will be extremely small or nil because of lack of domestic substitutes. In practice the internal consumer price index is likely to rise by the amount of the change in the exchange rate.[48] In other words, there must be considerable import-substitution possibilities for a significant price elasticity of imports to obtain, and this relates fundamentally to the structure of production within the region concerned. The same obtains for export price elasticity. For instance, if the cumulative decline of the region's exports has been tolerated for long, so that the bulk of the firms in the L.D.R.'s export sector are small-scale, relatively labour-intensive, and technologically backward, they may be producing goods which are effectively differentiated from those available in the M.D.R. in being lower in quality whatever their nominal price. In this case the devaluation necessary to make them competitive in the M.D.R. may have to be very considerable to improve export volume. Yet this can be an asymmetrical, one-way effect, since the quality of goods imported from the M.D.R. may render them less than proportionately responsive to higher import prices as a result of devaluation. In this way devaluation alone may prove insufficient to prevent a cumulative import-led decline process of the Whitman type if the region concerned has already become differentiated in structure and overall competitiveness from the M.D.R.[v]

For less-developed regions in single-currency areas there is little practical prospect of a unilateral declaration of monetary independence, even if it is estimated in the particular case that it could work to the region's advantage. The question is basically about the international policy instrument which the region has lost, rather than one which can be gained. As already indicated, it is mainly a practical issue in reverse terms: whether a less-developed country should integrate in a single-currency area including more-developed countries. This is a wide-ranging issue which, at least in anything less than the very long run, is not directly comparable with the problem of an L.D.R. which has suffered from cumulative backwash in a single-currency economy. Essentially the differences relate to the institutional, language, cultural and political barriers to perfectly free capital movements between countries. As is well known 'hot money' flows tend to be highly responsive even to relatively minor variations in interest rates. But there are considerable indications that there is less response to differentials in share earnings between countries. This partly relates to the fact that investment brokers know their national markets better than those markets with which their economies may be nominally integrated and tend to have a better appreciation of a home than a foreign company, except in those increasingly important cases where the companies concerned are already multi-national, with performance records which are well known or fairly readily evaluated. This is a different situation from that in which a national economy has already been integrated as a single-currency area for the period in which banking and investment institutions themselves developed. The development of comparable knowledge and confidence in the case of integration of previously separate currency areas into a single-currency area would take time, and not be likely to lead to a sudden outflow of portfolio investment from less-developed to more-developed members of the union.

However, while allowing for these qualifications, the previous analysis of cumulative divergence between regions of a national economy which is institutionally integrated, as well as integrated by a single currency, indicates that in due course major problems may arise for international economies which choose to integrate in a single-currency area. Basically, the more effectively they integrate, the greater the probability of cumulative divergence in their rates of growth of investment, product and employment on the lines already described. Again, the question whether monetary integration is desirable cannot be divorced from particular considerations including (1) the initial productive structure of the nation-states to be integrated as nation-regions in the single-currency area; (2) the level of unemployment or under-employment in particular regions; (3) the previous tendency to convergence or divergence between the growth rates and productivity of the nation-states; (4) the relative integration of the capital markets of the area before and after integration; (5) the direction, rate and consequences of interregional labour migration relative to capital migration in the integrated area; (6) the possible stimulus effects to investment and productivity growth to particular regions through monetary integration (reducing the risk element in foreign-currency transactions for small and medium firms which otherwise might not be able to afford the costs of forward cover); (7) the effectiveness of policy instruments adopted by the responsible authorities in the newly integrated area (either international or federal); and (8) the increasingly important extent to which multi-national companies qualify exchange-rate changes in pricing between their own subsidiaries.

As expressed by Mundell, 'the optimum currency area is the region', and the region is defined in this context as an area in which there is effective factor mobility. Mundell admits some problems in the concept, including the relative nature of factor mobility itself. As he puts it:

> factor mobility (and hence the delineation of regions) is most usefully considered a relative rather than an absolute concept, with both geographic and industrial dimensions, and it is likely to change over time with alterations in political and economic conditions. If, then, the goals of internal stability are to be rigidly pursued, it follows that the greater is the number of separate currency areas in the world, the more successfully will these goals be attained (assuming, as always, that the basic argument for flexible exchange rates *per se* is valid). But this seems to imply that regions ought to be defined so narrowly as to count every minor pocket of unemployment arising from labour immobility as a separate region, each of which should apparently have a separate currency. Such an arrangement hardly appeals to common sense.[49]

Perhaps not. But the arguments already considered in the present chapter indicate that the level of unemployment should not be the only criterion in determining whether an area should have it own currency. Basically, the advantage or disadvantage to a region from having a currency whose exchange rate can be altered will depend on its size, the structure of its export sector, and its potential responsiveness to exchange-rate alterations. Basically, devaluation alone will not ensure any region the benefits of cumulative export-led growth under any conditions, and

97

cannot be a substitute for structural adaptation and change. In other words devaluation cannot necessarily ensure the development of the region without complementary development policies. And the longer the initial process of cumulative decline, the more difficult such policies are likely to prove. In addition it would be naïve to ignore the political implications of separate currencies, just as these implications cannot be ignored in the case of integration of previously independent nation-states in a single-currency area. The main economic loss to an L.D.R. which decides to 'go it alone' is likely to be the reduced preparedness of the M.D.R. to finance and assist its economic adaptation and development under the new, independent-currency conditions. In principle the possibility of lower delivered prices in the M.D.R. through location in the L.D.R. might prompt a return of savings which previously had been drawn from the L.D.R. in the form of more direct investment in the region by M.D.R. firms. On the other hand, the pattern of multi-national trade and payments since the war, and especially since the 1950s, indicates that the Keynesian case for exchange-rate changes as a means of preserving full employment is increasingly being eroded.[w]

NOTES

[a] See further, Chapters 7 and 8 of this text.

[b] See later this chapter (pp.70–81).

[c] Such a multiplier effect from the expenditure on infrastructure by government agencies appears to have played a crucial part in the post-1950 growth of income in the South of Italy, despite a decline in the interregional output proportions of key private manufacturing sectors. Cf. later this text, Chapters 4 and 6.

[d] Cf. further the following chapter, which disaggregates the over-simple Harrod-Hicks production factors, and gives evidence on the relative 'spatial inelasticity' of labour in relation to portfolio investment.

[e] Cf. Chapter 4.

[f] Cf. further, Chapter 6.

[g] In her own exposition California (North) and Appalachia (South).

[h] There are clear indications that this has been the case over the longer term in

98

Italy, with the North-west region effectively integrated with the West European and wider world market rather than the South. Cf. later this section.

[i] Licensing, rather than indigenous innovation from regional R and D, has been typical in North-west Italy.

[j] In the long run it is possible that the South of Italy might also benefit on a large scale from a retirement population, which has the considerable benefit, relative to tourism, of being continuous rather than seasonal.

[k] Cf. the following chapter.

[l] See further the critique of Borts and Stein's analysis of U.S. regional growth in Stuart Holland, *The Regional Problem* (London: Macmillan, 1976) ch. 6.

[m] As examples they cite the cases of Denmark and New Zealand.

[n] For further analysis of the role of sectoral composition in regional growth with special reference to the Italian case cf. Chapters 4 and 6.

[o] Cf. further, later this chapter (see pp.95–6).

[p] Without unionisation, the inflow of labour from the L.D.R. to the M.D.R. would be likely to increase disparities in income distribution in favour of the share-holding class (while permitting maintained or increased investment in the M.D.R.), but this would not prevent rising real incomes for the labour employed in the M.D.R. and an upwards trend in the quality of consumption goods. The quality effect would tend to be more important for investment goods to the extent that the L.D.R. was unable to self-finance their relatively high capital requirements.

[q] Cf. the distinction between 'stagnant' and 'expanding' agricultural zones in the South of Italy in Chapter 4.

[r] Cf. further, Chapter 6.

[s] Southern productivity in iron and steel was 120 per cent of the national average in 1967 (because of the I.R.I. integrated shore-based steel plant at Taranto) and productivity in chemicals and chemical products was also 120 per cent (because of investment by the State hydrocarbons corporation E.N.I.).

[t] Figures derived directly from ISTAT data. For further analysis cf. Chapter 6.

[u] Cf. following section this chapter and later this text, Chapter 6.

[v] The argument assumes a free-market resource allocation without government intervention in favour of the L.D.R. In a federal situation in which the federal government both promoted structural improvement in the L.D.R and accepted a devaluation of its own currency or instituted a separate currency which could be 'devalued' *vis-à-vis* the M.D.R. the result clearly might be more favourable.

[w] Cf. further, Stuart Holland, *The Socialist Challenge* (London: Quartet, 1975) ch. 3.

CHAPTER 4

MIGRATION AND IMBALANCED RESOURCE USE

The previous argument has maintained that the unequal process of labour and capital migration – if unchecked by offsetting government policies – can aggravate rather than reduce the regional problem. The argument has been pursued mainly at a macro-economic level, without distinguishing different types of labour in the migration process, or the effects of migration on areas of labour outflow and inflow. An attempt is made to remedy this deficiency in the present chapter, while maintaining what may still be considered the macro-economic context of interregional labour migration. The available evidence indicates that there are quantifiable costs from unrestrained interregional migration of labour which can be expressed as costs to the national economy as a whole apart from personal costs to migrants.

Migration Self-Balance Mythology

It has been observed in Chapter 1 that the advocates of regional self-balance through the long-run working of the market normally fail to test their assumptions against reality. This can occur even when they take a particular country against which to put their case, as has happened in the case of labour migration models applied to Italy by Vera Lutz and Eckhaus.[1] Mrs Lutz's argument is developed mainly in her 1962 study, although some of her most important premises are outlined in earlier articles dating from 1958. Her argument assumes that there is a 'natural' process of interregional economic growth in which the factor proportions of an over-populated and under-employed agricultural L.D.R. will be improved relative to an initially more-industrialised M.D.R. The main instrument of this improvement is through out-migration from the agricultural sector in the L.D.R. which is supposed to raise land–labour ratios and thus output per head for the remaining working population in agriculture. The maintenance of previous agricultural output levels with a smaller labour force will mean raised productivity and the generation of a surplus of food products over local consumption needs. The export of this surplus to the M.D.R. will result in net savings in agriculture which can be invested either in improvements to techniques of production through mechanisation, or in industry within the region, or both. Investment of the agricultural surplus in industry will have twofold virtuous effects for regional agriculture through (1) increasing labour outflow from the sector through demand for more labour in regional industry, thereby further increasing agricultural productivity, and (2) increasing the demand for food in the expanded industrial workforce, where out-migrants from agriculture no longer produce food for their own consumption.[2]

This happy picture sadly conflicts with the facts in both the South of Italy on which Mrs Lutz bases her analysis, and in other major areas of labour outflow from agriculture such as the Deep South of the United States. In practice there is a major asymmetry between the responsiveness or spatial elasticity of labour and capital to both inter-sectoral and interregional differentials in factor earnings. Portfolio capital is highly mobile in a telephonic and telex world, and tends to respond in a near perfectly elastic manner to earning differentials in an institutionally integrated national market. Since the rate of return on capital in M.D.R.s tends by definition to be higher than in L.D.Rs., the result is a syphoning of L.D.R. savings towards the M.D.R. which in many cases occurs virtually as soon as L.D.R. savings are generated. If labour migration were as spatially elastic as this portfolio migration, this might not cause much of a problem. But in practice labour tends to be less responsive to potential income gains the further it has to migrate to secure them, and this spatial inelasticity can mean a faster reduction of a region's indigenously generated savings than of its unemployed or underemployed population. In fact the out-migration of labour from the region may not exceed its natural population increase, and with a net outflow of indigenous savings this will worsen its ratio between population and potential investment relative to a situation without freedom of factor flows.

But there are other over-simplifications in the Lutz theory of factor migration and structural adjustment which seriously compromise its relevance to actual regional problems such as those found in the South of Italy. For instance, (1) the M.D.R. may

101

have its own pool of under-employed agricultural labour. Out-migration from it is likely to be higher than from the more distant L.D.R. Assuming a similar agricultural structure in both regions in this first instance, this is likely to lead to faster productivity gains in the agriculture of the M.D.R. than in the L.D.R. and these may be sufficient for the M.D.R. to prove virtually self-sustaining in its food requirements without imports from the L.D.R. (2) The L.D.R.'s agriculture may be less efficient in the first instance than that of the M.D.R. both because of a lower initial industrial demand for food, and because of structural obstacles to increased productivity such as pre-capitalist forms of agricultural production and tenure which have already been eradicated or reduced in the M.D.R. because of its longer standing period of industrialisation; in the L.D.R. these obstacles may be sufficient to prevent the accumulation of a sufficient surplus to invest in capital-intensive production even if labour outflow is significant. (3) Labour may move from the land in the L.D.R. but mainly to areas of urban unemployment and under-employment in the same region which constitute staging posts for out-migration; the movement from the land therefore may not be accompanied by the creation of permanent and expanding demand for food within the region by the non-agricultural population, rather than relatively stagnant demand from a pool of urban under-employed which is itself simultaneously depleted by out-migration from the region and replenished by some out-migration from the region's agriculture. (4) The success of agriculture in the L.D.R. will depend substantially on the price structure of the demand for its products, and in particular on the terms of trade between agricultural and industrial goods; if the L.D.R. specialises in products whose prices increase more slowly than those of M.D.R. agriculture, its productivity and surplus generation potential will be more limited than that of the M.D.R. (5) The type of product and the price which they command may prove more important than land–labour ratios in determining productivity increases, particularly when nominally large land–labour ratios in terms of units of ownership are fragmented in terms of units of tenure, with non-contiguous strips of land held by peasants who have no security of tenure.

As is elaborated later in this chapter, it is for reasons such as

102

these that the neo-classical sectoral self-adjustment model argued by Mrs Lutz and others is powerless to explain the regional problem of the South of Italy. This impotence is well exemplified by Eckhaus, who has written that 'Southern Italy had relatively cheap labour, adequate rail transport, and was at no disadvantage to North Italy with respect to foreign metal and coal supplies.... Why the savings of the southern middle and upper classes did not turn into industrial investment to supply such markets as did exist is a problem for the social historian'.[3] In other words, the historians must explain why the South could not fit the neo-classical model, rather than the economist question whether the model ever should fit.

Emigration and Rural Poverty

The impact of labour migration on areas of labour outflow is complex, and not all its effects are uniformly positive or negative in terms of a cost–benefit type analysis. But the facts show a marked contrast with the self-adjusting equilibrium models of neo-classical theory. As has already been seen, the basic assumption of the Lutz–Eckhaus models is that emigration increases productivity in the area of labour outflow through raising either the land–labour or capital–labour ratio, or both; that this raises income per head over what it otherwise would have been, and promotes a self-sustaining virtuous growth circle of higher regional savings, investment and income. In practice there have been few regions since the war which have been subjected to 'proving' of this theorem, since even in less-developed countries, governments in most cases have undertaken some kind of expenditure in their problem regions to meet either national or international political pressures. But in Italy and the United States where there has been considerable government expenditure in L.D.R.s and also considerable evidence on the impact of labour outflow from them, it emerges that the neo-classical migration models are only in part correct, and, in substance, wrong.

One of the most important limitations in the neo-classical models is their failure to allow for the degree of spatial inelasticity in labour migration. Some of the statements of neo-classical theory are less than wholly clear concerning just how much migration they held to be necessary to begin the virtuous

103

self-sustaining growth circle of fewer people, high factor–labour ratios, and so on. But in both the U.S. and Italian cases it is notable that total out-migration from the South of the two countries since the war has either been equal to or has only slightly exceeded the regions' natural rate of population increase.[4] In other words, the total regional population in the South of Italy and the U.S. South remained effectively the same over the period of migration. In the Italian case this was despite a rate of growth of G.N.P. consistently in excess of 5 per cent per annum, with demand for labour in fast-growing engineering and chemical products sectors located almost exclusively in the North.[a] One trouble for the South – in terms of the neo-classical assumptions – was the unemployment and under-employment in other regions of the country, especially in agriculture in the North-east and Centre. Ackley and Spaventa have shown that more labour from these areas responded to the employment opportunities in the North-western cities (plus Bologna and Florence) than from the less-developed and more distant South despite the fact that income differentials between agricultural and non-agricultural employment in the Centre, North-east and North-west were less than between the South and the North-west.[5]

In the U.S. case there is considerable evidence demonstrating this spatial inelasticity of labour. U.S. Department of Commerce data show that from 1947 to 1967 migration movement (defined as a shift in the place of residence) was relatively constant as a percentage of total population.[6] But the bulk of the movement (five-sixths) was intra-state, and two-thirds of total movement was accounted for by intra-county moves. Only the remaining one-sixth was inter-state migration. This aggregate data is corroborated by a spatial disaggregation of migration patterns undertaken by Hathaway and Perkins, who found that the propensity to migrate was higher the closer the initial proximity to an urban area of 250,000 or more.[7]

Clearly the fact that labour migration from the Italian and U.S. southern regions has not exceeded the natural rate of increase of the regions' population does not mean to say that agricultural population in the regions has not declined in relation to total working population. In both countries inter-sectoral shifts in labour within the main under-developed regions have been substantial. In Italy, working population in agriculture in the

South declined by 950,000 between 1950 and 1967, against a total increase in regional employment in industry and services of 1·4 million. But total out-migration from the region over the same period was nearly double the out-migration from the region's agriculture.[b] Total registered unemployment in the region in 1951 and 1961 was over 11 per cent, and still was nearly 9 per cent in 1967.[c] Moreover total fixed investment in the region through the 1950s was more than covered by net imports, while as late as 1968 net imports still equalled more than three-quarters of regional fixed investment.[d] Therefore a massive 'slack' in the regional labour market was not reduced to frictional unemployment levels over nearly a twenty-year period, while the vast proportion of regional investment growth was covered by imports from other regions. In other words, regional investment growth was not due in any simple sense to a raising of factor ratios through a virtuous savings surplus and investment spiral initiated by emigration.

This is corroborated by a breakdown of the structure and composition of production and employment in the main areas of labour outflow. For instance, simple two-sector models of migration which are spatialised only in the sense that the L.D.R. is assumed to specialise in agriculture and the M.D.R. in industry neglect the fact that because of a variety of factors the L.D.R.'s agriculture may be less efficient than that of the M.D.R. and less capable of responding to potential productivity increases through labour emigration. Such factors can include (1) the structure of land ownership and tenure, which may militate against the efficient transformation of traditional into modern agriculture; (2) the lack of control over wholesale outlets for agricultural products, which may mean that productivity increases are syphoned off by non-producers; (3) differences in the type of agricultural product, and their price and income demand elasticities; (4) a spatial-inelasticity effect within the L.D.R. whereby the most backward agricultural producers may be furthest from the main regional markets and the least able to increase their income by selling unprocessed foods to major urban markets.

All of these factors militate against the accumulation of a surplus in the agriculture of an L.D.R. sufficient to permit it either to purchase capital equipment for modernisation, or invest that surplus in regional industry. In the Italian case agricultural investment has been facilitated through the concentration of development assistance in aids to agriculture.[e] In conjunction with the fact that southern agriculture was less capitalised and less developed than northern agriculture after the Second World War, these development policies contributed to faster rates of growth of investment and net product per worker in the South than the North over the inter-census period 1951–61.[8] On the other hand capital–labour ratios in southern agriculture remained only a third as high as in the North of the country in 1961.[9] Net product per hectare was only slightly more than half that in the more-developed agriculture of the Italian North-west in the same year, and since north-western productivity levels were only in line with those of the other main E.E.C.producers at the time this left the South at a marked disadvantage in relation to its main competitors in the developing common agricultural market of the E.E.C.[10] Also, despite major assistance to investment through the Cassa per il Mezzogiorno, agricultural mechanisation in the South measured in terms of tractors employed rose more slowly than in the North from 1951–61, as did the employment of chemical fertilisers as a proportion of gross saleable product.[11]

Expansion and Stagnation

The importance of disaggregating macro-economic models on the impact of labour emigration emerges very clearly from the pioneering work on southern Italian agriculture undertaken by Rossi-Doria and other economists who have followed his distinction of 'expanding' and 'stagnant' agricultural zones in the region.[12] Rossi-Doria's 'expanding' zones include 'intensive' farming and 'peasant mixed farming'. The intensive farming zone covered the Naples–Salerno plain, the coastal areas of Sicily, the Tyrrhenian coastal strip and southern Apulia. It therefore included not only the urban areas of Naples and Salerno, but also Palermo, Syracuse, Messina, Taranto, Brindisi and Bari – in effect *all* the major urban areas in the South. It benefited not only from the proximity of these markets, but also from the higher than average price rise of its principal products (vines, olives, and fresh and dried fruit).[f] The peasant mixed farming zone which constitutes the second of Rossi-Doria's two expanding agricultural zones in the South, shares the same kind of product breakdown and the same geographical advantages as the intensive farming zone, with the qualification that the holdings tend to be located in the more mountainous areas back from the coast where the scope for mechanisation is limited. The 'stagnant' zones in Rossi-Doria's classification include 'extensive peasant farming' in the mountain areas proper within the South – southern Sardinia, central Sicily, the Ionian coast of Calabria and northwards through Basilicata. This agriculture is again based on three nominally high-value crops (vines, olives and fruit), as well as cereals, but a combination of poor soils and drought in the more extreme mountain areas has meant that irrigated agriculture in this zone has been limited to lower lying areas nearer urban settlements which have lacked industrial employment. As a result population pressure has limited labour-productivity increases, and led to cereals production for local consumption rather than for livestock feed or for export to other areas. The second 'stagnant' zone in Rossi-Doria's classification is that of 'extensive capitalist farming', distributed in pockets on the Ionian coast, northern Campania and northern Apulia round Foggia. For centuries these were high-malarial areas. When malaria was brought under control through massive D.D.T. usage by the Allies after the war, lack of water supply still acted as one of the principal constraints to extensive cultivation of the main crop – cereals – which also suffered from a relative decline in wholesale price value in the post-war period.[g]

Certain qualitative anomalies stand out from this distinction of zones in the South of Italy. For one thing the extensive capitalist farming zone which, according to the neo-classical models should be a classic growth area, is one of the two main stagnant zones. Others emerge from a breakdown of the comparative performance of the two main types of zone made by Censis–Formez for the inter-census period. This revealed that in 1960–1 the expanding zones contributed 55 per cent of the gross saleable agricultural product of the South with an average return per hectare which was no less than 80 per cent higher than for the stagnant zone. In terms of labour productivity the differential was lower but still favoured the expanding zone by 25 per cent. As could be expected, the growth of gross saleable product in the expanding zones was consistently higher than in the stagnant zones throughout the inter-census period.[13] No direct correlation of size and productivity emerges from a comparison of the expanding and stagnant zones, despite the role of land–labour ratios in the neo-classical models. One of the principal reasons in addition to those already outlined has been the structure of tenure on the larger agricultural units. For instance, the *latifundia* – large units of ownership of more than 20 hectares – accounted for more than half the total cultivable area in the South of Italy in 1961, and among these, units of more than 100 hectares accounted for more than 30 per cent of total cultivable area. But the units of tenure are very much smaller, sometimes on non-contiguous pieces of land (*colonia parziaria non-appoderato*), which the tenant can hold only for a limited time period, which clearly discourages capital-intensive improvements. Even worse is the system of *compartecipazione*, by which the tenant shares with the landlord the risk of raising only one crop. If it is a poor one he may make less than he would have done as a day labourer (*braccianti*), while the decision whether or not to re-invest in the land remains with the landowner.[h]

But the most striking conflict between the self-adjusting structural change assumed in neo-classical migration models and the reality of southern Italian agriculture is in the fact that it is precisely the stagnant zones which have constituted the main areas of labour outflow in the South in the post-war period. The provinces which have included a net fall in population in the inter-census period have been concentrated in the stagnant agricultural zones, and in many of these cases the decrease was double or nearly double the natural increase in population.[i] The figures for average family income in agricultural and non-agricultural employment in the South show that income was lower in the stagnant, highest emigration zones, and that agricultural family income was without exception lower than non-agricultural income. In the expanding zones it averaged 57 per cent of non-agricultural employment families in 1959 and in the stagnant zone only 37 per cent of the average for non-agricultural employment. In both zones incomes earned in non-agricultural employment on either a full-or part-time basis by one or more members of the otherwise agriculturally employed family decreased the disparities, but in the stagnant zone the total income

108

of the families concerned averaged only 52 per cent of those wholly engaged in non-agricultural activity, against 80 per cent for those in the expanding zone.[14]

These figures are a far cry from the concept of a surplus for industrial development generated in agriculture through out-migration. In fact the stagnant zones have remained effectively subsistence farming areas, in contrast with the market-economy farming of the expanding zones. But while the stagnant zones have remained backward despite labour outflow, the expanding zones as a whole have grown while experiencing a marked labour inflow from stagnant zones, amounting to a total increase in resident population of 90 per cent over the inter-census period. In practice, the key to the growth of the expanding areas appears to have been the factor neglected in the neo-classical models which stress labour outflow rather than indus-trial demand for agricultural products and labour as the prime cause of improvements in agricultural productivity and income. For the expanding agricultural zones not only included the main urban areas within the South and thus the main markets for agricultural products, but also 90 per cent of the industrial investment which occurred over the 1951–61 period.[15]

Age and Skill Selectivity

Granted the low rate of increase or net decline in resident popu-lation in the main areas within the stagnant agricultural zone, it might be claimed that this zone at least was better off through labour emigration than it otherwise would have been. But in fact there is evidence qualifying this assumption, since the outflow has been highly selective between age groups, and in the areas of heaviest emigration has had a marked effect on the age composi-tion of the work force in the area. As Malfatti and Graziani have commented, 'the massive outflow from the area could be con-sidered positive if it could be controlled, but since it mainly con-cerns the young a pauperisation of the labour force is taking place'.[16] Also the outflow of male labour in many cases has led to a marked increase in the number of woman working in agricul-ture, with an increase as high as 60 per cent over the inter-census period 1951–61 in agriculture in parts of Sicily.[17] One of the principal results of this tendency to senilisation and

109

feminisation of the labour force in agriculture in the areas of highest labour outflow is a delay in the process of automatic raising of land–labour and labour–productivity ratios expected by neo-classical theory. In the case of senilisation this could be expected to amount to a once-and-for-all effect, even if delayed, since with the retirement from active employment of older workers the average age of the labour force could in due course be expected to rise again with a lower absolute employment level. A critical point might be expected to arise at which the enterprising young peasant will realise that it is in his own interest to stay and modernise his own and other families' units rather than emigrate. But in practice there are structural obstacles to such consolidation including the non-contiguous nature of many peasant holdings. In addition, it appears that what Giuseppe Galasso has called a 'psychological laceration' of the young in areas of outflow from agriculture has induced the potential capitalist farmer to join those of the young who have already found employment outside the stagnant area.[18] Certainly there is a marked coincidence between the low productivity increase or fall in productivity in the areas of labour outflow in the stagnant agricultural zone of the South and the migration of the young and middle aged.[19]

In addition to the age selectivity of emigration, there is considerable evidence on skill selectivity. However, it is not by any means uniform, and depends very much on the educational structure of the region of labour outflow, the pattern of the demand for labour in the areas of inflow, and so on. In the Italian case, Umberto Cassinis claimed that the climate of both social and economic under-development in the South promoted the outflow of the better-educated employed in urban areas as well as urban unemployed and under-employed agricultural workers, and that this better-educated category included technicians, university graduates, and professionally qualified persons.[20] Bruno Pagani, writing in 1960, argued that unless the emigration of both the young and the better-qualified from the South was stemmed it would be impossible to prevent its separation as a distinct region within Italy.[21] However, Cassinis does not give a breakdown of the proportion of technical and professionally qualified persons in total out-migration from the South of Italy, and it is not possible to say whether southern emigrants included a higher proportion of such persons than the regional population.

Considerable attention has been paid to the skill selectivity of emigration in the United States. In a pioneer study undertaken before the Second World War Wilson Gee drew attention to the fact that significant numbers of southern emigrants had achieved distinguished careers and made significant contributions outside the region.[22] The possible implication that emigrants were a group with superior skills and abilities was followed up by Van Sickle, who found that emigrants from the South had better than average health and education for the region as a whole.[23] Recent U.S. evidence is less conclusive with regard to the composition of 'skill loss' through emigration from the South. In a recent review of the literature Clarence Danhof identified four general hypotheses on the nature of migration and skill, including (1) that rural out-migrants are selected from the superior elements in the parent population; (2) that rural out-migrants constitute inferior elements; (3) that rural out-migrants include extremes of both inferior and superior elements; and (4) that rural out-migrants are a random selection of the parent population. He concluded that there was some evidence for each of the hypotheses, depending on the particular circumstances, and cited the conclusion of Thomas that it is probable that 'selection does operate positively, negatively and randomly, at different times, depending on a variety of factors that have not been adequately investigated'.[24]

Immigration and Urban Congestion

It is clear that modern urban problems are not caused exclusively by immigration. For one thing, internal scale economies in production can congest sites without notable expansion of labour. This will occur if the substitution of capital for labour has reached a point where output can be expanded without job expansion, which now is increasingly a feature of some sections of manufacturing industry. None the less, as well appreciated by Marx in analysing the urban problems of nineteenth-century England, the basis of urbanisation has been demand in non-agricultural employment for agricultural labour, or the unemployed and under-employed from other areas of the economy.

111

This can give rise to social and congestion costs after immigration has fallen or stopped.

Such costs will aggravate urban problems when the social-infrastructure needs of immigrant labour are not fully paid for by those firms which employ the immigrants. In practice firms will pay some of the costs of providing social infrastructure to the extent that they are reflected in higher local taxation. But the precise incidence of costs will depend on the relative share of firms and individuals in the local taxation system. In some cases firms are not obliged to contribute to local taxes and therefore avoid the costs of social overhead capital (S.O.C.).[j] Besides, while local authorities may be responsible for such S.O.C. facilities as transport, sewage, and power supply, they may not be responsible for housing or health facilities for immigrants, which the immigrants may have to meet from their earnings. In addition, from the viewpoint of interregional resource use, there is considerable evidence that the costs of providing S.O.C. facilities increase substantially with urban size. In other words, the S.O.C. costs for an immigrant and his dependents in a large urban area of labour inflow can be higher than in smaller urban areas in the region from which they have migrated.

The international evidence on this increase in S.O.C. costs with increasing urban size is impressive. In the early 1950s Gravier broke ground in this approach with a study indicating that annual public expenditure per inhabitant in Paris in 1949 had amounted to 25,000 francs, against only 8500 francs for Marseilles, 8000 francs for Bordeaux, and 4000 to 7000 francs for lesser urban centres.[25] In Italy a research project undertaken by SVIMEZ in 1957 estimated the average *per capita* cost of provision of public services and public utilities for three categories of urban size.[26] The standard of services and utilities provided was for new facilities, which thereby 'deflated' any quality differences in infrastructure in small and large urban areas. As is shown in Table 1(*a*) (p.277), the *per capita* costs of providing public services for communities of from 30,000 to 200,000 inhabitants was 40 per cent higher than for communities of less than 30,000 persons. For communities of over 200,000 persons its cost per head was almost double that for the 30,000 to 200,000 category, and nearly three times that for the less than 30,000 category. In the case of public utilities, the cost per person more than doubled between the first two categories, and rose again by about three-fifths for the third category.

A follow-up study undertaken by SVIMEZ in 1967 undertook a greater breakdown of both the size of urban area and the type of S.O.C. facility.[27] As is shown in Table 1(*b*), this distinguished the cost of provision of parks and open spaces, local government or communal offices, police services, urban cleansing, shopping facilities and urban wholesale markets. The *per capita* cost of these services was lowest for communities of 5000 persons, and only marginally higher (13,500 lire against 12,700 lire) for those with up to 20,000 inhabitants. But it more than doubled with the increase in urban size from 20,000 to 50,000 inhabitants, and doubled again with the increase from 50,000 to over 600,000 inhabitants. The lower cost figures for communities of less than 20,000 persons need qualification inasmuch as they make no provision for new shopping facilities and the provision of wholesale market premises. But even including such facilities gives a 'least cost' urban size in terms of S.O.C. provision of from 20,000 to 50,000 persons, or the range including the 30,000 least S.O.C. cost urban size according to the earlier SVIMEZ study.

A more detailed breakdown of S.O.C. costs by type of service was made in another Italian study published in 1963 by TEKNE, which considered the same categories of urban size as the 1967 SVIMEZ study.[28] The services included libraries, nurseries, primary and secondary schools, playgrounds for various age groups of children, clinics, general and specialised hospitals, psychiatric hospitals, fire, police, postal and telegraph services, law courts, cemeteries, and prisons. In contrast with the two SVIMEZ studies, as is shown in Table 2 (p.279), it was concluded that the costs of provision of the services concerned did *not* increase in communities with more than 50,000 persons, and were higher the smaller the size of urban unit, with costs of 300,000 lire per inhabitant for communities of up to 5000 persons, against costs of 220,000 lire for communities of 50,000 persons and more. However, the TEKNE study was based on the simple application of the cost of providing identical facilities to different urban size categories without consideration of congestion costs in larger areas from higher site and labour costs. It is a purely technical study in the sense of pointing out the unit cost of a service or facility operating at maximum capacity. The only services needing more than 30,000 persons for maximum utilisation were general hospitals (80,000), specialised hospitals (120,000) and psychiatric hospitals (160,000).[k] The rise in the cost of land in the second largest Italian city, and the first in order of magnitude of labour inflow (Milan) is given in Fig. 8, which shows the increase in cost in the city centre, the central urban area, the peripheral urban area and the suburbs from 1951 to 1963. As could be expected, the cost of land in the city centre was initially higher than in the more peripheral areas, and rose faster over the period as a whole than that in suburban areas, with a unit cost some four times that of the suburban areas in 1963.[29]

Evidence on average *per capita* expenditures of municipal governments in the Unites States is available from U.S. Bureau of the Census data reproduced in Table 3. This is a straightforward tabulation of actual costs in relation to urban size, and therefore does not take any account of qualitative differences between the services provided in the different urban areas. Clearly those available in a community of less than 2500 persons and those in a community of more than a million cannot be strictly compared. None the less, it is of interest that the *per capita* expenditure of communities of not more than 100,000 persons were only half those of communities of more than a million.[30] Further U.S. data which disaggregates *per capita* expenditure by type of service as well as by city size is available for Ohio, Texas and New Jersey.[31] The data reveals certain systematic relationships between size and cost, although relationships which are significant for some cities within the States concerned are not necessarily applicable to all three States. But, most notably, total current expenditure in all three States was some 50 per cent higher for communities of more than 250,000 people than for those of less than that number. In a study of possible economies of scale in the provision of S.O.C. in urban areas in the United States, Hirsch found evidence of such economies only in the cases of water supply and sewage, which accounted for only a minor proportion of total S.O.C. expenditures. He concluded that communities in the 50,000 to 100,000 range would be the most efficient in terms of least-cost S.O.C. provision.[32]

Up to a point, the increase in the *per capita* cost of S.O.C.

provision with increasing urban size can be employed as an index of the congestion costs of large urban areas. Up to a point only because the real resource cost of a given expansion of a particular urban area will depend on a variety of additional factors, possibly including what has been called the 'threshold' concept in urban growth.[33] This concept is based on the assumption that as an urban area expands it comes up against barriers due to geography, existing land use, and existing S.O.C. networks (sewage, transport systems, and so on) which represent thresholds of future development. These thresholds can normally be surmounted, but sometimes only at considerable capital cost. For instance, extending an urban surface or underground railway system may entail either a major land-clearance programme, or substantial extensions to the central junction and station systems, or both. The traffic congestion of a downtown area may necessitate the construction of an entirely new urban-motorway system if the road transport network of the suburban area is to be extended to link new suburban housing. A mountain-locked port such as Genoa may be incapable of continuous inland expansion without substantial transport engineering projects of considerable cost.[34] By contrast, urban areas such as Paris and Milan may be capable of indefinite outwards expansion on level agricultural land subject only to the constraints of additional construction costs on peripheral land which is relatively cheaper than that in the urban centre, and congestion costs in terms of traffic and travel delay in the downtown area. Urban planning for the metropolitan area as a whole may reduce some of these downtown congestion costs to the extent that service facilities such as some shopping services, deposit banks etc. are decentralised to suburban areas.[35]

In other words, both public policy and the land-use structure of urban areas will influence the rate at which S.O.C. costs rise with increased urban size. The historical pattern of urban expansion also is important in that a major city such as Paris which has been 'rationalised' at some date in the past in such a way as to provide wide boulevards, originally intended to facilitate the suppression of insurgents, may thereby provide a transport network capable of sustaining several decades of expansion of motor transport without the congestion costs which would occur for a medieval or renaissance city in Italy whose downtown road system was initially suited to feet rather than wheels. By contrast, a road system which may have appeared thoroughly rational when introduced, such as the grid or 'block' system in the United States, both may prove unsuited to a high volume of traffic flow, and raise net S.O.C. costs in the long run if new, high-density buildings are raised in excess of the capacity of existing services and utilities to supply them from existing S.O.C.[l] In addition, the rate of expansion of the particular urban area, as well as constraints on ease of expansion from geography or existing physical structures, is important in determining what S.O.C. can be provided at what cost.[m] Besides, S.O.C. costs alone cannot be taken as indicators of optimal cut-off points for urban size without consideration of other factors, such as increased social facilities for minority groups and tastes in major urban areas.[36] The bright lights of downtown areas may compensate some inhabitants for depressed living conditions in their immediate vicinity – and especially the young – quite apart from the opera-goers or foreign-film enthusiasts who may enjoy both the facilities themselves and the amenities of suburban or country house living. On the other hand, they may not, particularly if they are not opera lovers or do not enjoy foreign films. In this sense the wider social facilities of large urban areas cannot easily be included in a quantified cost–benefit analysis. Yet if it is to be at all comprehensive it must distinguish social classes and take into account which benefits for whom over what costs.

Despite the difficulties of taking such factors into account certain conclusions can be reached regarding congestion costs. In terms of least-cost S.O.C. provision, the evidence available from both the SVIMEZ 1957 study and from Hirsch indicates that communities from 30,000 to 100,000 persons are the most efficient. Projecting the TEKNE 'unit efficiency' cost range on to the SVIMEZ actual cost figures gives an 'optimal' urban size in S.O.C. .cost terms of just under 150,000 persons. In Fig. 9 this is represented by the intersection of the SVIMEZ actual costs and the TEKNE unit efficiency curves. In other words the figure indicates that point at which there are no net gains in terms of S.O.C. utilisation per unit for even specialist services such as psychiatric hospitals, which were not taken into account in the more basic S.O.C. facilities included in the SVIMEZ estimates. The intersection only gives an indication. It does not represent a universal optimum for 'cut off' in urban policy. In other words, it does not provide a basis for the depopulation of urban areas already well in excess of this size, even if it may give one parameter for restraining the continued or unlimited expansion of lesser areas over such a size. Also, it does not take account of the minority group facilities which may only be available in considerably larger urban areas, even if these are nominally of a private rather than social overhead kind. None the less, even allowing for an error margin of 100 per cent would indicate that communities of the 250,000–350,000 population mark entail S.O.C. congestion costs which would not arise in communities of only 150,000 persons, while the SVIMEZ and Hirsch figures also indicate that very much smaller population units can include essential S.O.C. facilities at a quarter to a third of the quarter million plus urban level.

The relevance of these S.O.C. cost differentials with different categories of urban size is very considerable in analysing both the impact on areas of labour inflow of interregional and interurban migration, and also the feasibility of a policy of dispersion of industry within an L.D.R.[n] In the present context of the impact of migration on inflow areas, for instance, it shows that there will be net costs in S.O.C. provision from the cumulative expansion through immigration of urban areas in the 250,000 plus population range. These social-expenditure costs will be reinforced by private costs to immigrants to the extent that the rate of construction of new housing is lower than the rate of net immigration into the area. The result will tend to be a sufficient pressure on accommodation for sub-standard housing to be let successfully at inflationary costs. There is considerable evidence of such trends in the U.S. case, where middle-class indigenous population has vacated downtown housing for suburban accommodation, and where immigrants have tended to replace them in downtown housing areas. The result of pressure on these areas has been an urban slum syndrome of a kind which does not enter into the neo-classical models of urban rent structure. As Robert Weaver has commented, 'ironically, illegal overcrowding of slum properties makes them more valuable in terms of capitalised income'. In effect, while *per capita* rent may be lower in the immigrant slum areas, the square foot rental is likely to be higher. As a result, the free working of the market mechanism tends to aggravate the urban core slum problem. It does not pay the owners to replace outdated structures whose capital costs may already have been amortised several times. As Weaver states, 'it would be convenient if we could rely on the textbook theory that private capital automatically flows where it is needed. The fact is that capital does not rush in and clear up slums; it rushes away from them, despite the heavy loss which they impose on community developments.'[37]

In the U.S. case the racial problem certainly has aggravated the already considerable problem of urban assimilation of migrants. Black migrants tend to concentrate in areas of declining employment opportunities in the central core of cities with populations already massively in excess of the 250,000–350,000 population level. But apart from the racial problem, it can be observed that migration in fact transfers the agricultural underemployed to urban unemployment in the main northern areas of labour inflow. As Kain and Persky have expressed it, 'the link between the rural negro core and the large northern metropolis is a very strong one'.[38] In fact the link between rural migrants to the core areas of the northern cities, and the migration of 'indigenous' northern workers to the unchecked sprawl of suburban areas across the north-eastern seaboard and Great Lakes appears as strong.[o] Yet it is precisely this link which appears to be neglected in most of the think-tank policies intended to cope with the urban crisis in the United States to date. Most of the policy analyses undertaken are made in a limited urban context, and amount to re-engineering the internal structure of the cities without consideration of limitations on employment opportunities through constrained space for plant expansion, and the income prospects of the immigrants. The result is purely cosmetic in the sense that small-scale green areas are introduced which are insufficient to meet the recreation needs of the local inhabitants, and in a short period re-emerge as the grey areas as which they had begun.[p] Well-intentioned authorities replace the slums with new housing which the previous slum occupants cannot afford, and therefore reduce the total volume of housing available for the lower-income immigrants. Comprehensive development programmes tend to be more comprehensive in the further reduction of low-income housing, simply displacing underprivileged immigrant groups from one area to another in the

118

urban core. There is relatively little awareness that a main cause of the urban crisis in the areas of labour inflow in the United States is the rural crisis in the areas of labour outflow.[39]

Without doubt the black immigrant problem in the United States is exceptional, and may not set the pattern for migration and urban problems in Western Europe. As is shown later in this chapter, there are significant differences as well as similarities in the nature of the migration process in Western Europe and the United States. At the level of the impact of labour inflow on urban structure, it is notable so far that in Western European cities such as Paris, the 'downtown' area has retained its prestige and high-income housing, with immigrant workers located either in poorer class suburban (or sub-central area) housing, or in shanty-town 'bidonvilles' in open spaces outside the main housing areas.[40] However, there also are similarities in the impact of labour inflow on the main Western European urban areas and those in the United States, and in particular the tendency for labour to migrate mainly to those cities which already are well in excess of the 250,000–350,000 population level at which S.O.C. diseconomies notably arise. As is shown in Table 4, ten Italian cities in 1961 had populations in excess of a third of a million. Among them, net immigration accounted for four-fifths or more of the increase in resident population from 1951–61 in Turin, Genoa, Milan, Bologna and Florence.[q] A fall in immigration to these cities occurred during the period following the mid-1960s recession in Italy, but net immigration still accounted for more than half of the resident population increase in Turin, Genoa, Bologna, Florence and Rome from 1961–9.

Turin registered the highest rate of increase of immigrant population from 1951–69, and has been one of the cities most clearly showing a trend towards U.S.-type congestion and urban-core adaptation problems. The city more than doubled its population over the period, with 92 per cent of its resident population growth from 1951–61 caused by immigration, and 61 per cent from 1961–9. Apart from the million plus population of the city itself, its surrounding hinterland includes some two million persons, directly linked to the city by employment or services, living in fifty-two communes. By the standards of the north-eastern seaboard of the United States this is still a small urban area, but the rate of increase of population has imposed

119

considerable strain on the social infrastructure of the city. As Giacomo Ghirardo has commented.

> Turin is exploding under the pressure of immigration from the South made possible through employment opportunities in an uncontrolled industrial growth. There are insufficient houses, roads, schools, hospitals, means of public transport, recreation areas. The mass of immigrant workers live in degrading conditions in the ghetto of the historical centre of the city and in the dormitory towns of the surrounding area.

He cites both local administration and local unions in claiming that Turin no longer is capable of sustaining further immigration because it already risks 'explosion' through pressure from past immigration.[41]

The 'ghetto' problem (italianised as *ghettizzazione*) is not only found in Turin. Calamida, Mori and Schiaffonati have drawn attention to the same widespread problem in the suburban areas of Milan, whose 'elephantine' expansion through immigration has subjected small communes within the immediate vicinity of the city to a s strain which they cannot properly support.[42] Granted the 'challenge and response' mechanism hypothesised in some of the more sophisticated neo-classical models of urban expansion,[43] it is interesting that these authors write of a chain-reaction process in Milanese growth which has led to a total un-balance between existing social infrastructure and the adaptive capacity of the communes concerned. As they say, this type of development 'combines the disadvantages of rural and urban life without permitting the advantages of either'.[44] As the Milan Committee for the Co-ordination of Services and Public Works has expressed it; 'these areas lack infrastructure, and public and social services and equipment'.[45] The result, as Umberto Melotti has said, is an increased strain on the infrastructure of 'down-town' Milan, which alone can provide them. From an environ-mental viewpoint, the periphery is 'shapeless, squalid and spoiled'.[46]

Without doubt one of the main problems for these areas of labour inflow in the North of Italy is the extent to which the pro-vision of additional social infrastructure is unplanned. The speculative building boom, which has characterised Italian construction since the war, and resulted in construction registering the fastest growth of value-added of any industrial sector, has not been accompanied by long-term planning on the part of the public authorities in the urban areas concerned. But in itself this indicates the difficulties of adaptation of a decision-making structure to a labour inflow which is largely uncontrolled. The urban authorities are not in a position to know with certainty what demands will be made for which services in particular areas. They could inform themselves on a current basis by obliging firms to inform them of additions to their labour force from immigration, the anticipated housing needs of the immigrants and their families, and so on. But such information alone would serve little purpose if the authorities are not in a financial position to meet the cost of providing the S.O.C. necessary to ensure comparable social services and facilities for the whole community. And for whatever reason – limited tax base, inflationary construction costs, or the political costs from lost support from 'indigenous' voters – S.O.C. expenditure clearly has lagged behind need.

The Migration Process

The migration process observable in capitalist economies such as the United States or Italy contrasts sharply with the harmonious self-balance assumptions of neo-classical theory. The facts simply do not support a picture in which migrants optimise their potential welfare by moving from regions where jobs or pay are low to high-pay and high-job regions. For one thing migrants lack the 'perfect information' assumed in such a model of inter-regional migration. For another they frequently lack the means to move large distances between regions even if they want to. Much migration is rational in the sense that the reasons to move exceed the reasons for not moving. But this rationality in many cases is not strictly economic. It includes the desperate out-migration of the young from regions which offer them no sure prospect of jobs and self-improvement even in the very long run; the escape from social exploitation by a dominant local class, and in the case of the U.S. Deep South, the escape from racial discrimination to the racial ghettoes of the northern big cities. Where economic gains are maximised in the U.S. federal

121

system, they frequently are the gains from higher unemployment benefits in immigrant cities than the benefits available in outflow areas. The choice is between different compensations for not being employed, not between a job and no job.

Much emigration is involuntary or quasi-voluntary. In many cases the young are shoe-horned from the home by temporary jobs and incomes which increase their local mobility and accustom them to independent life styles in local urban centres. Certainly U.S. and Italian evidence shows that migration occurs mainly by stages, with migrants from agriculture moving in the first instance to towns in their own regions, rather than to other regions. This has already been indicated by figures cited on the pattern of intra-state and inter-state migration in the United States and is corroborated by the work of Kain and Persky, who found that 'there is evidence that negroes moving North move in stages: first to a southern city, then a northern one'.[47] A similar staging process appears in the migration pattern in the South of Italy, where out-migrants from agriculture have stayed in the first instance in provincial capitals before moving out of the region. However, in commenting on this Italian evidence, Cafiero has drawn attention to the fact that those urban areas in the South which experienced the greatest increase in resident population through in-migration from agriculture between 1951 and 1961 were not necessarily areas of high growth of industrial or service employment, and in some cases were notably excluded from industrialisation. He suggested that in many cases the first 'break with the land' was caused by the local provision of temporary non-farm employment through public-works programmes in agricultural areas, particularly those of the Cassa per il Mezzogiorno. When this employment moved out of the area with the completion of a road, an irrigation system or some other construction project, some of the previous work force would move to the nearest sizeable town rather than follow it out of the home area, and would take lower paid work in services or other jobs, or remain unemployed. It would only be over a longer period in which expectations of improved income and employment had been frustrated that they would then move out of the region to the industrialised North, perhaps through a further staging post of a larger urban centre in the South.[r] In other words, the first move from the land was in many cases to a limbo

122

of local urban under-employment or unemployment, from which the further move out of the region or abroad could be made as much in desperation as h in hope of better things to come.[48]

In the U.S. case out-migration from the South clearly is very much influenced by racial factors, just as the pattern of urban immigration in the North is partly influenced by the higher welfare and public-relief services which the larger U.S. cities provide. On the other hand, it has been argued by Lindley that 'it has been the push of poor rural conditions rather than the pull of urban economic opportunities' which has been the main motive factor in northern urbanisation. The basic evidence is indirect – the fact that the black migrant moves to the inner core of the urban-inflow areas where employment in general is declining at the same time that population increases as a result of higher birth rates among immigrants.[49] But it certainly is clear that much of the white migration which occurs from the Appalachian states as well as black migration from the South is 'irrational' by the standards of neo-classical migration models. In a recent survey of the available literature Bishop concluded that 'few would contend that decisions concerning migration are made in a well considered rational manner. On the contrary, there is increasing evidence that most decisions to migrate are based on very incomplete information.'[50] Marsh found that the planning period for moves was under a month in a third of reported moves; that alternatives were not considered in two-thirds of all cases, and that in over half the cases heads of families who relocated consulted only one source of job information.[51] In the mid-1950s Smith found that the vast majority of migrants do not have a definite job offer at the time of migration, and that most have little or no information on living conditions in the areas to which they migrate.[52] In both the U.S. and Italian cases the presence of relatives or other social links in the areas of labour inflow tended to explain the movement of labour to particular urban areas.[53]

Evidence on the costs to migrants in cash outlay from migration and on earnings in new employment in the area of immigration qualifies the private cost–benefit return assumptions made either implicitly or explicitly by neo-classical migration models. Sjaastad claimed that spatial differences in earnings would lead

123

people in lower-paid employment in less-developed areas to invest in their migration to the higher-paid employment areas, and that this would tend to equalise differences in interregional earnings.[54] But in the United States Hathaway and Perkins found from a one per cent sample of total farm employment through 1957–60 that a high proportion of those who changed occupations (from farm to non-farm) did not improve their income in the short run by changing, and that more than 40 per cent of those leaving farming in one year had lower incomes in their non-farm occupations the following year. The mean gain in earnings averaged for the three years was less than $200 per person. As they expressed it. 'farm–nonfarm occupational mobility does not seem to close the income gap between the poor and those better off – indeed it may widen it.'[55] The insignificance of the mean gain is emphasised if the costs of moving are taken into account. In a pilot study of mobility in North Carolina, Johnson found that costs of movement plus the costs of forgone earnings and the costs of search for new employment were close to $300 per person for moves of only a hundred miles.[56] The force of the loss through migration in the U.S. case is indicated by gross rather than net migration movement from agriculture. In a sample analysis from social security data for 1956–7, Hathaway and Perkins found that the change in the farm labour force was —4·9 per cent, while the migration from farming was 15·6 per cent. In other words the backflow of emigrants to agriculture was 10·7 per cent or more than two-thirds of the outflow. If the migrant worker, under neo-classical assumptions, is rational in leaving the L.D.R., at least two in three appear rational in returning to it. In practice, of course, the hopes which prompted out-migration from one part of the economy are dashed by despair in another.[57]

NOTES

[a] Cf. further, Chapter 6.
[b] Cf. further, Chapter 6.
[c] Cf. Table 5, p.281. Registered unemployment in the North fell from 9 per cent

to 4 per cent from 1951–67. But a more marked indication of the employment problems in the South can be secured from active population (32 per cent in 1967 against 39 per cent in the North) and temporary employment as a proportion of the total labour force (30 per cent in the South in 1967 against only 7 per cent in the North). Cf. Paolo Sylos-Labini, Untitled Contribution to *Nord-Sud: I nuovi Termini di un Problema Nazionale*, ed. Club Turati (1970) p.345.

[d] Cf. Table 5, p.281.

[e] Over the 1950–65 period the main development agency for the South (Cassa per il Mezzogiorno) gave a marked priority to agricultural aids. Cf. Chapter 6.

[f] The wholesale price index for agricultural products in Italy rose by 11 per cent from 1953–64; that for olive oil rose by 37 per cent; fresh and dried fruit by 34 per cent and wine by 22 per cent.

[g] The wholesale price index for cereals in Italy fell by 4 per cent from 1953 to 1964.

[h] *Colonia parziaria non-appoderato* was estimated to account for 26 per cent of cultivated land in Sicily and 10 per cent of that in mainland southern Italy in 1961. Disaggregated data on *compartecipazione* is difficult to secure, but both it and day labour accounted for the type of contract in more than a third of the total cultivated area in the South in 1961. Cf. *Informazioni SVIMEZ*, 50–2 (1963).

[i] These included all the provinces of the Abruzzi and Molise region, plus the provinces of Avellino, Benevento, Foggia, Potenza, all provinces in Calabria, and the Sicilian provinces of Agrigento, Caltanisetta and Enna.

[j] For example, when offered local tax 'holidays' as an incentive to invest in less-developed countries.

[k] Cf. Table 2 (p.279) first column.

[l] Referring to the fast re-building to increasingly higher levels in U.S. cities Vernon has commented: 'the general tendency was to add to the ossification of the structure: to surface the public streets more permanently and to cram their sub-surface with more and more cables, mains and transit conveyances. Each re-building therefore tended to make the next one a little more difficult than the last.' Raymond Vernon, 'The Changing Economic Function of the Central City', in *Urban Renewal: the Record and the Controversy*, ed. James Wilson (Massachusetts Institute of Technology Press, 1966) p. 4.

[m] These factors contribute to explaining why some cities in the previously cited Ohio, Texas and New Jersey evidence have lower *per capita* social expenditure than others which have smaller populations.

[n] For the relevance to industrial dispersion cf. Chapter 7.

[o] The Washington–Boston suburban belt concept was dramatised by Jean Gottman in *Megalopolis: the Urbanised Northeastern Seaboard of the United States* (Massachusetts Institute of Technology Press, 1961) although largely in isolation from the question of South to North labour migration. The decline of inner urban population also, of course, reflects the need for space to exploit internal scale economies, for which manufacturing industry also has tended to find white labour in the suburbs. For the extent of inner urban decline of population in the United States see Fig. 12, p.298.

[p] In 1970 the New York City authorities were applying literally cosmetic policies in downtown slum areas, commissioning modern art external murals for buildings in the area.

q As the figures in Table 4, p.280, indicate, Genoa registered a net decline in 'indigenous' (non-immigrant) population from 1951–61. It is notable that Milan–Genoa–Turin were not the only centres attracting immigrants in either period, and that the impact on Bologna and Florence was strong, suggesting that the growth area in the North amounted less to the golden triangle, as it is generally known, than to a pentagon.

r Cafiero distinguishes a variety of additional factors initially pulling labour off the land into local urban areas, including the movement of families seeking to invest their small savings in tertiary rather than secondary activities in the local towns; the movement of women finding domestic employment, and the movement of families following men who have found work as porters, ushers, waiters as well as in other service trades. Cf. Salvatore Cafiero, *Le Migrazioni Meridionale*, SVIMEZ (1964), pp.13–20.

CHAPTER 5

UNEQUAL COMPETITION AND REGIONAL IMBALANCE

It has been seen that neo-classical location theory makes major assumptions about the nature of competition which affect the outcome of its self-balance models. For the most part such theory is in a perfect or pure competition framework which assumes away most of the structural imbalance which results from capitalist competition itself. In spatial terms such perfectly competitive firms behave with the discipline of a chorus line. They may advance, retreat or even disperse, but always under controlled conditions in which none threatens the survival or dominates the behaviour of others. Like the chorus they may look beautiful, but their behaviour is unreal and untypical of firms under modern competitive conditions. This is much more in line with the combination of leap-frogging, throat-cutting and devil-take-the-hindmost which characterises Marx's analysis of concentration. There is a need to extend the link between structural and spatial concentration as pioneered by Marx and developed in the post-war period by François Perroux, thereby demonstrating the relation between regional imbalance and the inequalities of modern capitalist competition.

The Banality of Competition for Space

In fact there were some noteworthy exceptions to such perfect competition analysis of the location of the firm in the inter-war period which paralleled the attempts of Joan Robinson and Edward Chamberlin to break new ground in the area of imperfect or monopolistic competition.[1] For instance, Otto Engländer criticised the general equilibrium analysis of the location of firms and maintained that any theory of competition in space should generalise from empirical data. The process should be primarily inductive rather than one of deducing general principles from general equilibrium assumptions. He claimed that entrepreneurs choose sites by considering alternative supply prices in different localities, plus the transport costs of delivery to markets. But he also stressed that, once they had chosen a site, their activity in turn influenced the structure and price of inputs and outputs in other firms and markets. These could not be generalised in any perfect competition, general equilibrium framework.[2]

Similarly, Tord Palandar criticised a general equilibrium approach and focused attention on the disequilibria caused by the location of a firm. He considered not only the changes in production and consumption patterns which a new firm's location would promote, but also the institutional changes which it would induce. He was scathingly critical of the assumption of perfect labour and capital mobility in general equilibrium models, and pointed out that such an assumption effectively eliminated real space from the analysis.[3] However, neither Engländer nor Palandar registered much impact on the development of location analysis in Europe or the United States between the First and Second World Wars. Their contributions reinforced the disequilibrium analysis which emerged from the later, synthetic part of Weber's pioneering work. But, as already stressed in Chapter 1, the neo-Weberians chose to neglect this part of Weber, and retreated from reality into the hexagon fantasies of Lösch.

The most influential contribution to inter-war location theory which worked from an imperfect or monopolistic competition framework was an article by Harold Hotelling published in 1926.[4] Hotelling drew attention to Sraffa's observation that any market commonly is divided into areas in each of which one seller is in a quasi-monopolistic situation.[5] He also criticised spatial equilibrium theory for its failure to take account of 'the destabilizing effect of masses of consumers placed so near as to have a natural preference for one seller or another, even when the firms concerned sold at different prices'. As he expressed it, 'of all the purchasers of a commodity, some buy from one seller, some from another, in spite of moderate differences in price'. Many customers will be influenced by non-price factors in their attachment to a particular firm. They will buy from one seller rather than another 'because he is a relative, a fellow Elk, or a Baptist'.

This certainly introduced a welcome degree of realism into the area of 'spatial competition'. But in practice Hotelling's advance was limited by the same factors which later neutralised Isard's alleged introduction of scale economies into spatial analysis, and was to compromise the Robinson and Chamberlin contributions to imperfect or monopolistic competition. Basically, all their progress in qualifying perfect competition stayed in a framework of equilibrium theory. They allowed for modifications of perfectly competitive equilibrium, but only within a general theory which was itself determined by equilibrium or self-balance assumptions. Unlike Marx, or the later analysis of Weber, they failed to appreciate the extent to which scale economies promoted a monopoly trend which would break up equilibrium theory itself, and result in both inter-firm and interregional imbalance.[a] The result in Hotelling's case became an artificial model of competition in space which amounted to competition *for* space. In this sense it has some application for the retailing firms which he considers, but little to none under modern competitive conditions for spatial competition between industrial firms for regional and national markets.

The limits of Hotelling's argument are not simply related to the size of the area in which firms compete, or the restriction of his case to local market areas rather than regions. They arise from his definition of monopoly or quasi-monopoly. In practice he reduced the analysis to duopoly, or competition between two sellers who operate, according to his own terminology, in a quasi-monopolistic sense. But in the context of his analysis, these firms in fact locate like the perfectly competitive firms of general equilibrium theory. Also, to develop a model in which firms finally locate at the centre of a given market area, Hotelling employs perfectly competitive assumptions such as (1) constant transport costs, (2) zero production costs, (3) zero costs for the seller's changed location, and (4) homogeneous products. He also has to drop his admission that consumers buy partly for non-price or non-cost reasons, and assume instead that no buyer has a preference for either seller except on the grounds of price plus transport costs (which the buyer is assumed to pay). These are only his explicit qualifications of imperfect or quasi-monopolistic competition. The implicit premises which also are essential for his outcome of stable location at the market centre include consumers with equal incomes and constant tastes and preferences over time.

As with most of the rest of neo-classical equilibrium theory, Hotelling's argument is not wrong in terms of his premises, but the premises themselves are incorrect. This is not simply a matter of playing by normal *ceteris paribus* rules, which have their function in permitting the isolation of some interrelationships within a general system. It is the more important matter of defining monopolistic competition in such a way that the essential features of monopoly are abolished. This is why the exposition is essentially banal, and why the analysis contributes little or nothing to our understanding of the real spatial implications of monopoly or oligopoly. As with central-place theory, there is a spurious reality in Hotelling's argument inasmuch as the two firms competing for his homogeneous market area ultimately decide to locate at the centre of the market rather than to place themselves in a more dispersed pattern which would minimise travel or transport costs for consumers. But it is the wrong explanation for a plausible general phenomenon. To get back on the right track, the underlying equilibrium theory has to be reversed in the first place.

The Dynamics of Unequal Competition

It has already been stressed that any escape from the straitjacket of neo-classical self-balance theory means more than loosening a few restraints through the introduction of product differentiation or quasi-monopoly solutions. The key neglect in this theory has been the failure to face the real implications of scale economies. The scale economies admitted by Marx, Myrdal and Perroux are not simply micro-economic phenomena which can be neglected or relaxed in playing with regional multipliers. They work through firms themselves to the level of the industry, the region, and the national and multi-national economy. They involve not only the production scale economies on which most micro-economic textbooks concentrate, but also economies from large-scale operations in distribution, access to favourable finance, higher rates of self-finance, greater application of technical progress in actual innovation, gains from a dominant hold over consumers and suppliers, increased bargaining position with national governments on State aid and location, and so on.

The trend to monopoly in the domestic markets of mature

capitalist economies such as Britain is now so marked that it might well be thought academic in the pejorative sense to consider whether scale economies bring cumulative gains to leading firms. But in terms of substituting an extended imbalance theory which will help replace the fantasy of self-balance mechanisms, it is important to expose the wrong-thinking and limited assumptions in much of the modern theory of the capitalist firm. A major contribution has been made in this area by Paolo Sylos-Labini, who has helped put the theory of oligopoly or domination of markets by a few leading firms at the heart of capitalist competition.[6] Interestingly enough in terms of regional theory, he traces the origins of this process to the reduction of local or regional barriers to trade through reduced transport costs. However, he emphasises that this penetration of hitherto 'protected' local markets did not promote an equilibriated distribution of trade and factors of production but 'at first gradually, and from a certain point on precipitately, more enduring monopolistic and oligopolistic positions'. This process benefited powerful social minorities who secured legal and political concessions to fortify their new economic hold. He describes this hold in terms which amount to an intra-sectoral counterpart of both Myrdal's spread and backwash effects: 'the modern process of concentration of firms pushes out of the market such small producers as make goods which have to compete with those made by the big firms, but the process is accompanied also by a mushrooming of small and satellite enterprises both in production and trade.'[7]

According to Sylos-Labini, the greater market share and financial base of larger firms allows them to derive greater advantage than smaller firms both from more extensive use of economies of scale at any given level of technology, and from a higher capacity to innovate. Only large-scale firms with wide markets will be able to take full advantage not only from mass production methods on the shop floor, but also from economies of scale in distribution.[b] Size brings further benefits in the form of monopsonistic or oligopsonistic bargaining power for factor inputs, and also the basis from which to effect vertical integration.[8] The advantage of size in permitting greater innovation works through both greater financial resources and easier access to technical progress. Citing Schumpeter, Sylos-Labini points out

131

that most innovations, and certainly major ones, involve the construction of new plant and equipment: 'If the new plant or equipment is within the reach of all firms, whatever their size, the cost reduction becomes general in a relatively short time. But this is not so if only the largest firms can afford the new plant.' In addition, only the large firms will be able to afford independent R and D establishments, and be likely to have the management structure capable of ensuring that technical progress is translated into innovation. This will be to their own immediate advantage given by patents. Such protection in fact may not last beyond a relatively short time period, as other large firms try to adopt similar methods and generally succeed, unless there are serious technical problems, or the innovation is altogether revolutionary. However, 'since success comes only after a certain interval, the initiators of the new production method reap extraordinary profits for some time'.[9]

Sylos-Labini points out that because they enjoy these cost advantages, various alternative tactics are available to the larger firms within a given sector which give them a degree of market control quite independent from the product-differentiation factors considered by imperfect competition theory. They are in a position either to prevent entry into their market, or even to eliminate competitors from it. To prevent the entry of smaller firms with more limited financial resources, the oligopolistic leaders within that sector can temporarily reduce prices below the level which would give new firms their minimum profit rate, that is to a 'no-entry' price. If this tactic is not successful, a more extreme variant can be employed which either would guarantee that a would-be entrant called off his attempt, or could eliminate a weaker competitor already established within the sector. This 'elimination price' would be fixed below the variable cost of the firm to be eliminated. It would quickly prove effective since 'a firm can survive for some time if the price is so low that fixed costs cannot be recouped, but it can remain in the market for only a relatively short period if the price falls below variable cost, requiring disembursements at short intervals'.[10]

Against this latter argument, it could be hypothesised that the smaller firm in such a contest could secure external finance to 'ride out' the elimination-price challenge. However, this would only be possible if the smaller firm could demonstrate to its potential investor that it had sufficient technical capacity to launch a counter challenge with a second-round innovation, or if it merged with another firm in such a way as to strengthen their joint financial and technical base in relation to the challenger. In either case it would to a greater or lesser extent become an oligopolistic firm like that which mounted the challenge. Further, would-be eliminators are able to mount a package of elimination tactics rather than in isolated measure. For instance, they may simultaneously choose to concede wage increases either under the pressure of trade union action or in their own interest. Inasmuch as this is offset by cost reductions unavailable to smaller firms it will 'tend to throw the small and medium firms in the same industry into a permanent state of crisis. These firms must try to survive by opposing wage increases for their own workers.'[11]

Sylos-Labini's analysis clearly parallels the main features of Marx's exposition of the crisis which leading firms cause smaller competitors.[12] Its expression in terms of oligopoly theory thereby helps extend the framework in which the dynamics of unequal competition can be shown to underlie main features of regional imbalance in modern capitalist economies. A distinction can be made in such theory between leading firms, firms which are led by them, and laggard firms. When the leaders move, some firms will be able to follow (for example, in adapting to a new market or innovation). But others will lag behind, lacking either the finance or organisation to follow the leaders. Even some firms in the wake of the leaders may find themselves backwashed by them and unable to follow. When they can do so it frequently is by grace and favour of oligopoly leaders who allow prices to settle 'at a level immediately above the entry-preventing price of the least efficient firms which it is to the advantage of the most efficient firms to let live'.[13]

But why do firms let others live? Why do they not invariably increase their market share in such a way as to end with an outright sectoral monopoly? One reason, according to Sylos-Labini, is the minimum plant size at a given level of technique necessary to fully employ available scale economies. Plant would be underutilised and it would not be worth the bother of establishing it to run at a higher unit cost than existing plant.[14] If the plant concerned are very large indeed this may well be of importance. Other factors could include the spatial dispersion of the markets of the 'tolerated' firms, or the qualitative differentiation of their products, commanding markets at lower price levels which may not be wholly substitutable with the products of the would-be eliminating firms. In economies with strong anti-trust legislation such as the United States, there is also the force of that legislation as a barrier to increased market share.[15] But the Sylos-Labini analysis suggests that the larger and technically more progressive a small firm grows the more difficult it will find not only its growth but also its survival, since its market would prove increasingly attractive to a sector leader in a position to eliminate it. And this has considerable importance in regional development policy, granted that much of that policy (especially in the South of Italy) is directed towards building up a fabric of small into medium and medium into large-sized firms, and has met with notably small success. It certainly is notable that Italy is one of the most highly concentrated modern industrial economies in terms of the sectoral share accounted for by the three largest firms.[16]

The regional implications of such oligopoly theory are elaborated in the following section of this chapter. However, one of the most important is that small L.D.R. firms cannot count upon an inbuilt restraint mechanism to hold back national sector-leading firms located in the M.D.R., and allow them to catch them up in terms of scale, productivity, rate of innovation, and so on. This is at variance with some post-war theories of the firm which have maintained that such restraint mechanisms do operate on at least the rate of growth of sector-leading firms. For instance, Jack Downie has admitted some of the arguments forwarded by Sylos-Labini, and allows that 'there is a tendency for more efficient firms to grow at the expense of less efficient firms'. He calls such a process a 'transfer mechanism', and states that 'if the transfer mechanism continued to be operated by an unchanged set of relative efficiencies the ultimate result could only be the concentration of the whole output of an industry in the hands of one, the most efficient, firm'. As with Sylos-Labini's analysis, the process works through the lower costs, the better access to capital and the greater capacity to innovate of larger firms.[17]

134

However, Downie maintains that there is a counter process to the transfer mechanism, which he calls the 'innovation mechanism'. The most important element in this process is the speed with which innovations are diffused within an economy. Innovation by leading firms, according to Downie, will cause other firms to re-examine their methods and experiment with new ones. But in imitating the sector leaders, the other firms will improve on them. Therefore 'the outside firm may be in a better position to improve on the best present practice than is the firm which originated it. The former suffers the disadvantage of less intimate knowledge. But it also is free from the distorting influence of the pride of creation.'[18] The same kind of argument has been put by Edwards, who argues that 'the less efficient firms have all that more incentive to do something. At the same time the tendency for the more efficient firm is to grow complacent, to reap the fruits of its current favourable position and to rest on its laurels. In this way the leader of one period becomes – often it would appear almost inevitably – the led of the later period.'[19]

Professor Penrose has suggested not that there is an absolute limit to the market share of an already dominant firm within a sector, but that there are limits to the rate at which a firm can grow. She allows that the existence of many small firms will depend on the policies adopted by their larger brethren, and that one of the reasons why some large firms will tolerate a 'price umbrella' under which smaller firms may shelter is simply public relations. Another is that the larger firms have not yet got round to 'mopping them up'. On the other hand, she maintains that the capacities of existing management impose a restraint on the rate at which any firm can grow and that for this reason already large firms cannot exploit all the opportunities for profitable investment which they themselves create in an economy.[20]

While there is some force to these arguments, they do not necessarily qualify the implications of the Sylos-Labini case. For instance, the observable levelling off in the *rate* of growth of many large firms which has encouraged the Downie, Edwards and Penrose conclusions may have more to do with the product composition of the firms than with their management capacity. This is implicit in the logic of the product cycle as analysed, among others, by Vernon. A firm which concentrates in a particular product line is likely in due course to find that its sales curve falls off as the product becomes 'mature', when the demand created by the innovation has largely been met and the fall off in its rate of growth is not wholly offset by replacement purchasing. For major modern industries such as refrigerator, radio and television production this may well explain why some large firms experience a fall-off in their rate of growth unless they are able to diversify into other or new products in the same or related sectors.[21]

In general the relationship between size and growth can be clarified by distinguishing necessary and sufficient factors. For instance, although there may be no necessary limit to the market share of the largest firm within a sector other than the combination of other firms into a larger or equal group (or their coordination of market tactics), this alone is not a sufficient reason for such an expansion to take place. But if size is not a sufficient cause of increased market share, this is not to say that a large firm necessarily cannot take advantage of its size through economies of scale in production and distribution, and by equally or more efficient management employ these scale advantages to increase its market share or its expansion into other markets.

Sargent Florence has put this very succinctly by pointing out that 'the contention is not that large organisations will inevitably be more efficient than small, but simply that it is *not* inevitable that larger organisations will eventually fail because of management.... Corporate management may become *more* efficient with size owing to specialisation of member managers or, if it becomes less efficient, its deficiency may in effect be counterbalanced by other factors.'[22] In fact this would now appear to be generally accepted by management itself. Not only has Ford learned from experience and followed General Motors' decentralisation by management division, but management outside as well as within the United States is increasingly prepared to pay for its junior members to be taught the art of delegation and decentralised decision-making in business schools. Otherwise, as far as motivation is concerned, it would appear that success in large companies can itself engender success rather than complacency, not least for the reason that the structure of management in such companies tends to be a differentiated pyramid, with the incentive of upward promotion for the management responsible for a successful innovation or increased market share.

Moreover, Downie's arguments tend to neglect the extent to which the introduction of major innovations depends on the structure of the firm. Although particularly imaginative entrepreneurs may increase their market share by simply taking thought and translating this into action (as with plastic in refrigerators, and so on) the application of major innovations involving entirely new products appears to be increasingly associated with size. The particular circumstances will depend on the sector concerned. Also, it is not necessary for firms in one economy to make the technical breakthrough themselves, rather than to import it under licence from another, as has frequently been the case with Europe relative to the United States. But even in this case, a large market share for related products will facilitate the introduction of the new product, particularly at the distribution level. Larger companies with specialised product divisions should be more able to cope with an entirely new product line. Also, successful innovation will depend on the labour relations of the company concerned, especially with regard to new production techniques, and these may well be poor if the company has not previously been able to compete with larger and faster innovating competitors except through small production-cost economies and wage restraint. In particular, smaller companies may not be able to offer the palliative of higher wage rates in association with innovations, and therefore will be doubly handicapped by the pace-setting of the larger firm or firms. This is in addition to the possibility that the innovator will simultaneously employ 'no-entry' pricing tactics with regard to the would-be entrant.[c]

Effectively, unless the later innovator of the Downie and Penrose type is comparably structured to the firm which leads with a particular innovation it may well find itself struggling to raise finance to cover its variable costs, and discover itself subject to bids for merger or takeover. Expressed differently, the only kind of company which will necessarily be able to withstand an oligopolist's price tactics during the innovation period will be an equally oligopolistic company. And even in this case the latecomer may find himself paying severe penalties for this lateness granted that the original innovator in Sylos-Labini terms will be able to draw on the reserve from 'super-normal' profits during the period in which he was first in the field, and use them if necessary to employ 'no-entry' pricing tactics on the would-be

137

entrant. Alternatively, the original innovator may be proceeding with an entirely new product or a major advance on the original innovation by the time the latecomer is introducing his own product, in which case the brand-attachment gains to the original company may help it maintain or increase its initial position at the latecomer's expense. There are no invariable rules in the game which obtain under all circumstances. Without doubt some large innovators become complacent. In addition, initially large firms in other sectors may have a sufficient market strength to be able to force entry into a field in which they have no previous experience through an entry forcing variant on 'elimination' pricing – setting their entry price below the variable costs of an already established innovator. They may 'buy in' their technology from abroad at a price which enables them to do this with little cost to themselves since they have no need to amortise their own R and D expenditure. On the other hand, it cannot be neglected that, with an observable trend to a 'speeding up' of the rate of innovation, the would-be late entrant will have to be able to call on larger entry resources and oligopolistic powers the later it waits, and even then may get its fingers burned. By the same token the successful entry of a small firm into an already established market becomes less likely the smaller it is and the longer it takes to attempt it.[23]

Meso-Economic Power and Regional Imbalance

The degree of unequal competition between big and small firms has now become so marked in the main capitalist economies as to fundamentally qualify all regional theory based on competitive micro-economic models and their synthesis with macro theory. What has emerged in practice amounts to a new meso-economic sector *between* the macro level of theory and policy and the micro level of the small competitive firm. (Greek *macros* = large; *micros* = small; *mesos* = intermediate). This can be illustrated from the rising share in manufacturing output and assets of the top 100 manufacturing companies in Britain. In 1950 the top 100 firms controlled only one-fifth of net output. By 1970 they controlled about one-half, and before 1985 they may control two-thirds.[24]

What this means is a situation in which a few very large meso-economic companies dominate the upper half of an industry,

138

with the lower half divided between thousands of small firms which still basically conform to the assumptions of micro-economic models. For instance, in the British case, less than six meso-economic (or big-league) firms controlled half the assets in twenty of the twenty-two main industrial and service sectors in the economy by 1970, while the assets in the lower half of the industry were divided between literally hundreds of thousands of small micro-economic (or small-league) firms. On average, less than four firms controlled the assets of the top half of these twenty industrial and service sectors. In the case of construction, five big-league firms dominated the top half of the industry, while 100,000 small firms scraped the morsels of the micro-economic market between them. The concentration of meso-economic power in the British economy parallels the United States and many West European economies. In 1970 the top 100 manufacturing companies in the United States controlled one-third of net output and one-half of industrial assets. In key manufacturing sectors from two to four firms control from two-thirds to nine-tenths of industrial output in West Germany, with comparable proportions in Italy, Belgium and France. In practice, this meso-economic power represents oligopoly concentrated on a massive scale in the heartland of the modern capitalist economy.[25]

The regional effect of unequal competition between meso- and micro-economic firms will clearly depend on the spatial distribution of the firms. For instance, if meso-economic leaders maximised locational benefits arising from higher labour availability or lower labour costs in less-developed regions, the result could be a situation which had no significant regional dimension. Some regions would gain in the short to medium term if they included either the parent or subsidiary plant of a meso-economic company which was able to protect or increase its national market share through increased scale, innovation, or inter-firm pricing tactics (where these resulted in new production and employment for the company itself rather than expanded production in a company which was taken over). Whatever the outcome of such intra-sectoral tactics, the long-term effects of maximising locational benefits would ensure that no particular region or area lost from them.

In practice, however, meso-economic firms do not necessarily maximise locational benefits in national economies, either because there are greater benefits from a multi-national location, or because transmitting lower location costs (including subsidies) through to lower prices would prompt protests of abuse of competition from small-league firms. The latter factor may play a part in the United States, where companies already earning 'super-normal' profits from a dominant position in the national market prefer to locate new ventures in the more-developed and faster growing markets of other economies, rather than in the less-developed regions in their own economy.[d] In other economies in which either the degree of oligopolistic competition is less strong, or where competition policies are less effective, most meso-economic companies which have secured a market lead through the benefits of an early start tend to supply that market either from plant on an initial home site, or from plant on the home sites of companies which have been taken over, from new plant located in the M.D.R. or from foreign subsidiaries.

This tends to promote a situation in which leading big-league firms and their subsidiary plant are located in, and continue to locate in, more developed regions. As a result, it is not surprising that most of the led small-league firms may do the same. Those micro firms which operate in practice as satellites to the meso leaders, and have grown in part through providing inputs for them, will tend to continue to expand in the M.D.R. in which the leaders initially located and grew. In principle, if the meso-economic leaders do not attempt to maximise possible locational benefits through higher labour availability or lower labour cost (or both) in a plant located in an L.D.R. some small-league firms within the sector might do so when their products are directly competitive with those of the sector-leaders. But in practice it appears rare that they do so. This could be for a variety of reasons ranging from inertia to admission of the retaliatory power of the big-league company (particularly where it is multi-national in operation and has access to lower cost foreign labour while the challenger does not). But it appears possible that one reason for the failure of many firms to maximise locational benefits is the low priority given to maximisation of profit in the general growth strategy of the firm – of which location is but one factor to be taken into account among many others.

For instance, Baumol has persuasively argued that firms maximise sales subject to a profit constraint, rather than profits *per se*.[26] But in any case their own overall profits relative to other competing firms concern them more than profits which they may be forgoing through not locating in less-developed areas in which either net location benefits or government assistance with equivalent effects could increase profit levels. Besides, increasing profits through reduced costs in an L.D.R. location could begin precisely the kind of price war which is resisted by big-league companies themselves. If a small-league firm challenges a meso-economic leader, it could be the challenger's signature of its own takeover, or, at a lesser level, the beginning of a period in which it finds itself squeezed by the sector-leader in a manner which cramps its freedom of action in other respects, such as the establishment of an international joint venture in production or distribution, which anyway might promise clearer-cut benefits over the medium term. In general, it appears plausible to assume that meso-economic companies are more tolerant of challenges to foreign firms from small-league national companies than challenges to themselves, even if this, in the longer run, may mean a stronger challenge to their own national and international position. If a fast-expanding medium-sized firm therefore has the perception to consider the location of a new plant anywhere other than just outside the city limits, it may well pay it to locate abroad rather than in the national L.D.R. Alternatively, it may prove beneficial to diversify into a type of product in which it is not directly challenging its principal competitor in its own main field.

Small-league firms which are sector-laggards rather than sector-led may not be able to indulge such a variety of alternatives. For instance, a small-league firm whose plant are exclusively located in an L.D.R. may benefit from a variety of locational advantages which a meso-economic leader may choose to ignore. These include readily available labour for fast expansion, lower labour costs, and a variety of government aids which the meso-economic leader discounts against greater gains from going multi-national rather than multi-regional. In addition, it may benefit from enterprising management of the classic entrepreneurial kind, anxious to expand at a rate which larger and more established companies might consider indecent, or at least hazardous. It may have been able to take advantage of a minor technical breakthrough, or imported a major technical breakthrough under licence. These factors may be sufficient in principle for it to undercut the big-league M.D.R firm in the leader's own markets, and cumulatively increase its market share at the expense of the more-developed M.D.R. firm. But in practice the greater initial scale of the big-league company in the M.D.R. will offset the potential gain of the small-league L.D.R. firm. Depending on the actual disparity, it may be sufficient to permit the big-league M.D.R. firm to forestall the expansion by the small-league L.D.R. firm through employing either 'elimination' or 'no-entry' price tactics before the new expansion is undertaken. The ability of the small-league firm in the L.D.R. to withstand these tactics would depend on the ratio of the total financial resources which it was able to mobilise through internal and external finance (including government assistance) in relation to the resources at the disposition of the big-league M.D.R. firm. The greater the initial market share disparity and the nature of the competitive challenge, the less the chances of success for the L.D.R. firm. If the 'elimination' prices tactic led to a takeover of the small-league L.D.R. firm this might not be to the disadvantage of employment and income generation in the L.D.R. to the extent that (1) the meso-economic M.D.R. firm chose to expand in line with the L.D.R. firm's initial programme; (2) continued to buy from other firms or plant located in the L.D.R.; and (3) did not restrict potential sales through higher prices than the small-league L.D.R. firm would have charged. But in practice the meso-economic firm may choose to focus expansion in the product line or lines concerned in its own plant in the M.D.R., purchase mainly from its own previous sources outside the L.D.R., and also allow prices to revert after the 'elimination' pricing period to the previous oligopolistic level.

However, the cumulative intra-sectoral disequilibrium process may have operated without restraint for so long that there may be very few micro-economic firms in a position to mount a competitive challenge against meso-economic M.D.R. firms, and which obliges them to resort to either 'elimination' or 'no-entry' pricing tactics.[c] The main elements in the cumulative growth of big-league firms will tend to ensure that such challenges are exceptional. Scale economies in production will tend to be reinforced by distribution scale economies of a kind which are less likely to be available to a micro-economic L.D.R. firm even if it manages to gain production scale economies which are comparable, plant for plant, with those of the meso-economic M.D.R. firm. Also, while lower labour costs in the L.D.R. micro-economic firm may enable it to secure a labour-cost advantage over the meso-economic firm based in the M.D.R., the more-developed firm may be able to destabilise the L.D.R. firm by a wage *increase* if that increase is met by wage demands and industrial action by unions in the L.D.R. – demands and action which are more probable the more successful the firm becomes. The process need not imply a demand for wage parity with the big-league M.D.R. firm, since even a lower wage increase by the small-league L.D.R. firm may prove sufficient to eliminate its competitive advantage if the big-league M.D.R. firm benefits from overall scale advantages when it does not. In addition the meso-economic M.D.R. firm may be able to match the labour-cost advantages of the micro-economic L.D.R. firm, or even undercut L.D.R. labour costs, if it is multi-national in operation, and utilises a high proportion of inputs from subsidiary plant in less-developed countries.

To the extent that a meso-economic firm located in an M.D.R. can take advantage of labour specialisation and scale economies through efficient division of management responsibilities it also may gain a competitive advantage unavailable to less efficient micro-economic L.D.R. firms. In fact, to the extent that resurrected claim of management indivisibility has any relevance to practice it probably is most relevant to the critical period of transition from owner management or individual management within firms to delegated or multi-divisional management responsibility. And by definition this is a problem which is more likely to handicap late-starting (or late-gaining) firms rather than leading big-league companies. If such problems coincide with the capacity expansion which would constitute a challenge to a leading big-league M.D.R. firm, they would facilitate pressure on the small-league L.D.R. firm of the 'no entry' or 'elimination' pricing tactic type. Similarly, productivity saving and market-expanding gains from innovation by big-league M.D.R. companies can in many cases be undertaken in a period of domestic market quiescence in which they either have the field to themselves or are strong enough to cope with oligopolistic pricing tactics, at least by leading national competitors. A later starting small-league L.D.R. firm may find its own innovation more difficult to the extent that its advance threatens encroachment on leading big-league M.D.R. firms. The later-starting firm also will tend to be handicapped to the extent that the technically more advanced big-league M.D.R. firm has already amortised its innovation costs, since under assumptions of administered prices this will allow the meso-economic leader of the M.D.R. a 'super normal' profit margin. When challenged it may only need to reduce this margin to 'normal' levels in order to reduce profit for the L.D.R. firm to a level which can deter entry. In this way there may be three dimensions to the expansion of the share of an L.D.R. firm on the national market which jeapordise its chances of success in relation to longer established M.D.R. firms, including (1) the adjustment problem with transfer from owner management to a more modern delegated management structure, (2) the capital costs of the expansion itself, and (3) the costs of innovation. It cannot be assumed that the growth of the small-league L.D.R. firm is in some sense a repetition of the growth of the big-league M.D.R. firm, only undertaken later than the M.D.R. firm's growth. It seems clear that the poor growth record of L.D.R. firms is to a substantial extent explained by the market tactics of more-established M.D.R. firms.[f] In this sense the key to regional growth lies not with the regional firm in the micro-economic sector, but with the meso-economic national and multi-national leaders.

This is not to say that no small, later-starting, L.D.R. firms ever catch up with early starting M.D.R. firms.[g] It has already been admitted that size is not a sufficient condition for competitive success. Thus the fact that larger M.D.R. firms may generally be in a better position to employ oligopolistic market tactics towards L.D.R. firms does not mean that this alone will ensure that those firms already located in M.D.R.s will necessarily increase interregional disparities through such market tactics and scale advantages. On the other hand, the mechanism of oligopolistic competition tends to increase rather than close such disparities, and also can mean that once large firms have started to expand in more developed regions their continued further expansion in those regions will 'backwash' smaller firms in L.D.R.s. The scale of the backwash concerned clearly will depend *inter*

144

alia, on (1) the initial national and regional location patterns in early industrialisation, (2) the force of other factors contributing to interregional divergence such as centripetal labour and capital flow, and (3) the time-period in which such divergence is not checked or offset by government policies.

Meso-Economic Structure and Regional Dualism

However, if that time-period is sufficiently long, a situation may arise in which most of the 'modern' meso-economic firms in the economy are concentrated in its more-developed regions, and most 'traditional' micro-economic firms in the less-developed. Alternatively, the large-scale, fast-innovating, multi-sectoral firms may expand to the point at which they dominate the regional market share in L.D.R.s. In general the L.D.R.s will be left with small-scale, slower-innovating, micro-economic firms which are not able to compete effectively with big-league M.D.R. firms in either national or international markets.[h] If the macro-economic interregional imbalance described in Chapter 3 has not also been checked by government policies, this will not only mean that the lower-profit and less-competitive L.D.R. firms continually suffer from a depletion of regional savings through portfolio outflow to the M.D.R., but also suffer from either stagnation or net decline in regional income per head. The result may well be major income per head disparities of a two-to-one variety at the end of a cumulative disequilibrium period, which major government policies once instituted will find difficult to close.[i] As a result of such income disparities expenditure patterns in more-and less-developed regions are likely to differ considerably, with different real incomes affecting the kind of product which can be successfully sold in the different types of region. Thus motor vehicle consumption, household durables consumption, new housing demand, and expenditure on utilities as well as recreation goods and services will be likely to prove lower and different in kind in L.D.R.s and M.D.R.s 'Consequential expenditure' patterns are likely to prove different in kind and scope, with lower regional scope for 'consequential investment'.[27] In general the qualitative differences between the types of product consumed in more- and less-developed regions will mean that some product sales are concentrated in M.D.R.s

145

with L.D.R. sales undertaken only as a bonus to M.D.R. sales. In addition, the price and profit schedules which M.D.R.-based firms can secure through M.D.R. and international sales may be such as to prevent major sales of their products in L.D.R.s. Rather than employ regionally differentiated pricing on a permanent basis, they therefore may well be content to leave L.D.R. firms to 'mop up' the lower-quality and lower-price L.D.R. market, thus allowing a regional counterpart to the intra-sectoral 'price umbrella' noted by Penrose.[28]

This disparate situation, with different types of firm concentrated in, and effectively serving, different types of regional market, provides a further dimension to the much advertised problem of interregional dualism. In effect, when different types of firm are located in different regions, inequalities in meso- and micro-economic structure will reinforce the interregional dualism problem. Dualism in this structural sense has been employed recently by Averitt, who has distinguished what he calls 'centre' and 'periphery' systems in the U.S. economy. The 'centre' system is composed of firms which are large in size and influence, benefiting from management scale economies.[29] Averitt defines it broadly by the top 500 U.S. industrial corporations, accounting for nearly three-fifths of all employment in U.S. mining and manufacturing. The 'periphery' system is composed of relatively small firms, which are usually dominated by a single individual or family. Its sales are realised in relatively restricted markets; its profits and retained earnings are commonly below those of firms in the centre system, and it finds long-term borrowing difficult. Production techniques and marketing are rarely as up to date in the periphery system as in the centre system. The firms concerned are often, though not always, 'technological followers'. Centre firms are in a position to employ research, innovation and advertising to allocate resources to themselves and to the industries under their control. Unions in centre firms are alleged to aid them through putting pressure on key industry competitors to pay uniform wage rates which they can less easily afford.[30]

The Averitt 'dual' classification therefore corroborates the meso- and micro-economic distinction and elements of the earlier oligopoly analysis of Sylos-Labini, Bain, and Galbraith.[31] Despite the fact that his analysis largely lacks any spatial dimension,

146

his use of the terms 'centre' and 'periphery' is highly suggestive for regional theory and analysis, complementing the spatial concentration of most economies in a centre region or regions and periphery regions. A quantified index of such interregional inter-firm dualism clearly is difficult to construct since (1) information on company size frequently is not disaggregated by region; (2) such information on size is only an imperfect index of the range of qualitative differences arising in dualistic intra-sectoral structures. None the less, data on Italian manufacturing company size by main region is available from the 1961 industrial census and yields sufficiently impressive results. Although the total number of firms in the least-developed region (South) and the most-developed (North-west) was virtually equal (177,500 against 179,800), the only category of firm in which the South had more units than the North-west was those employing less than ten persons. The South had less than one-quarter of the North-west total in the 11–100 employee category, and less than one-twentieth of the North-west total in the over 1000 employee category. This interregional disparity in the structure of manufacturing industry is underlined by the fact that more than two-fifths of industrial employment as a whole in the North-west in 1961 was in firms of more than ten employees against only just more than two-fifths in the South. In other words, allowing for the fact that size may only be a necessary rather than a sufficient condition for competitive success, the evidence indicates that the South of the country, with more than a third of national population, lacked modern meso-economic enterprise size in relation to the North-west (with a quarter of national population). And this was critically disadvantageous for the region, granted that it was mainly with north-western firms that southern firms had to compete for national markets and any kind of export-led growth.[j]

The problem for a major region such as the South of Italy is further emphasised if it is allowed that oligopolistic competition is increasingly characteristic of agriculture and services as well as industry.[k] Because of its relative degree of product homogeneity agriculture is frequently assumed to be a more or less perfectly competitive sector.[32] But inasmuch as this is held to be the case it appears to constitute a hang-over from imperfect competition theory which emphasises the competitive implications of pro-

duct differentiation, as against the dynamics of inter-firm oligopolistic competition which is only incidentally concerned with
differences between products. For even assuming that the agricultural product or the service in question is homogeneous in
character, the perfect competition model assumes a high degree
of freedom of entry and equality of entry terms. Yet this is not
the case either in the Deep South of the United States or in the
South of Italy. With regard to the Italian case Franklin has
appropriately commented that 'the pressure of population and
the perennial search for land has enabled large owners to take
advantage of their oligopolistic position and to establish types of
leasehold which are agronomically pernicious and socially de-
plorable in their consequences'.[33] In addition, in both agriculture and services, a large-scale producer will be able to provide
bulk products at lower unit costs the greater the extent to which
he mechanises his unit and employs modern production and accounting techniques.

Besides this, of course, the products of both agriculture and
services are differentiated, so that larger-scale and more highly
capitalised units not only are able to offer products and services
at lower unit cost, but also better products and services. In agriculture, if a peasant farmer is not able to secure the working
capital to purchase fertilisers, is insufficiently literate to understand the literature explaining their use, and cannot master the
technicalities of stock control and accounting, he will be unlikely
to compete with the modern capitalist or co-operative farms
which can. More importantly, the small peasant farmer will not
be able to process the product into a form in which it becomes
non-perishable and non-seasonal, through canning or bottling,
or transformation into packaged deep-frozen form. Perhaps
most importantly of all, he will not be able to distribute the products concerned to anything more than a local retail market (or
sell direct) without the intervention of oligopsonistic wholesale
and retail buyers. Stefanelli has drawn attention to such oligopsonistic practices in the Italian case, where the peasant farmer has
lost contact with the final market for his goods through the control of purchasing, processing and distribution by large-scale
capitalist groups. He cites an E.E.C. Commission study of the
olive-oil market in which it was shown that in the mid-1960s the
producer of olives received on average only 19 per cent of the

final value of his product, with not less than 52 per cent syphoned off by the extractor and 29 per cent by the retailer.[34] In this way the vertical structure of the agriculture market reinforces an intra-sectoral dualistic structure, with the peasant farmer unable to mobilise a sufficient surplus to capitalise his own production.[l]

The scale element in oligopolistic market growth also is important in modern services. Small-scale service units in the distribution sector will not be able to compete with chain stores or supermarkets.[m] Small banks and credit institutions will be less able than larger units to take advantage of high profitability investment projects not only because their credit capacity may be lower and below a critical minimum for high return large-scale projects, but also because their supplementary services to borrowers in terms of investment or portfolio appraisal and advice will tend to be less extensive and poorer in quality than that offered by their larger competitors. These advantages are independent of the extent to which greater scale permits not only greater labour specialisation but also employment of very large-scale computer and other facilities.[35]

Imbalance and Defensive Investment

Apart from these factors there is another important way in which regional backwardness can influence the structure of investment decision-making and operations within firms in a problem region. It has already been argued that the process of interregional disequilibrium, if unchecked by offsetting government policies, can result in a situation in which the overall rate of growth of an L.D.R. is either consistently lower than that of an M.D.R., or stagnates, or actually declines. But the difference between regional income growth rates even in the sense of consistently lower growth in the L.D.R. means not only less investment per head for the population of the region concerned but also less capital intensive and lower innovation investment. And this has considerable implications for the process of growth in the L.D.R. firms.

This process has been well analysed by Lamfalussy in relation to the Belgian economy in the 1950s, and the main elements of his analysis can be extended to a regional rather than national context.[36] For example, during conditions of low overall growth of demand, the growth of firms dependent on the regional market will, by definition, tend to be low, with low profits, low self-financing, uncertain market quotations, and so on. As a result the regional firms concerned will tend to undertake only minor modifications to their production techniques or products with the minimal aim of preventing a decline in their existing market share. In other words, their main policy aim will be to hold on to what they already have – in Lamfalussy's terms, 'defensive' investment. Various reasons apart from lack of internally or externally generated investment are likely to reinforce this tendency. In the first place minor process or product innovations can normally be carried out without bringing an existing product line to a complete standstill (unlike the entire replacement of existing equipment). Secondly, the value of scrapped plant and equipment will tend to be lower in a slow rather than fast growing economy or sector. Thirdly, there is a higher risk in large rather than small innovations, especially since fewer mistakes can be absorbed under low rather than high growth conditions.[37] Such 'defensive' investment patterns will tend to prove self-reinforcing and cumulative. This follows not only from the fact that small innovations tend to mean lower productivity gains than larger ones, but also from the fact that minor innovations increase entrepreneurial commitment to the plant concerned and thereby perversely delay the date at which it might be replaced by entirely new plant. In other words, there is an intra-firm dimension to the low, warranted-growth problem of the Harrod type which was previously applied to an L.D.R. Unless offset by government income transfers in favour of the L.D.R. sufficient to raise the regional warranted growth rate, the pattern of investment decision-making within firms will accentuate and strengthen a defensive reaction to low overall growth conditions, with initial caution leading eventually to not only a defensive but also a defeatist investment psychology. These problems will be additional to those caused for L.D.R. firms which are unable to invest in new products and techniques because of portfolio savings outflow to the higher m.e.c. schedule M.D.R.

Conversely, the M.D.R. not only benefits from capital inflow from the L.D.R., but, to the extent that it secures high overall income growth in the manner described in the previous chapter, will provide conditions which favourably influence not only the rate and level of investment but also the manner in which investment decisions are undertaken and carried out. In Lamfalussy's terms, high overall growth will encourage what he calls 'enterprise' investment. This is enterprising in the sense that management confidence in sustained high growth is sufficiently strong for it to aim deliberately at expansion of output entailing major innovations in new plant and production techniques. In this way innovating investment will tend to maximise both production scale economies and available technical progress, with direct sales benefits to the firms concerned through lowered unit costs, improved quality of existing products, and the introduction of entirely new products. At the same time there will be a stimulus to the growth of the regional economy through the demand for large-scale capital equipment, and indirect effects not only from standard pecuniary external economies (lower unit costs and prices for given goods) but also from innovation promotion (the same or lower prices for new use and higher productivity goods). The Lamfalussy 'enterprise' investment framework clearly gives a further dimension to the Sylos-Labini analysis of the impact of technical progress on company structure and inter-firm competition. Such enterprising investment patterns will tend to mean not only sustained but increasing profits, self-financing, market quotation, and so on, with an extended and strengthened company financial base for further investment rounds. At the same time rapid growth in the M.D.R. will reduce amortisation time periods, making resources more quickly available for second-and third-round investment in existing or new product lines.[38] In this way there is a cumulative self-reinforcing process linking management confidence in a high warranted growth rate to the actual structure of investment within firms, increasingly benefiting the fast-growth region.

Multi-national versus Multi-regional Companies

There is no unique definition of a multi-national company. These enterprises sometimes are called trans-national, international, or global firms. But there is general agreement that they are defined essentially by the characteristic of direct investment in more than one country.

In terms of our definition, they are also pre-eminently meso-economic firms, dominating the micro-economic sector. Multi-national production offers such companies a variety of financial gains which limit the effectiveness of government regional policy.[39] For instance, it gives companies access to low-cost labour in less-developed countries. Even excluding the special case of South Africa, such costs can be as low as a quarter of the price of labour in British Development Areas. For instance, the Burroughs company submitted to the Commons Expenditure Committee in 1972 that, in certain categories of labour-intensive work, it 'along with all other companies, is locating in Taiwan, Brazil, Mexico, the Philippines and Hong Kong, where the cost of labour is very, very low'. When asked how low, the Financial Director of Burroughs replied that it was about one-quarter of the cost of British labour, and agreed with a Committee Member that 'an employment premium would have to be very substantial to locate here' (i.e. in Britain).

This is true enough. The regional wage subsidy would have to be raised to 75 per cent of labour costs simply to close the gap between Britain and the countries cited by Burroughs. And this assumes that the foreign labour costs are only as low as one-quarter of British costs. Evidence from the U.S. Tariff Commission and other sources shows that Far East and Mexican labour costs range from one-tenth to as low as one-twentieth of U.S. costs, depending on the area and product.[40]

Corroborative evidence on the low-pull effect of the Regional Employment Premium (R.E.P.) was given by other multinational companies. Unilever submitted, in written evidence to the Expenditure Committee, that 'we are unable to produce evidence from our own experience that the Regional Employment Premium has increased investment or employment in the Development Areas'. I.B.M. submitted that the R.E.P. would be taken into account, but on a heavily discounted basis. Other multinational companies gave indirect evidence on the relative unimportance of the R.E.P. by failing to identify it as important in their written submissions on factors influencing location in Development Areas (for example Philips) and by submitting that

152

neither capital nor labour incentives played a major role in location (for example Cadbury Schweppes Ltd).[n]

In general, the evidence on the overall limitations of regional incentives on capital and labour in promoting a Development Area location was very clear cut. Univac (Sperry Rand) was not untypical in stating that 'we would have gone (to a Development Area) regardless of the grants offered'. G.K.N. submitted that 'the attraction of the incentives has so far been inadequate'. G.K.N. also showed the limited relevance of capital costs in total costs by submitting that 'the difference between creditors and debtors in our case, for example, is equal to the capital expenditure on plant and buildings'.

But for multi-national companies capital costs anyway are limited as a location factor by two main items. One is the relative weight of labour versus capital costs. For instance, if labour abroad is one-quarter its cost in Britain, and if the company can organise a less-developed country location, capital incentives simply will not enter into the location decision for relatively labour intensive plant. The second item is the relative gain from a capital incentive in Britain versus the cash gain through the transfer pricing of profits abroad. This is the mechanism whereby multinational companies can charge themselves high import prices to Britain from subsidiaries in tax havens or low-tax countries overseas. The enormous scale of the gains recently publicised in the case of Roche may be exceptional, but serve to illustrate the transfer pricing mechanism very clearly. The general importance of transfer pricing in balance-of-payments terms also emerges from the importance given to it by the British government's Counter-Inflation Bill of 1973.

The pull effect of a capital grant or allowance in Britain is compromised by transfer pricing in a basically simple way. If the capital grant intended to promote location in a Development Area constitutes x per cent of capital cost, but the scale of financial gain through transfer pricing constitutes x plus y per cent of capital cost, the regional grant or allowance is eroded. For most multi-national companies transfer pricing is not a conspiracy against the public interest, but a necessary means of maintaining a world competitive position once competing multi-nationals are transfer pricing. In extreme cases such as Roche, which in the early 1970s was selling librium and valium to the National

153

Health Service at a price several thousand per cent higher than Italian prices, the evidence indicates that the additional y factor not only could exceed *total* capital costs, but could do so by an astronomic margin.

Multi-national companies are in a weak position to claim that they cannot afford to locate major initiatives in Development Areas. First, many of them have a high proportion of their jobs in Development Areas – in several cited cases as a result of taking over firms which were already located there. Secondly, they trade a high proportion of their production multi-nationally, between subsidiaries of their own company in different countries. The difference between British and foreign labour costs, plus gains from transfer pricing, exceed multi-national transport costs by a wide margin. But apart from transport costs, the degree of market security enjoyed by these large firms enables them to manage global transport on what amounts to a pipeline basis. In other words, their own orders for the transported goods are regular and standardised, so that once a flow of goods has started (whether by air or sea), a flow process has begun in which the transport time becomes an insignificant factor.

Besides this, transport costs for the kind of high-value and low-weight products involved in most multi-national transactions are very low. The 1963 British Industrial Census showed that they totalled only about $2^1/_2$ per cent of total production costs. The costs of net distance (going to Scotland rather than staying in the South-east) are mainly a problem of persuading junior and middle-range management to move, and securing management access through frequent flight and rail schedules (Unilever, G.K.N. *et al.*). G.K.N. put the relative importance of transport facilities clearly in stating that 'up to now cost has also been important but flexibility is more important than cost'. Net distance costs are so small a proportion of already small total transport costs that many firms do not bother to isolate them in their own accounts for deliveries within Britain. The main reason is the difficulty of isolating the cost of travelling 200–300 miles on a motorway from the costs of waiting for 24 hours at a port before a load can be shipped, isolating the capital costs of transport equipment from net distance running costs, handling costs, insurance, and so on.°

In general large companies have shown that by going multi-

154

national they can afford to go multi-regional within one country. Their overall size and market security allow them to absorb risks of the kind which could swamp a smaller company. They are the most mobile companies in the most widely mobile sector in the economy – manufacturing. Moreover, the 'runaway' multi-nationals which are locating a high proportion of jobs in less-developed countries do so in those relatively labour intensive manufacturing sectors which are most suitable for job promotion in problem regions in developed countries such as Britain.

The claim voiced by some multi-nationals that they have to locate close to research establishments (for example I.B.M. at Havant) is highly suspect. First, there is substantial evidence that U.S. multi-nationals use European research establishments to monitor research undertaken by European companies and independent establishments rather than to develop their own R and D (which stays concentrated in the United States).[41] Second, the case for proximity to central management or research staff depends on the stage of the product cycle, or the degree of maturity of the product. For instance, in early stages of innovation, when the problems of production techniques and inputs have not been ironed out, proximity to skilled cost accountants, process engineers and research staff can be important. But for U.S. multi-nationals, this first stage of the product cycle is frequently completed in the United States. The second mass-production stage for a new product may be located mainly in the country where it is to be sold, partly for reasons of securing a national base for sales penetration. For electronics companies (for example Burroughs) the second stage of the product cycle anyway may be located in Hong Kong rather than Havant. I.B.M. unwittingly contradicted its own 'proximity' case by submitting in the same evidence that 'a particular computer installation in one country today might consist of some peripheral units made in Greenock and Sweden linked up with a central processing unit made in Havant, Germany or France linked up with some other equipment made in Italy perhaps. It is quite a complicated rationale but we do obtain economies of scale from that mode of operation.' In other words, I.B.M. secures cost savings from widely dispersed production, rather than from clustering all its production around research centres.[p]

There is a strong case for maintaining that the most important

155

factor in location for large companies is the manager's wife – especially when she is a university graduate and has a job in a developed area which might not be available to her in a less-developed region. Unilever was quite explicit on this. I.B.M. also put the general importance of social infrastructure higher than government incentives (that is to say communications, housing and schools before labour subsidies or investment grants).

But evidence on the importance of securing a close proximity between different plant and head offices differed between companies. For instance, Univac was asked whether public transport in Britain was adequate and did not take an unreasonable amount of the top management's time in travelling rather than managing. It replied: 'Not in Britain because of the very good rail service we have here. Britain is too small a country to have company transport in.' Dunlop also contradicted both the costs-of-moving case and the argument that dispersion increased problems of management. This was because of the *difficulties* of running a single-site, multi-product establishment. The company therefore located in Northumberland rather than Birmingham. It stated in written evidence that 'there is some lost time and travelling costs arising from necessary visits by senior management from Birmingham, but this is not really significant'.

Such evidence should cast doubt on the relatively high figures for transport and management costs submitted by other big-league companies in evidence to the Commons Expenditure Committee. In some cases the coincidence between such figures and a rounding up with available government aid should be open to question. For example, Tube Investments claimed that location diseconomies totalled £200,000 but also submitted that 'there are not many projects where regional policy is of critical importance to the strategic decision [to locate]'. Dunlop admitted that it actually made a surplus from regional incentives which were useful for investment elsewhere! (Written evidence from both companies). There undoubtedly are some costs for some companies. But these depend both on the type of product and its phase in the product life cycle. The more established the product and the more mature the production techniques, the less the need for specialised management to visit the plant. It is exceptional rather than general to disperse as many successive stages of construction between different plant as British Leyland have done. As Lord Stokes submitted in evidence to the Commons Expenditure Committee, it does not make economic or social sense to transport empty body shells vast distances by heavy transporter by night through urban areas. But the transport cost figures submitted later by British Leyland were rightly challenged by the D.T.I. on the basis that the finished vehicle delivery costs were not also taken into account in the calculation. Moreover, British Leyland's costs arise not from government policy so much as a gargantuan merger of several multi-plant companies. Lord Stokes submitted that he would prefer some half-a-dozen production centres to the seventy-odd from which the company at present suffers, and complained that he would not be able to rationalise his company profitably until the government took a firmer line with the unions opposing closures. But he neglected the fact that increased government intervention in regional development, however 'crazy' it strikes him from inside British Leyland, is his main hope of securing closures when alternative employment is brought to the areas from which he wishes to withdraw.

Strictly speaking non-multi-national companies should be defined as concerns without foreign direct investment. But in many cases companies may have only a minor proportion of their investment overseas and operate mainly in the domestic market. Such companies cannot be defined simply by a size criterion, but for the main part will be micro- rather than meso-economic. In British terms they will not come within the schedule of Category 1 firms defined in the White Paper on Phase Two of the British prices policy (Cmnd. 5267).

The main distinction between nationally and multi-nationally based companies lies in the different effects which regional incentives and I.D.C.s have for the former companies. Basically, national companies do not have access to very low-cost labour in less-developed countries and therefore are likely to pay more attention to a regional labour subsidy such as the R.E.P. Similarly, if they do not have operations abroad they are less likely to utilise holding companies in foreign tax havens or tax holiday areas, which will diminish profit syphoning through transfer pricing and increase the effect of capital assistance in British Development Areas. Further, for obvious reasons, national companies are more likely to be caught in the government's I.D.C. net than multi-nationals, since they cannot pressure for an I.D.C. relaxation by threatening otherwise to locate abroad. For example, they are not in a position to blackmail the government on I.D.C.s, unlike I.B.M. which felt able to admit in evidence that if the British Government says: 'I am sorry but you cannot go to Havant', (I.B.M.) will say, 'All right, we will not go to the United Kingdom'.

The Commons Trade and Industry Committee took evidence on the problems of medium and small national firms from the I.C.F.C. (Industrial and Commercial Finance Corporation)[q] and directly from Reliant. The I.C.F.C. submitted that the smaller firms with which it dealt were mainly 'one-man shows' in the sense that the chief executive took most of the decisions affecting the company. The firms were generally faced with the problem of finding a new location for plant when they expanded above the number of fifty employees and a £200,000 turnover. They normally did not have the expertise to evaluate the costs and benefits of alternative locations. Compulsion to move from the home area through refusal to grant an I.D.C. could impose serious costs of adjustment for such concerns. Reliant was adamant on the importance of government aid for a new location, the difficulties imposed by I.D.C.s, and the incidence of major costs from the spatial separation of plant. In other words, those factors which were marginal for larger meso-economic companies, or simply inconvenient (e.g. I.D.C.s) played a crucial role for a small firm in the micro-economic sector such as Reliant. In some respects Reliant's problems in coping with the location of a regionally distanced plant were exceptional. For instance, the motor industry is substantially an assembly sector in which the supply of components is important. Reliant claims to have 400 suppliers within 25 miles of its home plant, which is a number way in excess of most other manufacturing firms, however small.

But the problem of the small micro-economic firm is of considerable importance for an effective regional policy. It can be highlighted by a comparison with a large multi-national such as I.B.M., which can effectively hole the I.D.C. net when it chooses to do so by threatening otherwise to locate outside Britain. Reliant is in no such position, and may well find itself enmeshed to an extent which seriously affects its cost, profit and survival potential. Some of the costs are in terms of splitting management between different plant in a company which is so small that it will have only an embryonic modern management structure. A large multi-national will be a multi-company and multi-product concern. Its management hierarchy will be specialised, clearly defined, and offer job security with promotion prospects of a kind virtually unparalleled elsewhere (excluding government service). A good manager in a small company may risk his professional future by doubling his responsibility with a new regional initiative, and find himself joining the unemployed rather than creating regional employment.

NOTES

[a] As is well known, Joan Robinson was later to escape these limitations with impressive success.

[b] A related factor which is of considerable importance in the regional context (cf. following text) is the tendency of larger firms to internalise economies of scale and thus reduce the extent to which their own growth can spread to smaller firms through external economies.

[c] Danièle Blondel has stressed that the exploitation of technical progress depends very much on the structure of the firm in terms of scale and modernity, and that the more backward the firm the lower its capacity to innovate. In this sense there will be a leeway between firms of different size which entrepreneurship alone will not close. Danièle Blondel, 'La Transmission internationale des innovations', *Revue Economique* (May 1966) especially pp. 438, 440 and 462. On the basis of Belgian evidence, Lamfalussy has argued that smaller firms may respond to innovation by larger firms by 'defensive' innovations in production methods, and an attempt to maximise the small economies which these may secure, but that in the long run this will not stave off the 'enterprise' investment by the larger firms. Cf. Alexandre Lamfalussy, *Investment and Growth in Mature Economies: the Case of Belgium* (London: Macmillan, 1961) especially chapters VI, VII and X.

[d] Some U.S. companies have increasingly located new plant in the less-developed Deep South since the war, and in the case of the textile and food-processing industries this has included the closure of plant in the more-developed and higher labour cost North-east. But the process is exceptional and has not been the main factor in the inter-state *per capita* income convergence during the post-war period, as previously noted.

[e] Under inflationary price conditions a 'no-entry' price tactic may well take the

form of postponed price increases rather than actual price lowering. The wide-spread price stability of U.S. firms in the Western European market suggests that 'no-entry' effects are mainly registered in this way rather than by dramatic short-term price reductions.

f Such tactics contribute to explain the relatively high mortality rates of some firms in the South of Italy which have started operations with government assistance on a scale which superficially should ensure their competitive success.

g The southern located electrical consumer goods firms Ignis, Zanussi and Indesit are a case in point (despite the fact that they partly grew as satellite firms supplying oligopolistic multi-national companies outside Italy during a period in which these companies had not organised plant location in less-developed and lower labour-cost countries on any scale).

h The argument does not depend upon the assumption of single-plant rather than multi-plant firms, but only on the assumption that new plant by sector-leading M.D.R. firms are located within the M.D.R., or other M.D.R.s. In the U.S. case the division of the national market into more-and less-developed regions would make sense through distinction of the less-developed Appalachian states from the rest. In the Italian case the North-South division very clearly represents a major regional disparity of a similar kind.

i As previously noted such disparities in income per head are to be found for particular states in the United States, while in post-war Italy the South of the country, which constituted 37 per cent of national population, had an average income per head only 40 per cent of the North-west (25 per cent of total population in 1950).

j Cf. further Chapter 5 and Table 7, p. 283.

k In 1967 the South still employed 36 per cent of its working population in agriculture against 64 per cent in industry and services combined. Cf. further Chapter 5 and Table 3, p. 280.

l This, of course, is independent of whether disguised unemployment and surplus labour acts as a disincentive to the introduction of capital-based techniques.

m In the South of Italy the State-owned I.R.I. group has attempted in part to overcome this problem through a supermarket chain in competition with private groups, but it is not at all clear whether it operates in favour of southern producers.

n The counter evidence on the importance of the R.E.P. from Plessey was notable as an exception to the evidence submitted by other companies.

o For an in-depth analysis of distance, transport and location costs see Chapter 7.

p With the following analysis of management preference in location, these arguments on the product cycle and location are developed further in Chapter 8. The criticism of I.B.M.'s Havant location only conflicts with the product cycle factor in location policy, as to be outlined in Chapter 8, if I.B.M. can demonstrate that the bulk of development as well as research must be done locally, for the production at Havant.

q A small-scale financial agency established after the war by the Labour Government to assist medium-and small-scale companies. This was merged with the larger scale Finance Corporation for Industry (F.C.I.) in a new company, Finance for Industry, by the Conservative Government in 1973. Finance for Industry

(F.F.I.) played a role in the November 1974 Labour Government budget, where it was allocated £1000 million via the commercial banks and insurance companies for medium-term lending to industry.

CHAPTER 6

STRUCTURE VERSUS THE REGIONS

It is now commonly accepted that the structure of production and employment is one of the principal factors determining regional growth or decline. It is also relatively easy to distinguish extreme cases – for example natural fibre textiles on the one hand and electronics on the other. But it is more difficult to determine long-term growth prospects with precision. For instance, textiles and steel might both be considered 'traditional' industries, yet both are capable of qualitative modernisation through the introduction of synthetic fibres, or the establishment of integrated plant with continuous transformation of ore and scrap to finished sheet steel. Also, it is more difficult to determine the proportions in which development assistance should be allocated to one industrial sector rather than another. Investment in fast-growth, high-employment industries appears intuitively correct, but the inter-sectoral supply coefficients for such sectors presumably should be taken into account in a development policy if the expansion of such industries in the region is either to be possible (avoiding local supply bottlenecks) or is to benefit the region to be developed rather than the faster-growing regions in the economy. This, of course, is independent of the further important question of the proportions in which investment should be directed to industry rather than to industrial infrastructure, agriculture, or services.

Answers to such questions clearly will depend in part on the degree of under-development of the region concerned, the extent to which a self-sufficient growth process is thought desirable, and so on. If the region is depressed through dependence on, for instance, coal, and is also small, with a working population in coal of only some ten or twenty thousand, the question of self-sufficiency would not arise on any scale. It might be held sufficient to introduce more modern industries whose inter-sectoral linkages relate to the rest of the national economy, and the policy decision may relate mainly to the determination of which industries are most appropriate for the region or area concerned. If, however, the particular region is both effectively undeveloped and also large, the question of overall inter-sectoral allocation from the three main sectors downwards will be posed quite clearly, and will compare in principle with the investment strategy problem as debated for undeveloped economies. This certainly could have been said to be the case for the Mezzogiorno at the end of the Second World War, with a negligible industrial structure, substantially concerned with armaments production, partly demobilised by war action, and with a population effectively equivalent to that of Belgium and the Netherlands combined.[a]

The Limits of Stages of Growth Theory

Apart from the above, there is the critical question whether there is any inherent stages of growth type evolution in sectoral change, and whether the market mechanism alone can be relied upon to assure that it will occur. This was touched upon in the context of 'export base' theory in an earlier chapter, which considered the challenge to the Hoover–Fisher 'stages of growth' argument by Douglass North. It was emphasised that the differences between the Hoover–Fisher and North arguments depend considerably upon the size of region, the manner of its 'integration' with the rest of the national or international economy, and the productivity potential of its exports. North stressed the difference between the European and North American regional economies, and the extent to which regions such as the Pacific North-west had been able to achieve high productivity and income levels through specialisation in timber products and the exploitation of raw materials. This contested the case of Hoover and Fisher that 'if a region is to continue to increase both its total and *per capita* real income it must eventually *industrialise*', which they argued on the basis that the income elasticity of demand for agricultural products was insufficient to sustain *per capita* income increases in line with industry or services.[1]

In fact, as the earlier chapter pointed out, the Hoover–Fisher case did not assume that the transition from primary to secondary and tertiary sectors by stages would be automatic. They stressed that a region dependent on primary production may reach a limit to its total or *per capita* income growth and 'retrogress

163

or decay'. They paralleled Myrdal and Perroux by adding that such 'stagnation and decay too may be cumulative'. In addition, there is an element of unnecessary conflict between the Hoover–Fisher and North positions, since North's principal case (the Pacific North-west) is based upon exploitation of raw materials of a kind which is effectively industrialised (the forestry industry and its derivatives), besides being directly linked in growth terms to the demand for timber in industrial and residential construction. In other words, the forestry case does not refute the Hoover–Fisher argument concerning the limited income elasticity of demand for agricultural products.

In fact the Hoover–Fisher thesis amounts to little more than a sketch of possible implications for regional growth, using the Clark distinction of three main sectors. It was published before the encyclopaedic labours of Simon Kuznets permitted a general evaluation of the pattern of sectoral change in the main world economies, and is worth testing against that evidence.[2] In taking time-series data for the thirteen principal industrial economies, Kuznets found that the share of agriculture in total product showed a marked decline in all save one, Australia, where he assumed that agriculture was able to maintain a high share through the country's effective integration with the more industrialised and larger market of the United Kingdom. In general, the decline of agriculture in total product ranged from close to one-half (and in some cases as high as two-thirds) to less than one-fifth. In twelve of the thirteen countries the share of industry in total product rose from 20–30 per cent in the early phases of development to 40–50 per cent at the terminal dates. Australia again was an exception, with the share of industry on current price estimates rising and on constant price estimates falling, in each case by one percentage point. Thus the downward trend of agriculture and the upward trend of industry in most cases was very marked. By contrast, the movement in the share of services in total product was neither marked nor consistent, declining in Sweden and Australia and rising in Canada and Japan, with a trend on balance too small to be significant.[3]

As Kuznets emphasises, a decline in a sector's share in total product is not necessarily accompanied by a decline in its share of the total labour force (or total capital). If productivity has risen less in a given sector than in others, the sector may well

164

have absorbed a constant or even increasing share of total resources. The share of agriculture in the total labour force in fact
declined in each of the thirteen countries which Kuznets considered. The scale of the decline was invariably large in relation
to the initial level. He estimated that the share in the 'pre-
modern' phase for most countries was not below 50 per cent,
and that it then declined to less than 20 per cent. (His figures
clearly would be lower if they were carried to the 1960s.) He explains the principal exceptions – Japan, Italy and the Soviet
Union – on the basis that they were latecomers to industrialisation. This may well have been the case with the Soviet Union, in
conjunction with a policy of capital-intensive industrialisation,
and controls over the outflow of labour from agriculture through labour permits. Otherwise, neither Italy nor Japan was
markedly more of a latecomer to industrialisation than, for instance, Germany, whereas both economies have been classified
as 'dualistic' by several commentators.[4]

Kuznets found that the share of industry in the total labour
force rose in every country, although in many cases the rise was
absolutely and proportionately small, despite the long periods
covered. In France, Switzerland, Belgium, the Netherlands, Italy and Australia the share rose by only a few percentage points,
and even the more considerable rise in some other countries was
not as large as the relative rise of the sector as a proportion of
total product, which in most cases doubled. Only Britain, Sweden, Japan and the Soviet Union doubled their share of industry
in the total labour force. The share of services in the total labour
force either was constant or rose relatively little in Britain, Belgium, the Netherlands, Sweden and Australia. In other countries, however, there was a marked relative and absolute rise,
ranging from 10 per cent to nearly 20 per cent. Therefore, since
the share of services in total product either was constant or only
changed a little, the absolute and relative rise of services in the
total labour force was significantly larger than its increase in the
share of total product; that is to say the phenomenon to which
Kaldor, following Verdoorn, has recently paid attention.[5]

The Kuznets evidence therefore corroborates the Hoover–Fisher thesis in indicating that the international and inter-
temporal pattern of change between the three main sectors
shows a decline in agriculture during industrialisation in terms

165

of both total product and employment, followed by a fall off in the rate of growth of industrial employment with industrial product remaining relatively constant, and a rise in the share of services employment without any marked rise in the share of services in total product. In other words, the higher the stage of development of the economy as a whole, the lower the share of agriculture in total product and employment, and the greater the share of services in total employment.

Growth and Location Dependence

Other general conclusions can be drawn from Kuznets's evidence. One is the relative *growth-dependence* of services in relation to industry. This is to say that the growth potential of services appears to be limited not simply by the overall rate of growth of demand in macro-economic terms, but in particular by demand either directly or indirectly originating in industry. There is no clear-cut boundary here. The rate of growth of certain services will generate its own multiplier effect on other services – for instance an increase in hotel-based vacations will increase the services utilised by the hotels, as well as other local services such as entertainments, retailing of goods for tourist consumption, and so on. In addition, modern agriculture needs more services the more modern it becomes, including banking, insurance, utilities such as power, water and light, as well as specialist veterinary services, advice on soil chemistry, fertiliser use and so on. None the less, Kuznets's evidence on the relatively constant share of services in total product, and the relative decline of agriculture in both total product and employment, indicates that industry tends to constitute the principal source of demand for services, both directly through its own employment of such services as banking, insurance and other utilities and indirectly through their employment at either a personal or household level by those whose incomes are earned in industry. It also, of course, constitutes the principal source of supply for the intermediate goods employed in the provision of services.

If this conclusion is correct it is clear that any particular region specialising in the provision of services must be able to ensure, not only that it can provide these services as efficiently as other regions within the economy, but can provide them on a suffi-

166

cient scale to ensure continued *per capita* income increases in line with the rest of the national economy. Such specialisation may be sufficient to ensure the continued predominance of certain centres if they not only have traditionally constituted service centres for their regional hinterland, but also for the national and international economy – such as the commercial and financial centres of London and New York, which have been fortified in the provision of such services by their additonal role as industrial and trading centres. However, such centres for interregional and international trade by definition amount to exceptions rather than the rule, and their initial establishment as centres tends to become cumulative and self-extending through the oligopolistic nature of many of the service enterprises established within them. Therefore any region which is already backward in terms of income or product would be ill-advised to attempt to compete with them in these fields.

Perhaps more importantly for evaluation of the potential for regional growth of specialisation in services is the fact that many services not only are growth-dependent but also *location-dependent* in character. Despite the telecommunications revolution which has enabled telex links to reduce the time and distance gap between international branches of some service firms – particularly banks and finance houses – many services such as the retailing and distribution of goods, the provision of power, water supply and light are location-tied, with the result that no one region will be able to specialise in their provision to other regions.

It also appears clear from Kuznets's evidence that agriculture is *growth-dependent* in the sense that the growth of agricultural income is dependent upon the demand for agricultural goods by labour employed in industry and services. Moreover, despite the recent advances in the sales potential of agricultural products through food processing, the overall income inelasticity of demand for food is reflected in the decline in agricultural products in relation to total products, and in the agricultural labour force in all of the thirteen economies which Kuznets considered, with the exception of very small economies with particular climate and resource endowment advantages which were effectively dependent on demand from larger industrial markets (such as New Zealand in relation to Britain). In other words Kuznets's

167

evidence indicates that some regions can achieve high *per capita* income growth through specialisation in primary production, and to this extent thereby corroborates the North example of forestry in the Pacific North-west. But it also shows that *not all* regions can do so. Besides which, as with the case of established national or international service centres, it is worth remarking that both the Pacific North-west and the New Zealand economies are not entirely dependent on primary products. Both are to a large extent industrialised – with the Pacific North-West including one of the largest aircraft engineering and aerospace complexes in the world, and the New Zealand economy already highly diversified even if dependent on agriculture for the bulk of its exports.

In addition, there is the not unimportant factor that some of the principal services and agricultural products in which less-developed regions may have a particular advantage, such as tourism or viticulture or citrus production, are seasonal in their demand for labour, and give no guarantee of continuous employment of the kind offered by industry.

It therefore appears clear that, while a region may 'jump the gun' by concentrating on the provision of certain specialised services and thus miss the industrialisation stage, it would only be able to avoid a divergence between its own and the national *per capita* income growth rate if it could secure or develop firms of national competitiveness in those services which were not location-dependent. In a similar way, a region could only afford to specialise in primary products if it enjoyed a special advantage in their production relative to other regions which were industrialised. In the case of agriculture it also would need to be able to develop or secure a sufficiently high level of productivity and competitiveness to be able to secure and maintain an export flow to other regions in order to secure the industrial goods necessary for the attainment of living standards comparable to those in the industrialised regions. In addition, unless the level of national protection of agricultural products is sufficiently high, the region concerned may have to achieve a degree of international competitiveness which structural obstacles and supply inelasticities may prevent. For instance, in the Italian case, the climate advantage which the South enjoys has not been sufficient to prevent Californian and Israeli citrus fruits from prov-

168

ing more competitive in Milan than those from some of the principal southern areas.

In general, it may be concluded that while specialisation in either primary production or services *may* ensure that a region is able to maintain a rate of growth of *per capita* income in line with the rest of the national economy, it does not necessarily do so. Moreover, it will be less likely to do so the larger the region. In other words, the larger the region concerned the stronger the case for a strategy of regional development through industrialisation. This is independent of the additional questions as to whether an agricultural region which is integrated within an otherwise industrialised economy will be able to generate sufficient savings through agricultural exports to provide investible funds for its own industrial development: whether these funds, if generated in the first place, will be invested in the region of origin rather than in the more-developed industrialised region or regions; and whether the infant industrial firms in the less-developed region would be able to survive in national markets even if such funds were retained within the region itself. The previous chapters have maintained that the free working of the market mechanism in fact would tend to promote an outflow of savings to the higher m.e.c. schedule M.D.R.; that emigration from agriculture to other sectors in the L.D.R. may not prove sufficient to raise agricultural productivity to a level at which re-investible surplus can be generated, and that infant industrial firms in a predominantly agricultural region are unlikely to be able to compete effectively with mature national and international oligopolies except in those local, inferior quality and profit markets which the oligopolies leave to them. All of which increases the case for a policy of industrialisation the larger and more backward the L.D.R. in the first place.[6]

The Case for Priority Sectors

If the Hoover–Fisher case is corroborated by the Kuznets evidence, this does not indicate how a general policy of industrialisation can best be implemented, or in what proportions relative investment in industry, agriculture and services should be undertaken. Once more the size of the region concerned is important. The larger and less developed it is, the

169

more relevant is the balanced and unbalanced growth debate as elaborated in the theory of development. It is particularly relevant to the case of a major underdeveloped region such as the South of Italy in which post-war governments have opted for specific sectoral priorities in successive development programmes, without much practical effect. Both the Italian case and the choice of priority sectors *within* industry can be better evaluated in terms of the unbalanced growth strategy.

On the balanced growth side, Nurkse argued that most industries catering for mass consumption are complementary in the sense that they provide a market for and thus support each other. While a single investment project might appear impracticable because of the limitations of the pre-existing market, 'a wide range of pro)ects in different industries may succeed because they will all support each other in the sense that the people engaged in each project... will provide an enlarged market for the products of the new enterprises in other industries'. Expressed differently, Nurkse argues that 'balanced growth interests us mainly for the sake of its effects on the demand for capital'. A balanced demand (or 'diet') for industrial production will therefore be provided by 'a wave of capital investments in a number of different industries'. Nurkse qualified his original exposition of this case in a later lecture, in which he excluded both exports and intermediate markets from this recommendation of balanced inter-sectoral investment allocation through an investment package. His revised argument therefore amounted to the recommendation of a broadly based 'wave' of investment in basic industry as the condition for a self-generating growth process in intermediate industry.[b]

In commenting on Nurkse's case, Streeten argued that Nurkse in practice assumed a static pre-existing market for his broad investment wave. It could of course be argued that the multiplier effects from Nurkse's investment package would induce demand for final products, and that the availability of basic industrial goods would enable intermediate industry to secure the inputs necessary to meet this induced final demand. However, Streeten claimed that the most important complementarities in the growth process arise from the process of demand creation, which may be 'unbalanced'. That is to say that consumers will decide that they have new wants as innovation makes new products available. Such an 'anabolism' of wants would not become apparent through an investment strategy which concentrated on a wave of investment in basic industry, which might only satisfy existing demand patterns rather than promote a continuing, self-generating growth process. By contrast, the case for unbalanced growth, in the sense of concentrating investment in certain industrial sectors, lay in the stimulus which this could provide to the continuing generation of demand for new products. Therefore, the balanced growth case was correct enough in emphasising the need for an 'investment package', but it should be supplemented by concentration on certain growth sectors which have a higher than average capacity to induce a chain-reaction effect in demand for further products in new industries.[7]

Streeten has stressed that 'in so far as unbalance does create certain desirable attitudes, the crucial question is not whether to create unbalance, but *what* is the optimum degree of unbalance, *where* to unbalance and *how much* in order to accelerate growth; which are the "growing points", where should the spearheads be thrust, on which slopes would snowballs grow into avalanches?' That is to say that specific attention should be paid to the selectivity of an unbalanced investment strategy, 'to its precise composition, direction and timing'. He further emphasised that investment should not be the only component of the selected sectoral package, and that it also should contain actions to reform attitudes and institutions, including the desire to invest, the ability and willingness to work, to organise, to manage and to administer politically; a time-table showing the sequence of the various measures to be undertaken, with account of technological, political and sociological factors; controls checking undesirable or less-desirable investments, and policies designed to weaken or eliminate obstacles and inhibitions to development.[8]

Streeten's analysis in terms of an 'anabolism of wants' has been paralleled by Hirschman, one of the most emphatic advocates of unbalance. According to Hirschman the creation of pecuniary external economies plays a vital role in the process of growth through inter-sectoral complementarities: 'The expansion of industry A leads to economies external to A but appropriable by B, while the consequent expansion of B brings with it economies external to B but subsequently internal to A (or C or

171

that matter) and so on.' But, Hirschman stresses, the production complementarities concerned need not only be interpreted in terms of external economies, and that they arise in any situation where an increase in the demand for commodity A and the consequent increase in its output call forth an increased demand for commodity B at its existing price. This may be through a process 'where the increased availability of one commodity does not *compel* a *simultaneous* increase in supply of another commodity but induces slowly, through a loose kind of complementarity in use, an upward shift in its demand schedule'. Expressed differently, 'complementarity means that increased production of A will lead to *pressure* for increasing the available supply of B'. He admits that the effect of complementarity in this sense was anticipated by Veblen, who summed it up when he wrote that 'invention is the mother of necessity rather than vice versa'. He also follows Barnett in describing the process as 'entrained want'. None the less, he argues that the complementarity effect of investment in this sense gives a new concept of 'induced investment' which is more meaningful in the context of development economics than the more conventional Keynesian accelerator assumption that investment is directly related to past increases in output.[9]

In contrast with his use of the growth-poles concept, Hirschman's distinction of complementarity effects and external economies and his use of 'entrained want' appears to have led rather than followed François Perroux. In his earlier work Perroux placed considerable emphasis on the role of external economies in the mechanism of growth promotion but in an article in 1961 he contrasted them with the wider role of investment complementarities, and in 1965 he dismissed them as 'a crude and unclear expression of growth induction effects'.[10] His investment complementarities are primarily inter-sectoral. Growth induction (*effect d'entraînement*) is a process working either in terms of scale, or productivity, or innovation, or some combination of the three, rather than simply through cost reduction from external economies plus a Keynesian accelerator effect. The process relates sectors which are relatively active with relatively passive sectors, the former pulling the latter with them in a manner comparable with Hirschman's and Streeten's pressure for increasing supply from the passive sectors. To this extent it

172

is a disequilibriating, unbalancing process, with leading sectors inducing the growth of lagging sectors rather than inter-sectoral growth proceeding at a single uniform rate. However, it is not an automatic process. The active, growth-inducing sectors may be held back by supply constraints in the passive sectors (*effet de stoppage*). Policy therefore should be directed to promoting and sustaining the growth-inducinng process both by facilitating investment in those 'modern' industries in which innovation permits expansion, and ensuring that more 'traditional' industries providing inputs for the more modern can adapt themselves to a similar expansion rather than restrain it.[11]

The Choice of Priority Sectors

The balance versus unbalance debate may help policy-makers escape from the assumption that the offering of across-the-board incentives to industry in general will automatically induce an optimal growth process. The differences between particular versions of the respective theories may prove complexing enough to persuade some policy-makers that it is simply an economists' private dispute, but it appears evident enough that the differences actually are of degree rather than kind. They could only be taken to be the latter if Nurkse's 'frontal wave' were taken to include all industry, which his later lecture makes plain that it should not. However, if the weight of *a priori* argument would appear to rest with selective inter-sectoral unbalance, Streeten's question remains as to what unbalance, where and how much. Hirschman in fact has attempted to secure some conclusions by utilising international input–output comparisons made by Chenery and Watanabe.[12] In principle, he argues that those sectors to be selectively unbalanced would be those for which the network of input–output relationships is 'thickest' in that they buy the largest part of their inputs from other sectors, or sell the largest part of their outputs to other sectors, or both He distinguishes the relative merits of input provision or 'forward linkage' and output utilisation or 'backward linkage' in inducing growth, arguing that backward linkage is the result of pressure of demand which is essential for growth to occur: 'forward linkage could never occur in pure form. It must always be accompanied by backward linkage, which is the result of pressure of demand.' For this reason, in ranking Chenery and

173

Watanabe's data, Hirschman places those industries with high backward and low forward linkage ahead of those with the inverse characteristics.[13]

Hirschman himself admits that his exercise is something of 'a mental experiment', and that its conclusions take on 'a somewhat eerie flavour'. For instance, the largest value for backward linkage is to be found for grain-mill products, although it clearly is unrealistic to think of wheat and rice production being 'induced' by wheat and rice mills, rather than the reverse. Similarly, he points out that the ranking does injustice to particular sectors, which on a more intuitive basis would be rated more highly, such as machinery and transport equipment. In general, he concludes that such a ranking is useful to the economist-planner and 'something to be added to his criteria box'. On the other hand, he emphasises that 'excessive reliance should not be placed on these rankings, based as they are on a mental experiment subject to numerous qualifications'. For instance, he points out that industrial development should not be started everywhere by an iron and steel industry simply because this ranks highest in terms of both backward and forward linkage. He also claims that it is more useful to look at the structure of particular countries and to examine how linkage effects normally make their appearance than to translate such general international rankings into a policy of selective sectoral unbalance for any country.[14]

Part of Hirschman's difficulties are methodological. An input–output table can describe linkages, but it cannot fully explain the importance of particular sectors in the growth process since several of the most important factors in that process are not wholly inter-sectoral in character. For example, the mechanism by which a 'modern' sector may grow faster than other sectors relates significantly to the intra-sectoral arguments which were outlined in the previous section. In particular, innovation within a particular industry may be largely intra-sectoral in character, and its importance therefore 'disguised' by inter-sectoral linkage rankings. A further reason for not relying exclusively on linkage rankings in determining priority sectors for investment, of course, is the fact that linkage alone may not reveal other factors which may be of importance to the development policy concerned, such as the rate of growth of employ-

174

ment. Further, even studies of linkages in particular countries do not reveal 'norms' for a sequence of linkage effects for that or another country (or region). A given sequence may have been less effective in promoting growth than an alternative sequence which was not adopted. In particular, *ex post* analysis of the inter-sectoral linkage sequence in given countries does not mean that the causal factors in their growth should necessarily be repeated for another country at a later date, even if the sequence which emerged appears to have been 'optimal' for the countries concerned.

If such qualifications further handicap selection of priority sectors on a linkage basis, however, it does not mean to say that their selection need be purely intuitive, Nor does it mean that international or historical evidence is useless. Provided that it is evaluated qualitatively in terms of conclusions which can be drawn from other areas of growth theory, such quantitative information may provide a guide from which priority sectors for a particular national or regional economy can be determined. This is particularly the case if the relative growth rates of sectors and their changing share in national product and employment are taken into account. In itself this will not automatically indicate a strategy for selective sectoral unbalance in any circumstances. The causal relationships involved will have to be evaluated and related to the economy concerned. On the other hand, it provides a thread of some kind through the maze of policy options, and enables analysis of more factors in the growth process than does the linkage approach. For instance, granted that the measurement of innovation even within a sector is of considerable difficulty, some indication of an innovation effect can be derived from a ranking of rates of growth of product and productivity. Similarly, a ranking of rates of growth of employment for specific sectors will give some indication of the prospects of employment for a given region through the selection of particular sectors as priorities in investment allocation.

Again, the Kuznets data is of assistance. With Bain, Chenery and others, he has pointed to the fact that historical evidence indicates a marked upward trend of manufacturing within industry in terms of either employment or contribution to total product.[15] Comparing Britain, France, Belgium, West Germany, the Netherlands, Denmark, Norway, the United States, Canada

175

and Japan for the period 1954–6, he found that manufacturing accounted on average for no less than 62 per cent of industrial product, and for 63 per cent of the industrial labour force.[16] In disaggregating manufacturing, and presenting long-term trends, Kuznets analysed only two countries, the United States and Sweden, using data for the period from the nineteenth century to the late 1940s. He found that shifts in the structure of manufacturing in the two countries as indicated by shares in total output, value-added, labour force and capital invested were quite similar. The shares of food and of wood products declined. The shares of textiles and leather products (even including rubber with the latter) declined in the United States, but not in Sweden. Of the remaining groups, the shares of paper and printing, chemicals and petroleum products, and metal products all rose.[17]

A broader and more recent international comparison, for the period 1950–62 and including not only Western Europe and North America but also the Soviet Union and Eastern Europe, has been undertaken for the Economic Commission for Europe by Kuklinski. For what he calls industrialised Western Europe (E.E.C and EFTA plus Finland and Ireland), Kuklinski found that the three fastest growing industrial sectors in terms of average annual increase in production were chemicals (7·4 per cent), electricity and gas (7·4 per cent, and metal products (7·3 per cent). For what he calls Southern Europe (Spain, Portugal, Greece, Turkey and Yugoslavia) the rate of growth of production in these sectors was even higher (1.6 per cent, 12.1 per cent and 10.3 per cent respectively), with rates of growth ranging from 9 per cent to nearly 12 per cent in metal-mining and basic metals, non-metallic minerals and products, chemicals, including coal-mining and crude petroleum, and paper.[c] In addition, however, Kuklinski analysed the rate of growth of employment in these sectors. For industrialised Western Europe he found that chemicals and metal products clearly led in employment creation over other sectors, with annual average rates of increase of 2.7 per cent and 3.6 per cent respectively. For Southern Europe non-metallic minerals and products led with a rate of increase of 9.3 per cent per annum, but were closely followed by chemicals and metal products, with rates of growth of 9.0 per cent and 6.7 per cent respectively. This international evidence persuaded

176

Kuklinski to identify chemicals and metal products as priority sectors *par excellence* for the development of problem regions.[18]

Kuklinski's findings very much strengthen the more narrowly based information available from Kuznets's analysis of the United States and Sweden. Kuznets in fact offers a more detailed explanation of these shifts within industrial structure than does Kuklinski, and stresses the role of innovation, which 'not only increased productivity in turning out old products (thus possibly reducing their relative prices) but created new consumer and capital goods'.[19] The role of innovation in the particularly fast rates of growth of chemicals and metal products has also been underlined by Postan in an analysis of changes in Western European industrial structure up to 1964. Stating that 'there is a strong p esumption – a presumption bordering on the obvious – that in our period demand for capital was linked with technological innovations and the proneness of industries to innovate', Postan points out that 'the chemical and petroleum industries, with their joint offspring in petro-chemicals, plastics and man-made fibres, developed a voracious appetite for new capital as they grew and renewed their equipment. Equally voracious for capital were the engineering and metal-working industries, especially their newer branches such as electro-mechanical, electronic and motor-car.'[20]

Kuklinski's claims in favour of what amounts to a policy of selective unbalance for chemicals and metal products therefore secures corroboration from both Kuznets and Postan. On the other hand, it does not indicate that these should be the exclusive sectors to be unbalanced in favour of any problem region. Kuklinski's work was undertaken for the Economic Commission for Europe, and it may well be that the regional problems of the main member states of the E.C.E. could be substantially resolved through the concentration of investment in chemicals and metal products within them. But some regions in some of the member countries (e.g. the South of Italy or some of the regions of the Soviet Union) are so predominantly agricultural in character, and so under-represented in either industry or manufacturing as a whole, that a further ranking of priority sectors, and relative unbalance between manufacturing sectors, appears necessary. This could include a distinction between 'modern' and 'traditional' manufacturing industry, and between 'footloose' manu-

177

facturing as a whole which can be directed in given proportions to any region, and location-dependent industry (mining, construction, power, and other utilities) which cannot.

Any distinction between 'modern' and 'traditional' manufacturing clearly must be arbitrary in certain respects. The modern manufacturing sector of today is the traditional manufacturing of tomorrow. Moreover, today's traditional industry may be modernised through new techniques of production, greater capital-intensity, and so on. For instance, textiles production employing natural fibres and labour-intensive mechanised techniques may constitute a low-productivity 'traditional' manufacturing sector, yet may be transformed through the employment of combined natural and synthetic fibres and more highly mechanised production techniques. In addition, no distinction can be made between two such different types of manufacturing simply on the basis of relative rates of growth of employment or product independently of the level of development, capital availability and production techniques of the economy as a whole. The lower the overall level of industrial development, the greater the case for employing relatively labour-intensive sectors in a planned structural policy for problem regions. But these should not be in 'traditional' manufacturing simply because such sectors include more labour than 'modern' manufacturing. Such a policy is fated to catch up yesteryear tomorrow, with serious long-term consequences for the region concerned.

The question of a qualitative distinction between 'modern' and 'traditional' manufacturing can be clarified by re-working Kuklinski's data, and up-dating it from U.N. source material. This is reproduced in Tables 7 and 8 (see pp.283–4). The U.S. and Canadian evidence shows the general importance of taking long-term data as a guideline for any policy choice, granted the fact that the annual rate of growth increased in the 1950–62 to the 1962–9 periods both for individual sectors and for the broad categories of 'modern' and 'traditional' manufacturing as a whole. This was true for both product and employment. The evidence for industrialised Western Europe is more striking. This shows a greater employment decline than would be caused by any marginal slow down in G.N.P. growth in the member economies (most of which in any case either maintained or increased their previous annual growth rates).[d] In 'traditional'

178

manufacturing the fall-off was so marked as to go negative in non-metallic minerals, and nearly negative in textiles and clothing, with annual rates of increase of only about half of one per cent in food, drink and tobacco, and wood. In 'modern' manufacturing there was a similar marked decline in employment increase over the two periods for the same countries. Basic metals fell from 2 per cent to —0·6 per cent a year; metal products from 3·6 per cent to 1·1 per cent; chemical products from 2·7 per cent to 1·7 per cent, and paper from 2·5 per cent to 0·7 per cent.

Therefore the distinction between 'modern' and 'traditional' manufacturing in the case of industrialised Western Europe shows that only basic metals and chemicals (as opposed to chemical products) have a lower employment growth record than any 'traditional' manufacturing sector, and that basic metals manufacturing has a higher employment growth record than either wood or non-metallic minerals products. Moreover, *all* the sectors classified as *modern* manufacturing showed a higher product growth rate than any 'traditional' manufacturing sector with the exception of non-metallic minerals (which was as high as the product growth rate for metal products and paper).

In other words, the qualitative distinction between 'modern' and 'traditional' manufacturing is significantly corroborated in terms of quantitative differentials in product and employment growth rates, and indicates that there are grounds for giving priority to not only Kuklinski's chemical products and metal products in selective investment in a major backward region, but also to other sectors within 'modern' manufacturing as a whole. But it also shows that in the case of industrialised Western Europe there is a marked shrinkage of the rate of employment increase in both modern manufacturing, and in the spearhead sectors. In other words, policy-makers can count on fewer jobs being available for movement into problem regions and areas in these sectors, and in a relatively short time are likely to be faced with the need to undertake entire relocations of modern manufacturing plant if they wish to ensure a balanced job-mix in problem regions. This means that, at a time when the trend to multinational capital is increasingly undermining the effectiveness of government policy on location, there are going to be fewer jobs on which to exercise interregional leverage in the first place. In both senses, any policy hoping to improve on past performance in these areas is going to need new instruments of considerable power to cope with the problem.

The scope for such new instruments – especially new public enterprise as both a direct and indirect lever of new regional jobs – has already been indicated in previous chapters. Returning to the distinction between 'modern' and 'traditional' manufacturing, and the spearhead sectors within them, it is clear that this at least gives an indication of priority sectors for a policy of regional development. It is corroborated by considering both the degree of labour intensity and the rate of innovation in engineering and chemical products. For instance, evidence on the capital cost of investment per employee in the South of Italy for 1967–9 drawn up by Nicola Cacace shows an average *per capita* cost of 24 million lire for manufacturing as a whole. Steel, primary chemicals and their derivatives, cement and rubber involved a capital cost higher than the average, with massive *per capita* capital costs for rubber (280 million lire per employee) and primary chemicals (165 million lire per employee). At the other end of the capital-intensity scale came the labour-intensive and 'traditional' manufacturing sectors of shoes, clothing and miscellaneous manufacturing with a capital cost per employee of less than 5 million lire. In the intermediate category of capital costs per employee of between 5 and 25 million lire lay the broad range of those manufacturing sectors which by our previous definition can be identified as 'modern' manufacturing, with a concentration in engineering and chemical products.[21]

Cacace's breakdown is useful in showing the marked contrast between the capital-intensity of 'upstream' and 'downstream' sectors within modern manufacturing industry. By comparing her breakdown with evidence on R and D costs as a proportion of turnover in U.S. manufacturing in 1968 she also has demonstrated that the most capital-intensive industry within U.S. manufacturing is also that with the lowest technological advance. It is the more labour-intensive aircraft, electronic, electromechanical, automobile, and chemical products industries which include the intermediate and advanced technology sectors in which (prestige projects apart) employment opportunities in general are most assured.[c] Such evidence therefore indicates that there can be little doubt that priority for Kuklinski's 'spearhead' industries of engineering and chemical products, followed by those sectors which have previously been identified as 'modern' manufacturing, gives effective terms of reference for which sectors to unbalance in favour of a region such as the South of Italy. To this extent it indicates Streeten's 'what' to unbalance, even if it does not by itself help to indicate the equally important 'how much'.[22]

The answer to 'how much' cannot be generally specified without reference to the particular sectoral structure of the given region over a given time period. For instance in the Italian case, the South in 1967 included more than one-third of national population, but just more than one-tenth of national employment in engineering and chemical products, and less than one-tenth of national employment in 'modern' manufacturing. Its share of national employment in manufacturing as a whole actually declined from $19 \cdot 5$ per cent in 1950 to $18 \cdot 1$ per cent in 1967, with a decline from $13 \cdot 4$ per cent to $10 \cdot 3$ per cent in its share of national employment in engineering.[23] Granted that only a massive allocation of manufacturing investment to the region could improve its share of national manufacturing employment, and granted also the evidence available from Kuklinski's data on the faster rate of increase of both product and employment in engineering and chemical products than the rest of either total manufacturing or 'modern' manufacturing, target proportions for the region by three main sectoral categories could be specified. This might schedule 70 per cent (roughly double the region's share of national population) of national investment in engineering and chemical products for the South by a given target date, and 60 per cent of national investment in 'modern' manufacturing. A further target proportion for the region of 50 per cent of national investment in total manufacturing might also be established (granted the region's lower share of employment in total manufacturing than its share of total national population).[f]

Such precise objectives on the basis of only indicative evidence might appear highly evaluative. But while this is the case, they are not therefore either arbitrary or irrelevant to the region's needs. First, the need for a critical minimum industrial investment constituting a proportion of the national total in excess of the region's share of national population has already been indi-

181

cated. Secondly, it has been stressed that in order to offset advantages to the more-developed region (rest of the economy) from an inclusion of faster-than-average growth industries, it would be necessary to secure some offsetting inclusion of such industries within the less-developed region. Giving a margin of some breadth to the fastest growth sectors such as metal products and chemicals and 'modern' manufacturing as a whole would mean harnessing the forces of inter-sectoral disequilibbrium in favour of the less-developed region rather than against it. Thirdly, provided both public enterprise and locational controls are employed in a planning framework, such objectives should prove feasible, and may actually assist the companies concerned in their investment programming and resource utilisation. Fourthly, if there were any danger that fulfilling such objectives might mean an unbalance in national investment in the sectors concerned which disproportionately favoured the less-developed region, the percentage requirements could be revised accordingly. Provided that such revisions were not arbitarily sprung on the firms subject to locational controls, there is no reason why they should compromise their investment programming.

Some evidence on the feasibility of such objectives is already available from the Italian post-war development experience. In 1957 the two major state industrial groups, I.R.I. and E.N.I. were obliged by law to locate 40 per cent of their total investment, and 60 per cent of their investment in new plant, in the South. According to I.R.I. this specific obligation was initially regarded as a nuisance by the Group, since it was felt that the government could in practice oblige them to locate any given investment project in the South, and was therefore setting an unnecessarily arbitrary investment obligation. However, the economic advisory section within the Group soon found that the setting of a specific investment target both provided a fixed point for their investment programming as a whole, and also acted as a catalyst on management within the Group which had been persuaded of locational advantages from investment in the South but hitherto had lacked the necessary impetus for a successful hearing of their strategy. Further, and crucially, both I.R.I. and E.N.I. managed to fulfil these obligations by the target date of 1964,[24] and to adapt successfully to a later raising of the obligation to

182

100 per cent of new plant in the South or depressed areas in the Centre–North.

A further important benefit from specifying precise targets for the location of investment in industry, manufacturing and fast growth sectors within manufacturing, if this is combined with locational controls, is the higher degree of precision which this allows in the forecasting of investment requirements in infrastructure and agriculture. In the case of post-war Italian regional development up to 1957 almost exclusive reliance was placed on a combination of public investment in these sectors and the offering of incentives to industry in the South. With regard to infrastructure, Rosenstein-Rodan appears to have been one of the foremost advocates of providing a minimum of social overhead capital as a basis for both indigenous and incoming industry.[g] Such investment would create a minimum quantum of infrastructure without which firms could not be expected to locate in basically undeveloped areas. Also, apart from this, it could have a significant effect by raising demand in the areas concerned to the extent that the required inputs were provided from within the region, and that the labour employed would spend a proportion of its wages on additional goods produced within the region. On the other hand, as Rosenstein-Rodan further pointed out, the effects of infrastructural investment are both indirect and uncertain. The induced investment expected may not take place at all, or may take place outside the region. In this case, there is no point in indefinitely increasing the proportion of available public investment funds allocated to infrastructure. As he expresses it, 'if one proceeds to install a second dynamo besides the first, instead of making the transmission belt function, the induced current of industrialisation would not ensue and the installation of a second dynamo would be wasteful. A whole system of different policy measures may be required to make the transmission belt function.'[25]

It is precisely here that target proportions for location in given industrial sectors, focused on meso-economic firms, could prove more effective. The pattern of location – whether concentrated or dispersed, or a combination of both concentration and dispersion – is an element of development strategy which must be decided on other grounds. But once such a pattern is decided upon, the degree of certainty in location for the incoming or indigenous firms necessary to fulfil the overall sectoral targets means that sufficient infrastructure for those firms can be tailored to their specific needs. This not only could reduce the major wastage of resources on infrastructural investment to which Rosenstein-Rodan has pointed in the Italian case, but also would mean a gain in the time period during which a policy of industrialisation could take effect. Instead of undertaking a massive infrastructural programme in the hope that the impression of a qualitative change will finally penetrate board rooms in the more-developed region, which either will take several years before location decisions are influenced, or may not take place at all, the development authorities could secure their infrastructural requirements from the meso-economic leading firms liable to controls and evaluate both specific and general infrastructural requirements from them.

Similar benefits could be expected for public investment in agriculture in the less-developed region. As locational factors would have to be taken into account in determining the spatial distribution of industry and appropriate infrastructure, so the particular characteristics of given agricultural areas would have to be taken into account in assessing their long-term development potential. But inasmuch as it is rightly assumed that the improvement of agriculture depends essentially on industrial demand for both agricultural labour and products, and also that a stimulus is given to both by the proximity of industrial employment to under-employed agricultural areas, the degree of certainty in providing industrial employment through specific sectoral targets and locational controls could yield similar advantages for investment in agriculture as in infrastructure. The expectation of a given quantum of investment in modern manufacturing through harnessing meso-economic firms could enable the planning authorities to estimate the overall employment creation effect for the region from new industry over the planning period. The use of locational controls could further ensure that a higher degree of certainty was introduced into the estimates of labour outflow from specific agricultural areas into industry. Demographic trends could be taken into account in evaluating the short- and long-term needs of particular areas. Trends in emigration of labour from the region to industry elsewhere in the economy would be affected both by the new employment possibilities in the region, and by the effect of controls on the rate of industrial expansion in the more-industrialised region. But these too could be more precisely estimated if the specific location as well as the total quantum of industrial investment and employment over a given time period were known in advance.

To this extent the establishment of precise locational targets for industry and given industrial sectors could have major advantages for the process of development planning as a whole. As manpower requirements within the region were made plain by firms subject to locational controls, government training centres could immediately undertake training of labour within the area in which the firms were to locate, and in the skills which the firms specified that they would require. Similarly, inasmuch as government policy anticipated any need to rationalise the structure of firms in services, the precise location of industry could provide a basis for such rationalisation which would be more effective than general exhortation to modernise. Granted that such service firms could be informed with precision which firms (on what scale) would be located within the area which they could serve, they would have a clearer incentive to adapt themselves to meet forthcoming demand than in the event of the government only offering incentives to firms to locate, and of neither it nor the firms in services knowing where that location might ultimately take place. In general, the more precise the locational controls, the more efficacious the policy, and the greater the extent to which the planning process could prove comprehensive in its effects.

False Hopes from Input–Output Analysis

Granted that such benefits could follow from the specification of targets for given sectors within industry, what reliance should be placed on other techniques of inter-sectoral analysis, and, in particular, on interregional input-output analysis? In fact, of course, the difficulties of determining priority sectors for unbalance from input–output data have already been seen in the Hirschman attempt to secure evidence on forward and backward linkages from Chenery's data. The simpler rate of growth of product and employment method has its own limitations in

185

terms of inter-sectoral linkages, but is not handicapped in the first instance by this fundamental problem. Secondly, while input–output techniques have considerable usefulness in specific instances in enabling the policy-maker to trace particular intersectoral supply and demand effects, they suffer from major handicaps which the simpler growth method does not – in particular, the scale economy problem, and technical change. For instance, while the 'modern' manufacturing sectors already identified may appear unsophisticated because relatively broad in range, this range itself means that they include many of the external economy and innovation effects which input–output analysis cannot.

Some of the most ardent advocates of interregional input–output analysis have admitted such major limitations even when the technique is used only as a supplementary programming or planning method. Thus Isard and Smolensky have allowed that 'it is recognised that one of the major shortcomings of input–output analysis and similar techniques in linear economics is that they fail to take account of scale and external economies'.[26] Edith Thorne has spelled out what this means somewhat more fully:

the input–output approach... abstracts from almost all the complex problems that are associated with the simultaneous expansion and contraction of industries: even if explicit provision is made for capital requirements the problem of surpluses and shortages of specific men and machinery are ignored. The implications of these assumptions for regional analysis are important. They imply that economic differences between regions could not have arisen because one region benefited particularly from economies of scale or because it developed new technologies producing cheaper products; the differences must have arisen simply because of the effect of a change in the pattern of final buyers' demand on the industrial complexes of each region... Even at its most sophisticated, input–output can only provide information about the state of affairs which actually exists or would exist in the future if present trends were to continue.[27] [h]

That is to say that input–output techniques neglect precisely those effects which this and the previous chapter have claimed to be the main constituents of the regional growth process. In addition, there are major practical difficulties in input–output estimation at a regional level which further qualify its usefulness and the hopes which should be placed on it. Vera Cao-Pinna has drawn attention to the practical difficulty of setting up an inter-regional trade matrix, which arises from the fact that 'no precise information is available or can be collected about the proportions of competitive imports (i.e. imports of materials which are also produced in the country or region under study) to the total amount of individual inputs required by each productive sector'. She stresses that 'actually, this is the main reason why an input–output table should never be considered as a real body of facts, or as a consolidated statistical system, but rather as an approximation to the reality which is arrived at through a complex set of estimates'. Emphasising that this is a crucial handicap, granted that the fundamental set of information required for setting up a regional input–output table is the quantitative data on import and exports of goods and services between the region under study and the rest of the national economy, Cao-Pinna comments that 'the fact that such a fundamental lack of information has not restrained the pioneers of regional analysis from attempting to establish regional accounts is rather alarming'.[28 i]

Perhaps the most eloquent additional argument for not placing false hopes on input–output techniques in regional intersectoral resource allocation and planning is the fact that one of its principal pioneers, Isard, has rejected it in favour of a far more limited technique of 'industrial complex analysis', which is considered in the following chapter. Granted, however, that the application of input–output techniques at a regional level continued to attract attention and study and that it may well arouse interest in regional policy circles, even with its limiting assumptions, as more quantitative data becomes available through extensions in regional accounting, it may be worthwhile to reiterate the highly evaluative nature of the technique as admitted by practitioners such as Isard and Smolensky. For instance, writing of the Italian case, they have stated that in Italy national goals must yield at least in part to regionally orientated goals. . . . At the outset goals may be defined broadly so as to reflect basic national aspirations such as equality, liberty, justice, security and social welfare. From such broad objectives must succeed a chain of successive specification. . . . Intermediate goals *might* concern such items as the level of *per capita* income, the proportion of the labour force in agriculture, the intensity with which particular resources are to be developed, a steel plant or some heavy industry in every region, a school in every village, etc.[29]

That is to say that a specification must be undertaken independently of the technique. The technique itself is no economist's stone which can indicate which sectors should be selected as policy variables.

The limits of the technique and the continuing need for evaluation has been stressed by Klaassen. Referring to the fixed coefficients problem he states that

this means that it is assumed that all regions will expand or contract out of any national industry in proportion to changes in national demand. Such an assumption might hold good for large regions, less good for smaller regions and only to a limited extent for local areas. *But this is not the main limitation.* In the (regional) context, the emphasis is on depressed areas that are trying to *change* their industrial structure. This aim is incompatible with the assumption of fixed allocation coefficients.[30]

Giving due credit to 'the contribution of unquestionable importance' which has been made by regional input–output models, he adds that 'the limits within which the model builders must operate are very narrow. . . . It is not surprising that hardly a country can be found in which economic policy is based upon econometric models alone, and where due weight is not given to the intuition of policy-makers and to the counsel of expert critics of government policy'.[31] He stresses that his own approach to the identification of sectors for regional development is based on (1) comparative studies of the structure of the area and that of the rest of the economy, and (2) *simplicity.*[32]

In the comparative study which he gives as an example of this method in his earlier work he in fact only uses employment data, declining to utilise data on production. Allowing for the fact that there is not always a good correlation between the two, he undertakes a 'structure index' for the area. First, he expresses employment in branches of industry and agriculture as percentages of total employment for the nation and the area. Assuming that 'industry' in this context can be considered to be growing, and 'agriculture' to be stagnant or declining, and assuming also that forecasts for the national growth of industrial sectors are available in terms of both production and employment, he suggests that the structure index to be calculated should be the weighted average of the growth potential of both sectors. This potential refers to the probable future growth of demand for labour in the area. The probable future supply of labour can be projected from demographic data, and if the rate of growth of employment in the area both is likely to be higher than the national average yet lower than that sufficient to ensure full employment, some emigration should be encouraged.[33]

In the Italian context as well because of his major contribution to the technique of analysis reference must be made to Chenery's input–output studies on the Italian economy, particularly the South. This has appeared in various forms over more than a decade, with his first (joint) work being an estimation of the effects of a 25 per cent increase in G.N.P. on the sectoral structure of the economy over the 1951–6 period, a goal adopted at that time by the member countries of the O.E.E.C.[34] Since the methodology of that study is the same as that for his later work on the Mezzogiorno, it is worth considering both its technique and its success. It included three main elements of a feasibility analysis: (1) a final demand projection; (2) a matrix of input coefficients and other parameters; and (3) the constraints on availability of primary factors. Its aim was to secure information which would answer six main questions: (1) what expansion of investment and government expenditures would be required to generate sufficient demand for fulfilment of the O.E.E.C. goal; (2) what individual industries could be expected to have the most favourable development prospects; (3) what capacity limits, if any, was the economy likely to encounter; (4) what increases in imports were likely to be required; (5) what would the probable

189

fuel balance of the economy be in 1956 through the substitution of natural gas for coal; and (6) what would be the probable effects on the volume of industrial employment and the number of man-hours worked.[35]

The final demand projection started with a conventional national accounts analysis. The probable expansion of exports was estimated independently, considering recent trends. Consumption was estimated on the basis of 'a roughly calculated marginal propensity to consume', and imports on the basis of a marginal import coefficient, with the latter revised upwards in the second approximation to check with the total detailed commodity imports indicated by the inter-industry solution. The increase in investment and government expenditures needed to provide sufficient aggregate demand was then calculated as a residual. These aggregated final demands were broken down among the 200 product classes distinguished in Italy's national accounts, and these reduced to eight major categories of final demand. With regard to the inter-industry matrix, 'the study followed the usual input–output practice in deriving most of the input coefficients directly from the base year (in this case 1950), using an unmodified proportionality assumption'. A few adjustments were made, Chenery states, for technological changes under way such as the blast-furnace expansion undertaken as part of the Marshall Plan, the increased use of pig-iron relative to scrap in the steel industry, and the substitution of natural gas for coal. Marginal import parameters were calculated at a maximum level of disaggregation for each of the 200 product classes, measuring the fraction of additional requirements expected to come from imports rather than domestic consumption. With respect to constraints on the supply of primary factors, it was estimated on the basis of yields per hectare that the marginal import parameter for eight groups of agricultural products should be raised to 100 per cent. Constraints also were calculated for some twenty basic industrial materials by estimating the shortage of existing capital equipment rather than natural resource scarcity, using data for 1953. But these 1953 capacities were *not* incorporated into the input–output calculation itself. They were only used *after* the calculation to consider whether investment during the rest of the period seemed likely to be adequate.[36]

In making his own estimation after 1956 of the accuracy of the

190

projections, Chenery was limited to summary data for that terminal year, since it proved impossible to construct even a rough input–output table to check the results. But the results themselves were qualified by other factors. Firstly, the O.E.E.C. goal for the economy was revised upwards from a 25 per cent to a 32 per cent increase in G.N.P. This was met with a small margin to spare. As Chenery himself expressed, it was made possible by 'a substantially larger growth of investment, government expenditures and exports than had been anticipated, offset by a smaller growth of consumption and an even sharper rise in imports'. With regard to his own projections, he admits that the national accounts projection and the detailed final demand projection were 'too proportional', and that there was insufficient The pro)ections certainly included wide margins of error. For the production of individual industries the average percentage error between the projected and actual production indices was 16 per cent; for imports it was 31 per cent (excluding wheat, which was 402 per cent). Disaggregating the industry production targets also showed wide divergences within the average, and in particular for the modern and advanced technology industries whose growth was substantially *under*-estimated. For nine industries the error was less than 10 per cent; for five between 10 per cent and 20 per cent; for four between 30 per cent and 40 per cent, and for one 56 per cent. The 56 per cent underestimation was for petroleum refining. Cellulose and artificial fibres were under-estimated by 12 per cent; mechanical engineering by 14 per cent; metallic minerals by 16 per cent, ferrous metals by 34 per cent, chemicals by 38 per cent.[37]

One very clear conclusion emerges from this study. Although it was not differentiated regionally, it is quite evident that, if production and import targets had both been set for the less-developed region and, through policy measures, achieved, the under-estimation of the feasible sectoral targets for the rest of the economy would have meant that it increased its lead over the lagging region by a substantial margin. In practice this would appear a realistic assumption granted that the industrial capacity of the L.D.R. would have increased less than the increase in demand, with or without 'appropriate' policy measures. It is of some interest that, in his 1962 study of feasible growth rates for

191

the Mezzogiorno, Chenery in fact reduced his level of disaggregation and distinguished only four main target sectors: agriculture extractive industry, the food industry and other industry. He then delineated three different options for the South of Italy over the 1959–70 period: (1) a 'pure and simple "demand projection" ', based on the assumption that increases in production would be determined by existing demand elasticities for the existing structure of production, maintaining fixed 'regional supply coefficients' (the share of the region in national production, excluding imports); (2) the structural modifications necessary to guarantee a growth rate of gross product in the South of 5 per cent per annum, with an 'optimistic' assumption of the growth potential of Southern agriculture, considerably higher than the national growth rate, and (3) the structural modifications necessary to secure an increase in *per capita* product in the South of 5 per cent per annum without increasing the rate of emigration.[38]

The limitations which Chenery admitted for these estimations included: (1) that demand could be calculated only on a national rather than a regional basis through lack of data; (2) the only data on supply available for the South was for agriculture and extractive industry; (3) the projections were calculated at constant prices 'because of which any effects from variations in the terms of trade between regions was excluded *a priori*'; (4) no account was taken of the utilisation of factors.[39] His summary of results is extremely brief, and are almost entirely listed as follows. For the first option, the South would experience a fall back from the rate of growth of G.N.P. of 5 per cent per annum, due to the assumption that the rate of emigration would be equivalent to that of regional gross product, whereas it had been higher during the 1950s. The extent of the projected fall back is not specified. In order for a rate of growth of *per capita* income of 5 per cent per annum to be achieved, a tripling of the 1950s emigration rate would have to be secured. For the second option, the proportion of national manufacturing value added provided by the South would have to amount to 15.7 per cent by 1970, and, for the third option, to 18 per cent.

But as with his national projections, Chenery's regional projections in fact proved to be substantially incorrect. For instance, income *per capita* in fact grew by just more than 5 per cent per annum from 1960 to 1969.[40] But this was achieved with a net fall in the rate of emigration from the South rather than the tripling of the rate of emigration assumed necessary for such an income growth by Chenery.[41] Also, it was achieved with a Southern proportion of national manufacturing value-added in 1969 of only 12·9 per cent, rather than the 18 per cent hypothesised as necessary by Chenery in the event of a constant emigration rate.[42] In other words, Chenery's emigration assumptions were more than 300 per cent wrong, and his assumption for manufacturing value-added was wrong by nearly 50 per cent. Moreover, despite the greater sophistication of his technique of analysis, Chenery's regional model was more highly aggregated than our own more simply devised sectoral targets of the previous section in this chapter, and in this respect alone less useful for policy evaluation. This is perhaps surprising for, in a review article of development policies in Southern Italy published the same year, he criticised the failure to disaggregate policy ob)ectives, pointing out that one of the major reasons for the poor performance of southern industry in the 1950s was the region's small share of output in those sectors which had contributed the bulk of national exports in the decade. These included metals and metal products, chemicals and chemical products – i.e. those sectors which we have indicated (following Kuklinski) as priorities for selective unbalance in favour of the South.[43]

Chenery's failure to link his model and his policy recommendations is perhaps understandable in view of the intrinsic limits of the techniques which he employed. To some extent he appears to have been undecided himself about its practical use, writing in 1965 in a further but similar study on the South that 'it is too soon to say how much formal programming methods can contribute to the work of economists and government policy-makers concerned with economic development'.[44] But in his 1962 model he clearly holds that such models of regional growth 'throw light on the manner in which an increase in national income is translated into increases in production in each region', and that 'once the model has been chosen it will be possible to analyse the effects which effective or potential economic policy measures will produce on the actual structure of demand and supply'.[45] Yet this is patently what his models cannot do, not least because he makes an implicit equi-proportional or strict balanced-growth assumption concerning the regional distribution of the national income increase. The rate of growth of supply in the sectors in each region is determined by existing supply and demand elasticities, and these are simply projected to fulfil the given increase in aggregate demand. In other words, the sectoral composition of production in the region in the 'planning' period is simply an extrapolation for its sectoral composition in the base period.

NOTES

[a] Cf. further this chapter.

[b] As previously mentioned, an industrialisation policy for the South of Italy has been disputed on arbitrary grounds by Mrs Vera Lutz, whose case is criticised in Chapter 5.

[c] See Table 6, p.282.

[d] Among the E.E.C.'s six orginal member countries only Germany registered a marked fallback in average annual G.N.P. increase in the 1960s relative to the 1950s.

[e] Cf. Table 9, p.285.

[f] For smaller regions the proportions problem clearly does not arise on the same scale. The general guidelines in this case would be 'modern' rather than 'traditional' manufacturing.

[g] In his capacity as economic adviser to successive post-war Italian governments.

[h] Edith Thorne also emphasises the extent to which regional input-output analysis is unable to take account of the entrepreneur: 'by ignoring the effects of scale and technical progress and the problems of adaptation to change, the analysis omits from consideration the role of the entrepreneur who responds successfully to changing conditions by changing production methods, products, markets, etc.' In effect, input–output analysis could be said to improve on purely macro-economic projections, but as a complete explanation of the changes in the regional growth process it does not disaggregate enough. On the other hand, despite the particular shortcomings of interregional input–output analysis as outlined by Vera Cao-Pinna (cf. following text), there is no reason in principle why more disaggregated information should not be secured by planning authorities from leading firms, within sectors, and an attempt made to incorporate extrapolations from their estimates of changed production methods, products, etc.) into a national projection. Cf. later, Chapter 8.

[i] In attempting an input–output model for Sicily Cao-Pinna emphasises that this was largely made possible through Sicily being administratively an autonomous

island region, with trade statistics between not only the region and the rest of the world but also with the rest of the Italian economy.

CHAPTER 7

SPATIAL CONCENTRATION VERSUS DISPERSION

The Role of Locational Economies

It was suggested in a previous chapter that some of the disillusionment which has recently been felt with growth-pole policy reflects a fundamental misunderstanding of the role which external economies can play in the polarisation process. It has been seen that Myrdal initially stressed the role of external economies 'interpreted in the widest possible sense' in the cumulative disequilibrium process, with the concentration of such economies in the areas in which growth historically began reinforcing further concentration.[1] Perroux also stressed their importance in his initial exposition of the growth-pole concept,[2] yet later demoted them in favour of the concept of 'growth-promoting' investment, interpreted in a different sense to include the force of innovation in entirely new processes and products, again concentrated in those areas in which growth had initially taken place.[3] But in fact his later treatment does not argue the case against reliance on external economies in polarisation. It simply asserts it. As a consequence, it is perhaps not surprising that so many of his own followers have continued to employ the external economies concept in a growth-pole context, and that this fashion has been extended in the United States in 'industrial complex' analysis.[a]

Granted the disappointing results from growth-poles policy, a revision of the nature of the external economies concept and its role in promoting (or not promoting) a self-generating and sustaining growth process in particular locations is overdue. This indicates that while there may well be two main concepts of external economies, only one of those identified by Scitovsky should be considered a properly filled economic box, that is to say 'pecuniary' economies. The second of Scitovsky's two concepts – 'technological' external economies – is largely an illusory phenomenon, arising either from a confusion of locational and technological factors, or also of external and internal economies themselves.

In proposing the distinction between pecuniary and technological external economies, Scitovsky was attempting to clarify the use of an already overloaded single concept.[4] He pointed out that a confusion had arisen from its use in two entirely different contexts: equilibrium theory on the one hand, and industrialisation theory on the other. As an explanation of the former he cited Meade's definition,[5] which was that such economies exist whenever the output of a firm depends not only on its own factors of production but also on the output and the factor utilisation of another firm or groups of firms. He points out that, as defined in this way, external economies are a peculiarity of the production function. They arise because of *direct interdependence* between producers. For this reason they are 'the villains of the piece' in general equilibrium theory which, of course, is a theory of *in*direct interdependence through the market mechanism. He draws attention to Viner's use of 'technological' to describe direct external economies.[6]

Scitovsky maintains that it is not easy to find examples of such economies from industry, and claims that in going through the literature he can find only two which fit the definition: the case in which a firm benefits from the labour market created by the establishment of other firms, and the case of more than one firm using a resource which is free but limited in supply. As examples of the latter (as a diseconomy) he gives the oil well whose output depends on the number and operation of other wells in the same field; the fisherman whose catch depends on the operation of other fishermen in the same waters, and the firm which uses a public road or another publicly-owned utility, and is partly crowded out of it by other firms using the same road. Reference to Meade's article, he continues, will convince the reader of the scarcity of industrial examples of technological external economies, since most of those which Meade cites are 'bucolic' in nature, for example the economies accruing to a bee-keeper from the proximity of an orchard which sustains his bees, and of the bees to the orchard-owner in that they pollinate his trees. He concludes that external economies of this type fail to account for the main category of external economies which exist in practice:

those which arise because of *indirect interdependence* of producers through the market mechanism. As he expressed it himself:

external economies are invoked whenever the profits of one producer are affected by the actions of other producers.... This definition of external economies obviously includes direct or non-market interdependence among producers, as discussed above and defined by Meade. It is much broader, however, than his definition, because, in addition to direct interdependence among producers, it also includes interdependence among producers through the market mechanism. This latter type of interdependence may be called 'pecuniary external economies' to distinguish it from the technological external economies of direct interdependence.[7]

There is little doubt that Scitovsky has helped to clarify the concept of external economies by distinguishing those which are 'pecuniary'. On the other hand, it seems evident that the non-pecuniary external economies which he dismisses as relatively unimportant are of considerably more significance than he admits. For instance, from the point of view of regional analysis and policy, the benefits accruing to some firms from the labour market created by the establishment of other firms, or from the existence of transport facilities, can be extremely important. Also, his adoption of Viner's terminology of 'technological' to describe non-pecuniary external economies probably is misleading. In the first place, there clearly is a sense in which *pecuniary* external economies are 'technological' in that they concern reductions in unit costs for an individual producer in securing inputs from technologically related firms whose internal economies of scale permit them to produce the inputs at lower cost than the producer who purchases them. There is a more evident 'technological' link here than in the external economy to a producer from the availability of labour and transport facilities. In fact, it is not so much technology which distinguishes non-pecuniary external economies from those which are pecuniary, as the fact that such economies arise from a particular *location*.[b]

Probably one of the best ways to make this clear is to 'go back to Marshall'. In introducing the external and internal economies concepts he stated that 'we may divide the economies arising

198

from an increase in the scale of production of any kind of goods into two classes – firstly, those dependent on the general development of the industry; and, secondly, those dependent on the resources of the individual houses of business engaged in it, on their organisation and efficiency of management. We may call the former *external economies,* and the latter *internal economies.*'[8] This statement – the most frequently cited – clearly is consistent with and can be held to support Scitovsky's emphasis on pecuniary external economies. However, Marshall immediately continues the same paragraph (concluding Bk IV, chapter IX of the *Principles*) by stating: 'in the present chapter we have been chiefly discussing internal economies; but we now proceed to examine those very important external economies which can often be secured by the concentration of many small businesses of a similar character *in particular localities*: or, as is commonly said, by the localization of industry.'[9] In the following chapter Marshall outlined the principal external economies from location analysed extensively by literature on location since his time, such as labour and employment availability, savings in transport costs and ease of communications.[10] If we add socio-economic infrastructure to these, we have four of the principal categories of external economies from location indicated by some of the most recent empirical evidence on the subject.

The most useful way in which to consider Scitovsky's 'technological' external economies is as pecuniary external economies of location or, more briefly, 'locational economies'.[c] Some of the literature on location and regional analysis to appear in the last decade has focused attention on the spatial juxtaposition of technically related industry in industrial complexes, which might superficially appear to amount to 'technological' external economies. The most sophisticated example of this so far has been the Schooler study of a single-plant complex in which crude petroleum would be refined, and the by-products processed into fertiliser and manufactured into synthetic fibre on site.[11] The other most notable case is the integrated steel plant, in which the production of pig-iron, steel, steel tubing and steel plate are undertaken as a continuous process.[d] In fact, however, it is apparent that the economies secured from an integrated complex are only extreme (and highly logical) examples of locational economies. It is principally the pecuniary saving in transport from on-site production which promotes the juxtaposition concerned. It is feasible enough to transport pig-iron from a foundry at one location to a steel plant at another, or to transport the gas containing ethylene from the refinery site to a fertiliser plant elsewhere, but integrated production in a single location, by saving transport costs and generally improving communications between the different stages of production, is more economical. In most cases, moreover, such integrated plant are owned by single private or public companies, and therefore anyway amount to *in*ternal rather than external economies.[12]

Ultimately, of course, the terminology employed in identifying such external economies as labour availability, transport facilities, communications and infrastructure is not of crucial importance provided that the analytical consequences of such economies are clear. It has already been pointed out that Perroux has recently reduced the importance which he initially attached to them in contributing to the spatial concentration of activity. His disciples, however, in some cases have not followed him, and argue that such concentration alone can maximise the economies concerned. This emphasis may be understandable enough in view of the continued output of neo-classical models of balanced spatial distribution of the type outlined and criticised in the opening chapter. On the other hand, it is increasingly evident that some firms can secure greater economies, in the sense we have described, by locating away from large urban concentrations. Moreover, dispersion of this kind is different from the dispersion of neo-classical theory, with its assumption of perfectly competitive firms producing homogeneous products for spatially fixed and unchanging patterns of demand. By contrast, it depends very much on differences in the structure of firms and the type and stage of production in which they are engaged. Because of these differences, and their evident importance for regional policy, the following two sections distinguish between the contribution of locational economies to spatial concentration and spatial dispersion.[c]

The Case for Concentration

Labour. Traditionally, most analysis of the factors contributing to the concentration of economic activity in urban centres has placed great emphasis on the role of labour in the dual senses of its availability to producers as a factor of production, and the availability of employment in such centres for labour itself. The principal reason for the migration of rural population to urban centres clearly are the higher earnings to be obtained in industry and services than in agriculture plus, in many cases, the escape from seasonal unemployment. The larger the centre and the greater the absolute number of firms, the greater are the possibilities of employment. The more diverse the type of production (frequently, although not always, varying with the size of the centre), the greater the possibility for a worker finding alternative employment in the event of his becoming redundant as a result of declining demand in the industry of which his firm is part. Conversely, the constant inflow of labour to a large urban centre masses reserves of labour for employers in those centres. As Hoover expresses it: 'a shoe manufacturer in one of the big centres like Brockton or Chicago can normally get additional or substitute help at a few hours' notice, whereas an isolated shoe manufacturer cannot.'[13] To this extent, it pays the employer to wait for labour to come to him, rather than going to the labour in agricultural areas where it will probably be more thinly distributed. An additional factor reinforcing this is the fact that labour immigrating from rural to urban areas tends to be 'preselected' for the urban employer, in that it constitutes the fitter, younger, more adaptable element of the population from which it is drawn.[f]

A further factor whereby an urban employer may benefit from an urban as against a rural location is what Marshall has called the 'constant market for skill'. Thus, 'the owner of an isolated factory, even if he has access to a plentiful supply of general labour, is often put to great shifts for want of some *skilled* labour.[14] In a large centre where a particular trade has become established, such skill may be acquired by subsequent generations. Marshall may be exaggerating by claiming that 'the mysteries of the trade become no mysteries; but are as it were in the air, and children learn many of them unconsciously'.[15] What the children learn for the main part probably is an attitude towards a particular type of work, and a preparedness to accept it, whether it be coal-mining, working in a steel plant or in an automobile factory. On the other hand, they may also learn the principles of the work before they actually encounter a coal-cutter or an assembly line, and be more adaptable to specific instruction on entering employment. The importance of skilled labour in promoting urban concentration was emphasised recently by Parodi: 'it might be thought that the abandonment of certain activities in the primary sector would be a consideration favouring the industrialisation of rural areas. In fact, the need for highly qualified personnel limits the possibility of setting up industries to large towns and constitutes one of the reasons why the Paris area is found to be attractive.'[16]

Transport. It has already been stressed that one of the principal locational economies from production in an integrated plant is the saving in transport costs. Like Weber, but without restricting himself to Weber's assumptions, Hoover ascribed primary importance to transport costs in determining location, distinguishing between 'material' and 'market' orientation. In the former, there is a high 'weight loss', either in the processing of a raw material (for example the waste from iron ore in pig-iron production), or in large fuel requirements which do not enter into the product (for example cement, glass, calcium carbide and synthetic nitrates). This makes it more profitable to locate production near the material concerned, and transport the product (where necessary) to markets elsewhere. Conversely, in a 'market orientated' industry there is a high 'weight gain' in the production process, so that distribution costs per ton of final product are greater than the cost per ton of inputs coming from any single location to which it would pay the producer to move. As examples of this Hoover cites fragile, cumbersome and perishable products (for example bread, beverages, confectionery and ice cream). But he also makes the more widespread claim that, with later stages of production approaching and reaching final demand, 'the customers buy in smaller and more varied lots and are more insistent on prompt delivery of goods ordered at short notice. Demand reflects more and more the passing whims of the final consumer, and goods not closely tailored to market trends and rapidly produced and delivered are likely to miss the market.'[17]

As later argued, it seems evident that plant size enters importantly into the extent to which market orientation need contribute to the location of later stages of production in urban centres. If a single plant may serve a substantial proportion of a national market, and if the geographical distribution of concentrated market areas includes several large urban centres, it would seem clear enough that (other locational economies being available) it may pay the company to locate such a plant between two or more such centres rather than locate at either of them. On the basis of a purely *a priori* analysis, Hoover denies this, and maintains that 'the best location will ordinarily be found either at the materials source or at the market and only exceptionally at any intermediate point.'[18] Clearly the size of the urban centre will be important. On the basis of a study of the New York metropolitan areas for example, Benjamin Chinitz has argued that 'all in all, the forces pulling manufacturing employment into the metropolitan areas seem to be increasing rather than diminishing in strength'.[g] In such a case the massive concentration of final demand attracts the later stages of production to itself rather than to an intermediate point between New York and other urban areas. An additional transport factor with so large an urban area is that the transport network leading to several other urban centres concentrates and intersects at New York, so that the advantages of an 'intermediate' location between Boston and Pittsburgh coincide with the largest centre of final demand in the North-east of the country.[h]

Communications. Hoover has drawn attention to the benefit for producers in being able to deliver varied quantities of goods adapted to special consumer requirements at short notice at later stages of production. In the case of relatively small firms, it seems clear that proximity between producers and consumers is an advantage in this case not only in the sense of quicker and cheaper transport, but also in facilitating communications and thus making the order possible in the first place. A small-to medium-sized concern in a large urban area can more easily make contact for inputs with particular specifications needed at short notice with a producer in the same area than with a producer outside the area. They probably will know each other and have built up personal contact (perhaps belonging to the same trade association) with a degree of confidence based on previous transactions. If necessary, pressure can be brought more easily

203

in the event of failure to meet an agreed time schedule. The closer the two concerns in this sense, the more their related production approximates to a single unit, with 'internalised' economies from regularly placed orders. The availability of stocks at short notice in an urban area also is evidently important for small firms.

Marshall has emphasised that local communication may have what amounts to a 'spread effect' in facilitating the introduction of new technology or other forms of innovation: 'good work is rightly appreciated, inventions and improvements in machinery, in processes and the general organisation of the business have their merits promptly discussed; if one man starts a new idea, it is taken up by others and combined with suggestions of their own; and thus it becomes the source of further new ideas.'[19] For small firms without independent R and D departments, or without management in touch with those innovations made public in management and other journals, this probably is still largely the way in which innovation is achieved. An isolated small producer might stay 'out of touch' indefinitely, or until he found his own local market undermined by more progressive urban producers of his own scale. Vernon has recently claimed that there is 'good reason to believe that the antrepreneur's consciousness of and responsiveness to opportunity are a function of ease of communication; and further, that ease of communication is a function of geographical opportunity'. He has also pointed out, following Stigler, that in the early stages of introducing a new product, producers are especially concerned with their degree of freedom in changing inputs. Since the price elasticity of demand for new products tends to be comparatively low in initial stages of production, 'the need for swift and effective communication on the part of the producer with customers, suppliers and even competitors is high'. To this extent, in the initial stages of innovation price factors tend to be less vital than location.[20]

Vernon appears to have originated this analysis from his findings from the New York metropolitan study undertaken with Hoover and others. In that study he identified just under one-third of total manufacturing employment within the New York region (600,000 from 1,900,000 jobs) as including industries whose location was governed by some overriding special need. Among them he particularly identified 'communication-oriented' industries, and especially the clothing and printing business of downtown Manhattan. These industries offer customer-tailored products and services which frequently depend upon face-to-face contact (clothes of a certain design, or financial prospectuses, of which the customer wishes to see a sample before confirming the order). This would not matter so much if it were not also for the pressure of time in many of the orders concerned. As he says 'the firms are not offering as their stock-in-trade the products themselves but the products-by-a-certain-time'. However, he also emphasises that there are particular additional reasons which encourage such central clustering in the Manhattan area (and in the clothing trade a few street blocks within it). The first is the unstandardised nature of the products concerned, and the uncertainty of the market. The second is the small size of the firms concerned and their low degree of market power. Thus, 'if the industries we have discussed so far were dominated by large firms, we might envisage a different locational pattern. If the firms were large enough, dominant brand names might emerge, and superior bargaining power might accrue to a few firms. If so the producer might be free to select his location with more freedom.' In other words there tends to be an interrelationship between product uncertainty and small micro-economic manufacturing establishments. Moreover, he stresses that the communications-orientated industries, like others in the New York metropolitan region, have recently begun to show a dispersive tendency, leaving the core of the region for other, more peripheral locations.[21]

Services. As with the sale or supply of products in which time and a degree of unpredictability are important, it is evident that replacement and repair services are of considerable importance to a producer in enabling him to avoid serious production stoppages. The smaller the plant, and the less the extent to which he can provide such services himself, the greater the benefit may be from location near them. As Greenhut states: 'proximity facilitates repair of machinery and replacement of broken parts, thereby shortening the time period of bottlenecks in production.'[22] Similarly, the proximity of a bank with sufficiently senior staff, knowing the firm, and with independent authority to offer short-term facilities at short notice, may affect whether or not a relatively small producer undertakes a particular production decision, especially where this affects variable costs which he otherwise might not be able to meet. Proximity again may determine whether or not such a firm employs specialist engineering or technical advice since, as Aydlot writes, 'an engineer's or expert's time is expensive'.[23]Lombardini has emphasised that there are indivisibilities in the provision of such services. They are not uniformly available throughout geographic space, but available only in areas which are large enough to support them.[24] To this extent, it pays small firms to locate in the relatively large urban areas in which they can be found.

Infrastructure. It has been widely held that infrastructure (in the sense of housing, health, education, welfare and cultural facilities, access to main transport routes, power and water supply telecommunications and sewerage) is highly indivisible. This has been stressed by Hirschman,[25] and has been well put by Lombardini: 'a conspicuous example of indivisibility due to technical factors is given by the economies promoted by the decisions of local authorities with regard to infrastructure, which can only be realised at a certain level, and which is effective only if undertaken in an organic complex.'[26] The case for the 'minimum level' argument has been stressed by Gavin McCrone: 'small units of 30,000 or so can scarcely justify frequent rail services or technical colleges, let alone airports or universities.'[27] Even if it may be argued that not all economic activity *needs* technical colleges, universities, airports or railways, there is considerable force to the further argument that many of the facilities of social overhead capital are mutually complementary, in the sense that they are all considered necessary to the achievement of a given standard of living. In this case the minimum population density necessary for economies of scale in any single facility would influence the desirable minimum size of the urban centre as a whole.

Further, there are cumulative, self-reinforcing effects between the provision of urban infrastructure and other locational economies. A relatively small firm may not be able to afford the construction of an access road in an isolated area, or be able to wait for the extension of power, water, telecommunications or sewerage facilities which could be more readily available in an urban complex. The higher standard of housing which may be available in urban rather than rural areas may be an additional inducement to higher incomes in promoting immigration. The health facilities provided in an urban centre may not only maintain but also improve the fitness and productivity potential of the labour force. The higher education facilities normally available in urban areas should mean a higher standard of education for at least the second generation of immigrant labour. If technical colleges and universities are available, some of them may become the 'highly qualified personnel' cited as of such importance by Parodi.[28] In addition, the higher standard of 'social' facilities in a large urban area clearly tends to attract (or retain) both unskilled and skilled labour, technical personnel and management, whether such facilities amount to 'blue' movies or art films, strip clubs or theatre, league football teams or the country club. Not least, the manager's wife will be able to buy the latest in-fashion clothes, household goods or whatever, without grudgingly conceded and infrequent visits to a larger urban centre. All these factors contribute to explaining the continuing, massive attraction of large urban centres as against more isolated locations.

The Case for Dispersion

Labour. Two principal factors may offset the benefit to urban employers from the spatial concentration of labour in urban areas: (1) higher wages, whether contractual *minima* or effective, and (2) greater unionisation. The two factors may interact. Stronger unionisation may mean a higher agreed rate in urban areas. On the other hand, the same multiplicity of producers in an urban area which, it has been argued, contributes to attracting labour because of the greater ease of alternative employment, may itself promote a rise in urban over rural wages. The ready availability of alternative employers either obliges an individual employer to respect the going rate for the type of labour involved, or may reinforce his readiness to offer more in order to secure it, thus contributing to wage drift.[29] In a more isolated location in which there are fewer employment alternatives this tendency to wage drift will be reduced or avoided, and both minimal and contractual rates are likely to be lower. The degree of availability of labour in such a location will depend partly on the degree of its isolation from the main urban areas of labour inflow, which appears to influence the rate of emigration and thus the degree of unemployment and disguised unemployment.[30] The Italian evidence indicates that many small communes in both the South and the North have been able to provide a working force for medium-sized firms which have been rational enough to locate there rather than in one of the major centres. In such cases it appears that the firms concerned have been persuaded that they can secure sufficient labour for both their present and future needs. Clearly the potential labour force for such plant could in due course be drawn not only from under-employed agricultural labour, but also from under-employment in retailing, distribution and other services, and from hitherto unemployed female labour.[31]

The further important benefit which may occur from the concentration of labour in large urban areas is the requirement of 'skill' stressed by Marshall, Parodi and others. It has been argued by Coront-Ducluzeau (as with Parodi, from French evidence) that the rise of labour costs in regions or areas with a high degree of labour concentration is offset both by higher productivity and by labour economies resulting from innovation.[32] On the other hand, Hoover has pointed out that, with the maturing of almost any industry, technical and managerial innovation (which will tend to be labour-saving with increased mechanisation) also permits the 'routinisation' of work, so that 'ordinary labour without special training can be used'. On the basis of North-American evidence, he argues that 'the normal result is that industry spreads or moves to other areas, its dispersion from the original centres being sped by the relatively high wages and inflexible conditions that have become established there by the skilled elite'.[33] Hoover's argument is corroborated by Italian evidence. The plant managers of the Alfa-Romeo automobile company and the Taranto steel complex maintain that illiterate southern labour can and do learn to perform the manual labour tasks required by their plant within a month, and at the outside within six weeks.[i] Olivetti is said to find the same even for the assembly of office machinery.[j] On this evidence, the labour-skill argument clearly is not a sufficient case for the location of plant in large urban areas. Further, this evidence may not conflict directly with Parodi's argument, since it appears from his own ter-

208

minology of 'highly qualified personnel' that he is concerned with technicians, engineers and draughtsmen rather than manual labour. The unavailability of such personnel may be an important limiting factor in the choice of locations for small-to medium-sized firms with 'immature' production processes requiring constant adaptation. A large firm with such production. however, may be able to provide such personnel internally. Further, many medium-sized firms do appear to have 'routinised' production in Hoover's sense. Where they do not, the expansion of technical education in the region concerned may contribute to 'closing the technical gap' and thus widen their locational choice.[34]

Transport. One of the principal features of high transport costs in the past is generally agreed to have been the protection of local or regional markets, with the cost of long-distance hauls acting in effect as tariffs. However, the reduction of transport costs, and especially the wider range of road, as opposed to rail, networks, has increased the locational options available to firms operating from a single plant, and thereby has enabled many to take advantage of economies of scale in production which previously would not have been available. This has been argued from British evidence by Luttrell: 'economies of scale of a single large plant may outweigh possible transport savings of a regional pattern'.[35] Florence has pointed out that the widened location available from such reduced transport costs may include several material and market areas: 'Localisation has been the child of cheaper transport since it has made procurements of materials and distribution of products to and from a wide area less costly, and given the economies of large scale production in one or a few localities a greater chance to prevail over transport costs.'[36] This is particularly the case if the type of production in the plant concerned is relatively 'mature'. If orders are regular, and allowing where necessary for seasonal fluctuations in demand, more efficient use can be made of vehicles in loading and distribution.[k]

This argument clearly conflicts with Pottier's claim that transport axes in particular have the effect of concentrating growth at the urban agglomerations which they interconnect.[37] On the other hand, Pottier's argument amounts at least in part to a case

209

of *post hoc ergo propter hoc*. Urban agglomerations were intensified in the early period of industrialisation by high transport costs for 'weight gain' and in many cases also for 'weight loss' industries (when either raw material deposits coincided with an existing urban centre, or attracted population and promoted urban growth). Further, relatively few firms decide to establish new plant rather than expand existing ones, since the expansion justified by increased demand may not be sufficient, or may not be thought sufficient, to justify the cost of an entirely new plant incorporating available internal economies of scale.[38] However, in terms of least transport costs, the optimal location in terms of distribution for a plant serving two main market areas would be somewhere between them, with the precise location being determined by the relative size and frequency of delivery to each. This attraction of one or the other centre would be reinforced (or conversely, offset) by whichever centre was the major source of inputs for the plant. But in the event of both centres coming within the economic area of supply and distribution, and other locational economies being available, it would not benefit the firm concerned to locate at either centre as opposed to somewhere between them.[39] In general, the same argument would apply for more than two such centres, except in the rare case that such a least-cost intermediate location happened to coincide with a single market centre or trans-shipment point. Even in such a case the traffic congestion within such a centre could increase distribution costs to other markets, and could promote a location actually outside the centre itself.[40]

Chinitz and Vernon corroborate the intermediate location solution from their analysis of plant location under changing transport conditions in the United States. They distinguish a 'transport cycle' which is an advance on Hoover's two-stage distinction between initially raw-material orientated and later market-orientated locations. As they point out, the initial impact of the twentieth-century transport revolution through the introduction of motorisation was to promote the decentralisation of industry rather than its further concentration near raw materials. Its effect was to reduce the cost of short relative to long hauls, with truck rather than rail transport encouraging the producer to obtain proximity to his market. But they emphasise that recent developments in transport such as (1) the spread of co-

210

ordinated services such as 'piggy-back' (container) transport, (2) the growing use of air freight, and (3) increased co-ordination of railroad freight structures (in the United States) can be thought of as reversing the earlier trend by which the cost of short hauls had been declining relative to long hauls. Thus,

> the new developments are likely to strengthen the position of distant producers – provided they are not too distant relative to local producers. A manufacturer on the East Coast may not find his position much improved in competing with a manufacturer on the West Coast for the California market. But the position of, say, a Chicago producer or a New York producer in relation to a competitor in Dallas for the Texas market may be decidedly improved.[41]

Communications. In stating the case for concentration it was emphasised that small firms stood to benefit considerably from the ease of communications in urban areas. Personal contact could play an important part in identifying market trends, the placing of an order and securing the necessary inputs at short notice in the event of such an order changing previous production patterns. However, the larger the firm and the more meso-economic its structure, the less important personal contact becomes. The more 'mature' the product and the production process, the more likely that orders will be regular and constant in specification. In the event of any variation, telecommunications can be as prompt as or more prompt than personal contact. The more established the firm and the greater its general reputation, the less the need for pressure and bargaining in guaranteeing that the change in specification can be met. Similarly, telecommunications or occasional travel can ensure the effective transmission of most senior management decisions in the event of the parent company being located elsewhere. In the event of the decisions being structural or exceptional, the plant manager's role can be deputised while he travels to attend the meeting at which they are taken.[42]

Similarly, the benefits accruing to a small firm from 'being in touch' with innovation by location in an urban area are likely in practice to be extremely limited. Technical progress and innovation are increasingly associated with internalised economies

211

from R and D undertaken in specialised departments in the meso-economic companies which can afford them, rather than gathered over a trade association lunch table. As the rate of technical progress and the scale necessary for innovation both increase, the small urban producer is more likely to hear of such innovations rather than introduce them. In this event his chief resort probably will be 'defensive investment' of the Lamfalussy type, permitting minor economies from adaptation of the existing technique of production but inadequate to safeguard his market position in the long run. By contrast, larger firms with a degree of oligopolistic market power are in a better position to phase the introduction of innovations at plant level, with previously established orders, or more probable markets, for the innovated product.[1] In the event of multi-plant companies having located some plant outside urban areas, the more likely it is that they will have available low cost or pre-purchased land for the introduction of a major innovation. In other cases major expansions associated with innovation may prompt a major decision to relocate outside congested urban areas.

Services. The indivisibility of certain services has already been cited as a locational economy for small firms. On the other hand, the indivisibility concerned is only relative to the size of plant. Whereas a small plant may not be able to support an internal specialist for repair, a large plant is very likely to do so, if not to maintain a repair team. A very large single plant may also be able to support the full-time employment of the engineers and 'experts' whose time, as Aydlot has pointed out, is expensive.[43] If this is not the case for a single medium-sized plant, it may well be cheaper for a multi-plant company to employ engineers and other specialists for several plants throughout a given area rather than bring in outside specialist help. If the breakdown in a plant is attributable to design failure, it may well be necessary to bring in specialists for an independent evaluation, but the addi-bring in specialists for an independent evaluation, but the additional time taken for such specialists to visit a relatively isolated plant would be inconsequential in terms of the production loss sustained, and in some cases may be recoverable from insurance. But in any case, as argued previously, the more regularised and established the type of production, the less probable that there would be serious design problems in the first place, and the greater the probability that such breakdowns as might occur could be dealt with on the spot without serious production losses

As far as benefits to small micro-economic firms from location near to more general services such as banking and insurance are concerned, there would appear to be little or nothing which cannot be secured more easily by larger meso-economic firms at greater distance. The larger the firm, the greater its creditworthiness with a given bank or finance house, and the more regular its normal transactions. Payment of employees at plant level does not necessarily involve or require a bank branch in the vicinity. Similarly, insurance for a large plant, with approved fire and theft prevention devices or supervision, tends to be routinised, and should not add significant service costs in a relatively isolated location. In the case of a multi-plant firm, moreover, the central office may be located in a national financial centre and be able to deal directly with banks, finance and insurance houses for urgent, high-priority business, leaving the plant to concern itself with directly productive activity alone. In general, the more specialised the divisional management in meso-economic companies, the more evident that it is possible to decentralise production operations to lower-cost, non-metropolitan or even rural areas.[m]

Besides, there is considerable evidence that repair and service facilities are following the out-migration of small- and medium-sized plant from congested urban centres. As Hoover and Vernon have commented on their findings in the New York metropolitan study,

> repairmen and subcontractors for a considerable range of services are now found almost anywhere in the (greater New York) region. Sewage, fire protection, police protection, adequate power and adequate trucking services also are penetrating the undeveloped open spaces between old cities. The early city monopolies – their ability uniquely to provide an environment in which small plants may settle – are being broken. And in time small plants will have almost as wide a geographical choice as their larger competitors in selecting a site for their activities within the region'.[44]

Infrastructure. In outlining the role claimed for infrastructure in promoting spatial concentration the concept of 'infrastructure'

213

was not disaggregated into its main 'economic' and 'social' capital components. Very frequently, 'infrastructure' is used synonymously with 'social overhead capital'. In analysing its role in encouraging spatial dispersion, however, it is useful to disaggregate the concept. Hirschman distinguished what he called a 'hard core' to the subject, and suggested that this 'probably could be restricted to transportation and power'.[45] Hansen has gone further, and distinguished between social overhead capital, by which he means (rather broadly) 'the provision of satisfactions which have generally been regarded as non-economic in nature', and economic overhead capital, in the sense of 'roads, bridges, harbours, power installations and similar undertakings'.[46] If we are more specific in defining 'social' and 'economic' overhead capital, we could also make a clearer distinction between the two, and classify the former as including housing, health, education, welfare, social facilities (including cinemas, sports facilities, and so on), and general infrastructure essential for domestic use, even if also used in directly productive activity, such as roads, power and water, communications facilities, sanitation services and sewerage. This would mean that the concept of 'economic overhead capital' would refer to that infrastructure essential for the directly productive activity of firms, such as available land and buildings, access to transport routes (either urban or non-urban), on-site power and water supply, on-site communications facilities, sanitation and sewerage.

Distinguishing between economic overhead capital (E.O.C.) and social overhead capital (S.O.C.) in this way helps to clarify several issues, not least the fact that E.O.C., as we have defined it, is the only infrastructure for which a firm is likely to pay directly and in full.[47] For this reason, its constituent elements are among the major factors which firms are likely to take into account in assessing the costs or benefits in continuing the location of plant in major urban areas rather than decentralising. The costs of such alternative locations clearly will vary for the factors concerned. For instance, the difference between charges for power and water supply, on-site communications and sewerage may not be significantly decreased by location outside a major urban area, depending in particular on the pricing policies of the national or local authorities concerned.

214

However, the cost of land and buildings clearly does vary widely between major urban and more isolated locations. Moreover, while a firm may be able to sustain such additional costs for a relatively long time period in an urban location by maximum utilisation of site area, or even shift work, this is likely to be more costly in itself than normal labour housed on a less-restricted site (particularly if a considerable proportion of the site must be used for stocks, loading transport, etc. or if production cannot easily be undertaken in multi-level buildings). Further, an existing site in an urban area may be quite inadequate for the expansion of capacity at a scale which would be sufficient to permit technical economies in production. Evidence by Luttrell, and Cameron and Clark indicates that this factor has been crucial in promoting the decentralisation of production in Britain.[48]

Conversely, it was outlined in the previous section that the generally greater range and higher quality of existing S.O.C. in large urban centres makes them more attractive to many firms, since it will tend to attract and retain younger, more adaptable, better qualified labour. This has been said to offset higher costs to the firms concerned. A further factor reinforcing the growth of such large centres is that the relocation of all production in a smaller, lower-cost centre outside commuting distance of the original location will mean losing that qualified labour which the firm does not undertake to house in the new location and compensate for the cost of movement. This may well prompt the firm concerned to relocate production on a lower-cost site within commuting distance for the existing labour force. On the other hand, a smaller urban centre outside commuting distance of the original location may have sufficient S.O.C. to retain and make available an adequately sized, cheaper labour force for the migrant firm or plant than would be available nearer the original location. From a social welfare standpoint, the standard of this S.O.C. may be below that of larger centres and may also be below the national minimum held to be politically desirable. The health facilities may be only sufficient for the prevention of disease; housing may be outdated, overcrowded and relatively under-equipped in terms of modern sanitation facilities, electricity supply, and so on. The standard of literacy may be below the nominal legal minimum, with a high proportion of the

215

potential labour force actually illiterate. On the basis of the evidence already cited, however, whereby efficient modern firms with relatively routinised production have not found illiteracy a handicap to training labour to the required standard within four to six weeks, it would appear that literacy is not essential to the employment of labour at high levels of productivity. Further, it is not *essential* that accommodation should include air conditioning or central heating before the unemployed qualify for employment.

In effect, however desirable it may be from a social welfare viewpoint to increase S.O.C. in relatively backward areas, it is increasingly evident that S.O.C. infrastructure is not essential for the efficient undertaking of directly productive activity, and that the provision of E.O.C. alone is a necessary condition for it. This distinction naturally does not mean that S.O.C. should not be simultaneously increased with the provision of E.O.C. In fact, while the provision of S.O.C. alone does not necessarily result in the attraction of industry to an area, the location of directly productive activity utilising available E.O.C. will increase income and thus local taxation receipts from the firms concerned and employees, which can be utilised for the improvement of S.O.C. in addition to any central government grants available for such improvement. This 'spread effect' will be reinforced to the extent that increased income in the area attracts social facilities such as cinemas, modern retail outlets, restaurants, and so on. It will have a 'feedback effect' for the firms concerned inasmuch as such S.O.C. improvement will offset the disparities between the local area and major urban centres, and thus tend to reduce the given rate of labour outflow from the area, thereby increasing the likelihood of a balanced age structure in the potential labour force for plant expansion.

Evidence and Evaluation

It is apparent that concentration and dispersion need not be mutually exclusive options for a national locational policy. Their desirability depends upon the kind of firm, the type of production, the distribution of market and supply areas, the nature of the transport system, labour availability and cost, site and congestion costs, and so on. In fact, as with Streeten's proposals for inter-sectoral unbalance, the question for locational policy should not be whether but *what* to concentrate and disperse, *where* and *how much*.[49] Such policy clearly should take macro-locational criteria such as cheaper resource utilisation into account, and where possible indicate the extent to which the micro-locational criteria of firms fail to do so, and for what reasons. In this case, the evidence cited in an earlier chapter on the increase in S.O.C. costs with increased urban density provides an important guideline, as could differences in effective wage rates between alternative locations. The extent of irrational or insufficiently rational locational decisions made by firms should also be taken into account. On the other hand, such a policy would be ill-advised to neglect available empirical evidence on the criteria employed by firms in determining relocation or the location of plant for expanded operations and should where possible advance on the impressionistic view that concentration benefits some small firms and that dispersion may benefit larger firms. One of the principal factors which therefore should be taken into account in the determination of locational policy is the ranking of what we have called 'locational economies' as available from empirical evidence.

U.S. Evidence. In a major study published in 1964 Bergin and Eagan undertook to rank criteria for plant location on the basis of replies to an enquiry from 1180 firms in the United States.[50] From these replies it is apparent that the role of labour was of primary importance not only in the sense of availability (ranked first), but also lower cost (fourth) and less unionisation (sixth). Convenience to markets and raw materials ranked second and fifth respectively. E.O.C., in the sense of 'availability of buildings and other property', ranked third. Transport costs ranked low (tenth out of sixteen factors). Decentralisation of operations ranked only fourteenth, with 'home of management' eighth. The criterion of location at the 'centre of a particular industry' ranked only twelfth.[n] In general, bearing in mind that this enquiry was concerned with firms locating either in the home area or outside it, it is interesting that so few of the criteria listed could *only* be served by the expansion of plant in the home area. It would appear that only criteria 8 and 12 ('home of management' and 'centre of a particular industry') support the

217

case for concentrated location, while even in these cases the home of management need not necessarily have been in a major urban area. By contrast, important categories which could only have been served by dispersion ranked very much higher: that is to say all the labour factors, which came first, fourth and sixth. In other cases it would appear that the criteria could be served in either a dispersed or a concentrated location. Therefore, on the basis of the evidence of these 'micro-locational' rankings, it appears that more new plant would be better served by dispersed locations than by expansion in the area of original location. From a 'macro-locational' resource allocation viewpoint, this case would be reinforced wherever the area of original location involved higher unpaid-for S.O.C. costs than elsewhere.[o]

British Evidence. We have already cited Luttrell's study to the effect that the major impetus to relocation or the location of new plant was the expansion of capacity.[51] Luttrell's evidence, based on an analysis of some hundred British firms betwen 1945 and 1952, revealed that the two principal factors restricting expansion in the original location were lack of labour availability and lack of available factory space in that order, closely corroborating the Bergin and Eagan rankings for these factors (first and third respectively). He found that cheaper and less-organised labour was more often a factor in the choice of a new site, once the decision to relocate had been taken, than a factor in the original impetus to movement. He also found that. whereas lack of factory space rather than lack of labour had been the chief driving force towards relocation in the pre-war period, with the consequence that firms often went to the suburb of the same town, the reversal of priorities in the post-war period has meant that firms have had to relocate farther away from the original location in order to find the necessary labour.[52] The maximum distance moved by the firms studied, with one exception, was about 400 miles from the original location. Most movement was to the Development Areas – at that time including South Wales, North-west and North-east England, South-west Scotland and Northern Ireland.[p] These areas were 'industrial districts which had been depressed in the previous decades, had then been fully employed during the war, but again showed signs of flagging

218

when armament orders were reduced'. New industry could therefore be introduced more easily than it could have been, for example, into a peasant community with no industrial basis, as basis, as would be required in the under-developed regions of some European countries.[53]

Although Luttrell's ranking of factors determining location includes only the three categories of labour availability, factory space and 'other' factors, he found that 'the distance from sources of materials and markets was unimportant in the choice of location for most of our cases'. The only exceptions were heavy industry which needed to have shore-located plant for the importation of bulky materials from abroad, and firms in the packaging and food industries whose products were best delivered over relatively short distances. In terms of the wholesale price of output, or factory turnover, the additional costs of new over old locations for self-contained plants making complete products averaged 'well under one per cent'. Higher additional costs were incurred in subsidiary branches undertaking an intermediate process in a chain of operations, 'but as a proportion of the value of the parent factories' output, the cost in this category would be negligible'. With regard to the management of dispersed subsidiary plant, Luttrell found that they could be operated quite effectively by joint 'parent' and 'subsidiary' management up to a distance of 100 miles of the parent plant, but that for moves of more than 100 miles the subsidiary should be fairly self-contained in terms of both management and technical personnel. Although he found a 'service element' in some of the manufacturing firms considered, where the fitting of products to customers' plant or the regular need for subsequent maintenance work encouraged firms to adopt a 'regional pattern' of small manufacturing units, he found that small plants were limited in their range of location by the need for specialist services, and that plants of 200 to 300 workers were frequently necessary to internalise such services. On the other hand, he found that larger, self-contained plants employing upwards of 300 workers were not restricted by transport costs, management communications, or the need for services, and 'can go almost any distance within the practical limits of Great Britain'.[54]

In cases of complete relocation, Luttrell found that firms

employing from 500 to 1000 workers had 'a big advantage' over those employing 100 or so. Most such 'complete moves' were made by firms which had financial links with a larger concern, or activities of their own elsewhere, which strengthened their position. The advantages of such a move, as opposed to setting up branch plant, were greatest where the type of production to be relocated was in a fairly homogeneous range of products which would benefit from technical economies of scale in a single plant. All but one of the firms undertaking complete relocation were successful, with the revivifying effects of making a completely new start based on reorganised production methods playing an important role. On average, such firms took skilled personnel amounting to a tenth of their previous labour force with them to the new location, where they were engaged in training and supervising labour, but the proportion was lower for firms with a high degree of 'repetition work' in standardised manufacture. Such firms were in a minority among the cases of relocation which he studied, and the benefits accruing from complete relocation therefore were exceptional.[55]

For both 'complete moves' and the location of subsidiary plant Luttrell found that the time period for the training of labour in new locations varied between industries. In the metal industries training for simple repetitive jobs took from four to six weeks, spinning and weaving took three months; 'closing room' work in footwear took four months or more; 'linking' in hosiery took four to six months, and six months or over was found necessary for a narrow range of work in skilled engineering. He drew attention to the fact that the time taken varied with the training policy of management. In some cases it was argued that the priority should be on careful and thorough training and in others, provided major blemishes were avoided, workers should be encouraged to earn piece rates as quickly as possible and learn the finer points later. He also pointed out, however, that 'it would be an exaggeration to pose speed and quality of work as alternatives. On the whole, the better organised of the new factories achieved a high standard in both, while the poorly organised ones lagged, especially in speed of output, for several years, and often turned out a higher proportion than average of imperfect work.' In a selected study of thirty-six firms, and in some cases making a hypothetical

220

comparison of the new factory's output and the cost of the same additional output at the old plant, Luttrell found that it took fully three years to overcome relocation costs and reach the cost per unit of output achieved at the old location. On the other hand, in several cases which he studied, the full premises were not available in the first year of working because the buildings had not been completed, because the previous tenant was moving out in stages, or because of licensing and other difficulties.[56]

Some two-thirds of the ninety-eight plants on which Luttrell based his study were in what can be called 'traditional' industries (hosiery leather, clothing, footwear, food, drink and tobacco, manufacture of wood and cork, and paper and printing). Most of these firms at the end of the war found themselves with an acute labour shortage, not least because light engineering and similar manufacture had been located and expanded considerably in their area during the war. Most of the firms in hosiery, clothing and footwear had only one-half to two-thirds of their pre-war labour force, and were forced to relocate in order to bring their labour force up to par. This post-war phenomenon clearly was exceptional, even if the factors involved in firms securing and operating a new plant are of more general validity. The more interesting firms from the point of view of international comparison were the remainder, more 'modern' industries which, by contrast, not only were recouping pre-war employment and production levels, but continuing an expansion of demand and capacity interrupted by war production. These included not only light engineering such as vehicles and their components, electrical goods, precision instruments, small machine tools, plastics, etc., but also heavy industry such as chemicals and oil-refining.[57]

In the conclusion to his study Luttrell wrote that 'it has been shown that various kinds of industrial movement can be accomplished successfully, and that within a wide range from medium-heavy to light engineering the degree of success depends not so much on the inherent nature of the industry as on the organisational methods of the firms and the type of factory (in relation to its location) which it decides to establish'. He continued by pointing out that in terms of employment the manufacturing industry to which this potential freedom of

221

location or 'footlooseness' applied was very considerable, granted that manufacturing in Britain in 1954 accounted for some two-fifths of total civilian employment and some two-thirds of total industrial employment. In general, his analysis strongly corroborates the argument of the previous section to the effect that it is the established meso-economic firms with relatively routinised production, divisible management, and financial reserves which can most easily relocate or locate subsidiaries in less-developed areas and, in so doing, can benefit from more-available and cheaper labour and site without significant locational disadvantage from higher costs. He also pointed in his conclusion to the fact that the degree of industrial movement in many cases was less than optimal from a resource allocation viewpoint precisely because no government machinery existed for distinguishing between firms in an area of labour shortage where it would pay only some rather than all to move, and selecting some for relocation. Taking a hypothetical case he argued that

> if in a high employment town there were a dozen firms, each employing 500 people, which wanted to expand by 20% (and there were examples not unlike this) then each would have to found a branch of 100 workers; whereas a better pattern of plant size, for the most economical working, would perhaps have been attained if two had moved completely and the others had grown in their home town. But few firms were willing to face the upheaval and risk of a complete move, and there was no special machinery whereby they would be assisted to do so either by the Government or the industry.[58]

Italian Evidence. Luttrell's evidence clearly is of relevance to the Italian regional problem inasmuch as the high importance attached to labour availability and the low importance attached to transport costs to 'almost any distance within the practical limits of Great Britain' would indicate that the South of Italy should be at least as suitable for the successful location of new plant by northern firms as were the British Development Areas to Luttrell's firms. A much more relevant and more recent study, however, was undertaken by the Società Autostrade of I.R.I. into the effects on industrial location of the continuous four-lane motorway (Autostrada del Sole) from Milan to Naples between its opening in 1957 and 1964.[59] This revealed that, in this time, 544 firms located 583 new establishments within 5 kilometres of the route, providing employment for 37,000 people. It advances on Luttrell's findings by showing that a broad range of manufacturing industry actually can secure locational benefits from either relocation or the location of new plant. More than one-quarter of the total number of establishments in 1964 were engaged in metallurgy, mechanical engineering and electrical engineering, 12 per cent in construction materials and cement, and 8 per cent in chemicals and plastics. On the Rome–Naples section of the route more than half the establishments were engaged in production of these types. Some 35 per cent of the establishments on the route as a whole were engaged in food, clothing and textiles production.[60]

The ranking of the criteria according to which the firms chose to locate on the motorway very much emphasises both the qualitative improvement in transport facilities offered by it, and the influence on firms of the fiscal incentives available for locations south of Agnani on the Rome–Naples section of the route, where southern regional development aids are available. 'Proximity of access to the motorway' was ranked first, followed by the 'presence of fiscal incentives'. 'Availability of labour' ranked third, followed by E.O.C. in the sense of 'reasonable cost of site' and 'good transport infrastructure'. Thus, although labour- and site-availability costs follow the relative ranking in Luttrell's findings, transport factors appear to play a much more important role. On the other hand, the contrast may be more apparent than real, since it appears that the vast improvement of the motorway as against the previous trunk-road system (which was based on medieval and Renaissance road patterns, linking every main commune between the principal cities) widened the market area available to firms, increasing the range of locations available to them and making it possible to benefit from more available and cheaper labour and sites in less-developed areas, as well as from fiscal incentives for locating south of Agnani. This certainly is indicated by the fact that only 26 per cent of the markets of plant located on the Rome–Naples section of the route were within 100 kilometres of the plant themselves, and that the bulk of the rest were in 'the entire national territory'.[61]

No official Italian figures are available on unit transport costs by industry classification, either for trunk roads or for the new motorway.[q] None the less, the above evidence indicates that the construction of a continuous, high-quality motor transport system acts as a catalyst in favour of dispersed location, not only reducing transport costs by reducing the time taken for a given distance, with consequent savings in labour and vehicle utilisation, but also indirectly making available locational economies from dispersed locations which otherwise would be too remote to be attractive to the firm concerned. What also is of particular interest in the results of the Società Autostrade study, however, is the size of firm which has chosen to exploit such economies from dispersed location as a result of the opening of the motorway. Of the total 583 establishments locating from 1957–64 within the immediate vicinity of the motorway, but outside the main urban areas of Milan, Bologna, Florence, Rome and Naples, 45·8 per cent employed only up to 25 persons; 30·5 per cent employed from 25 to 50 persons; 12·4 per cent from 50 to 100 persons, and 11·3 per cent more than 100 persons. That is, some three-quarters of the plants concerned were less than one-tenth the average size of the plant in Luttrell's study, and nearly 50 per cent less than one-twentieth that size.[62]

Again, this evidence does not necessarily conflict with Luttrell's findings. It appears that firms establishing larger plant also made more radical locational decisions. Some 22 per cent of the plant located on the Rome–Naples section of the route were in the 100-worker-plus category, against 9 per cent on the Bologna–Florence section, and plant of this size accounted for some two-thirds of total employment on the former section, compared with less than one-half on the latter. Further, British road transport in the 1945–52 period from which Luttrell took his evidence not only was lacking in motorway quality, but was suffering from under-investment during the war. Had it been otherwise Luttrell's smaller firms might have found their range of location less restricted. In addition, the more recent the location, the more mechanised production techniques could be expected to be for smaller firms. However, what is remarkable about the Società Autostrade evidence is how very small was the average size of plant which the firms concerned freely chose to locate on a dispersed pattern, and the modernity of the industry concerned. In this respect, although the evidence may be 'compatible' with Luttrell's findings, it opens an entirely new dimension for the theory and policy of dispersed location.[63]

False Hopes from Industrial Complex Analysis

A further interesting revelation of the Società Autostrade study is the very low ranking given to 'the existence of other complementary firms'. This ranks twelfth – precisely the same as 'the centre of a particular industry' in the Bergin and Eagan study.[r] It conflicts sharply with the priority ascribed to such complementary effects by the school of industrial complex analysis, based in effect on the concept of technological external economies. For instance, the E.E.C. Commission's project for the development of the Bari–Brindisi–Taranto area, undertaken by Tosco, and recommended to the Italian government by the Commission in 1964, assumed the existence and power of the attraction of technological external economies in promoting spatial concentration and maintained that 'localisation of activity takes place not only because of demand, but also because of complex, reciprocal technological relations'.[64] It admitted that 'it would be very interesting to distinguish those industries whose localisation is the direct effect of technical interrelations, and those whose localisation is the direct effect of dependence on a local market, apart from industries which are located in these regions for other reasons', but concluded that enquiry 'which can give systematic and detailed information on this subject... would go beyond the limits of this report'.[65]

Tosco did claim to have undertaken a 'general examination' of the attractive power of 'technical interrelations' in promoting spatial concentration. This appears to have drawn substantially from Perrouxist growth-pole theory before Perroux himself demoted the external economies concept. Tosco referred to the historical evidence that secondary industries have tended to grow in the area of exploitation of raw materials, and claimed that 'the creation of great steel centres provoked the development of growth poles'. His conclusion from this in fact very general examination was that 'the fundamental objective of policy in favour of the Mezzogiorno is to form industrial concentrations in which external economies may be progressively created, that

225

is the economies *because of which* economic concerns prefer to invest in the North'.[66] To implement the policy he recommended the simultaneous by in Bari, Brindisi and Tarantoa dozen large firms and a few dozen smaller firms in nine mechanical engineering sectors – structural steel, domestic appliances, pumps, agricultural equipment, cranes, lifts, machine tools and scales. The bulk of his study was concerned with an input–output calculation indicating the production coefficients which it was estimated would maximise inter-firm linkage. Infrastructural and labour as well as investment requirements were estimated, with the conclusion that investment of 100 mld lire would provide employment for 10,000 persons.

It is evident enough that the Tosco study begs the whole question of concentration or dispersion in favour of concentration. In practice, this might not have been particularly important. If the study had actually led to the location of 100 mld lire's worth of investment in mechanical engineering in Puglia, this undoubtedly would have given a shot in the arm to a sector which is critically under-invested in both Puglia and the South as a whole. However, the study not only opted for the concentration of this type of activity in a given area, but also demanded very specific investment and production coefficients for that activity. As Tosco himself stressed, the justification of so elaborate an input–output projection would require the simultaneous establishment of all the plant concerned on precisely the scale specified by the projection. This itself reflected a remarkable lack of appreciation of the extent to which existing Italian policy instruments would have to be transformed to implement the proposal. To secure the simultaneous establishment of precisely tailored plant would have required a much more specific control over the location and structure of firms than that exercised anywhere inside the Common Market at the time. Even the British I.D.C. policy, which may refuse permission to firms to expand plant over a given number of square feet of factory space outside the Development Areas, does not specify either the precise location or size of that plant within those areas. So far no Italian government has been able to introduce any form of negative control over location – which would necessitate a revision of the constitution – far less introduce the effectively Stalinist degree of control which would be required to translate the Tosco project into reality.[67]

From a theoretical point of view this failure to relate a particular policy proposal to the available instruments of policy might not be crucial. As it happens, the Tosco study took four years to complete, and represented the main proposal made at that time by the E.E.C. Commission to implement the general provisions of the Rome Treaty calling for a reduction in the disparities between different regions in the Community. From the Italian viewpoint, it might have been more useful if the Commission had undertaken a study of post-war regional policy in Italy on something like the O.E.C.D. country survey basis, with particular reference to the consequences for the South of E.E.C. integration. The Tosco proposal was quietly shelved by the Italian authorities, no doubt in part because of its impracticability. If they had been sufficiently informed in advance of what its form was likely to be, it is possible either that they could have secured its revision, or could have envisaged some revision of existing policy instruments to implement it, particularly if the Commission itself had recommended and supported them. But even apart from the divorce of the project from the policy instruments then available, the assumptions, terms of reference and technique of the Tosco project have serious shortcomings.

Reference has been made to the fact that the project assumes that firms located near each other in some way benefit from technical complementarities. By contrast, it was argued earlier that such complementarities are not strictly locational, but amount either to *internal* economies of scale, or to market growth transmission of the Scitovsky cost-reducing or Streeten–Hirschman growth-inducing types. The Società Autostrade evidence further indicates that the markets of even very small modern firms are not highly localised, and that on average some three-quarters of their production is directed to the national market over and above 100 kilometres from plant. This evidence seriously compromises the Tosco assumption of a strictly local market in Puglia for the firms concerned since, if there were no significant cost in the securing of inputs from and the provision of outputs to the rest of Italy, there would not be any essential need for the employment of an elaborate input–output table to ensure the location of the relevant production in Puglia. In addition, if the employment of the technique were to be justified in terms of research and administrative time and cost, it would be necessary to ensure not only that the firms located on precisely the scale indicated by the project, but also that none of them 'broke the rules' and bought from other firms elsewhere either in the South or nation-wide. This itself would mean that, in the event of one of the dozen major firms running behind schedule in establishing production, the whole group would have to wait for its completion or establish input–output relationships outside the complex. If these were with other southern firms, it would be difficult to justify government refusal either to let them establish such markets and supply sources, or to compel them to abandon them once all firms had completed their investment programmes.

These qualifications raise the question whether a project of the Tosco type is to be fundamentally a self-contained sub-system, or is intended to act as a stimulant to the growth of mechanical engineering in the South (or wider problem region) as a whole. If the elaborate input–output technique on which it is based is assumed to be a necessary condition for the establishment of the firms concerned, it presumably would be desirable to extend the model to other projects elsewhere in the South. In this case one problem posed rather than resolved by the technique is whether one sub-region (Puglia) is to lead the wider region in a purely temporal sense of starting a 'self-sustained' growth before the rest, or whether it should lead it by providing markets for output and sources of inputs for the wider region as a whole. If a polarisation of activity within the wider region comparable in due course to that between the North and South of Italy is to be avoided, it presumably would be important to ensure that other projects were started simultaneously elsewhere in the South. But this itself not only raises the question of whether the sectors concerned should be restricted to mechanical engineering rather than extended to other sectors, but also whether it would be desirable to initiate separate self-contained local market and supply areas as opposed to more integrated markets for the South as a whole. The latter alternative has particular force if the feasible degree of dispersion of activity, as evidenced by the Società Autostrade study, is taken into account.

However, if the wider objective of integrated inter-sectoral and intra-regional markets for the South as a whole is agreed to be desirable, further strains are imposed on the Tosco input–output technique not only in research and administrative terms, but also in terms of the limitations of the technique itself. Any extension of Tosco-type projects would be unlikely to justify itself if it did not allow interaction between the new subsystems and the wider manufacturing economy already operating before and during the drawing up of the new systems themselves. If it did not it would be neglecting the growth potential for the South as a whole by establishing a dual, two-class system of production on a separate development basis, depriving existing industry of markets and sources of inputs from the new subsystems. Yet if it attempted to integrate the new systems with those already existing it would run up against the general limitations of interregional input–output models as appreciated even by the most enthusiastic supporters of the method. Thus Isard has written that

> unfortunately the use of a general technique such as interregional input–output is not without opportunity cost. The gains scored by being able to cut more into the interrelatedness of society must be weighed against the sacrifice of certain elements of reality, that is the need to work with such unrealistic postulates as constant cost production and unchanging supply channels. As a consequence, on a number of occasions the analyst, after he has completed an elaborate general interdependence study, comes to question whether the returns from such a broad framework justified its cost.[68]

In this case, does input–output analysis have any application to locational policy? Isard believes that it does, and continuing the above quotation on the difficulties of interregional (or regional) input–output analysis he claims that 'it is at this point that (the analyst) is led to scrutiny of the industrial complex techniques'. At first sight, this looks rather like Tosco's own approach, since he defines such a complex as 'a set of activities occurring at a given location and belonging to a group (sub-system) of activities which are subject to important production marketing or other interrelations'. As evidence for these interrelations, like Tosco, he rather sweepingly claims that 'crystal clear is the fact [sic] that the location of many activities is directly linked with

229

the location of one or more other activities. Examples range from fish canning and the fishing industry, to the intricate network of activities found in the garment centre of New York City or the metal trades complex of Birmingham, England.' Assuming that this largely *post hoc ergo propter hoc* argument has established his case, he gives general examples of the type of activity concerned as the coal, iron-ore, pig-iron and steel production sequence, that of food, fertiliser and industrial products from livestock production, a 'nucleonics' complex, and petroleum refining, chemicals and synthetic fibres.[69]

There is little doubt that Isard overstates his case concerning production complementarities through location. For instance, he claims of the petroleum refining, chemicals and textiles production sequence that 'none of the activities could be considered *a priori* as having an independent production location pattern'.[70] In the Italian case, however, this sequence is not concentrated, but considerably dispersed. The E.N.I. Gela and Syracuse refineries mainly refine crude oil transported by tanker from the Middle East and Eastern Europe, which is then retransported by sea to markets elsewhere in Italy and abroad. Because of the loading and unloading economies from shore-based plant, this proves highly economic. The plant also process various chemical by-products such as hydrogen, which can be reprocessed to produce fertiliser; methane, to produce plastics and synthetic fibres; ethylene, to produce plastics, synthetic rubber, antifreeze, detergents, and so on. But these products also can be reloaded and shipped elsewhere at a cost which appears to be a relatively insignificant proportion of the unit cost of the final output, and lower than the cost of transport of final products manufactured from the chemicals would be. As mentioned above a considerable proportion of the production in small-scale plant on the Autostradà del Sole is in plastics manufacture. In this case it appears that dispersed, independent location patterns in fact are possible in the production sequence.

This is not to say that the technique of analysis which Isard employs to estimate the cost–benefit of particular locations for industrial complexes is unhelpful. So far Isard has given only one concrete example of such a potential complex – a petrochemicals plant located in Puerto Rico. In selecting those branches of production which would prove more economic in Puerto Rico than elsewhere, he employs two main types of analysis: first, engineering studies and, secondly, the neo-Weberian analysis of which he has been the principal post-war advocate. Engineering studies enable him to identify the range of products which can be derived from petroleum refining, and also indicate the minimal technical economies of scale in this production. His neo-Weberian analysis enables him to identify the labour-cost differentials of Puerto Rico as against U.S. mainland locations, the size of local Puerto Rican markets for the alternative types of product as against mainland markets, and the transport costs of Puerto Rican production to the mainland. On a 'comprehensive dollar and cents' computation he estimated that, for a given pattern of markets (the Eastern mainland seaboard for refinery products, the textile South for fibre, and Puerto Rico for fertiliser), the minimum transport point for the location of a full oil refinery–petrochemical–synthetic fibre complex would be the Texas–Louisiana Gulf coast. On the other hand, this location would suffer a labour-cost disadvantage relative to Puerto Rico greater than the transport-cost advantage. This would be reinforced by a balance-of-payments saving to Puerto Rico from local production of fertilisers, almost all of which were previously imported.[71]

Isard's application of neo-Weberian analysis to Puerto Rico certainly is of interest, and might appear to justify location there of a complex of this type. On the other hand, it is evident that the choice of a relatively small island region, with markedly lower labour costs than the rest of the economy with which it is formally integrated, considerably facilitates the application of the technique. Location has to be either in Puerto Rico or on the mainland. Any intermediate location would be in the sea! To this extent the question of concentrating rather than dispersing location is artificially simplified. If the same technique were applied to the location of a similar complex in the South of Italy (or western and southern France, for example) the conclusions would be less clear cut, and indicate a far wider range of alternative locations. In the Italian case the location of the E.N.I. refinery and I.R.I. steel complexes give an indication of what the location criteria in fact would be. According to Finsider (the I.R.I. steel company responsible for the Taranto plant) the legislation of 1957 requiring state-aided companies to locate 60 per

cent of new plant in the South meant that the next plant to maximise technical economies of scale in the continuous production
of pig-iron, ingot steel, steel sheeting and tubing could not be
located in the North. In choosing a location in the South, the *only*
essential criterion was a shore-based plant. Finsider maintain
that the same was true of E.N.I.'s refinery location.[s]

I.R.I. is a group with considerable vertical integration, controlling over 90 per cent of national pig-iron production and two-
thirds of steel production, plus some 80 per cent of shipbuilding
capacity, about 20 per cent of machinery for the steel industry,
aircraft production and assembly, with comparable proportions
of railway engines and rolling stock, metalworking machine
tools, and of the motor vehicle market, with interests elsewhere
in the economy.[t] Granted the force which Tosco and Isard attri-
bute to the attractive power of technical interdependence in
related types of production and production sequences, it would
appear remarkable that the group did not initially locate much
of its related investment in these industries in the vicinity of the
Taranto plant. But, as with E.N.I.'s refineries, shore-based plant
means that sheet steel can be transported by sea to main
distribution points throughout the country at negligible cost (in
fact less than 2 per cent of the unit cost of output). Therefore
the new I.R.I. Alfa-Romeo plant can be economically located
near Naples while utilising Taranto I.R.I. steel. In fact the only
additional I.R.I. investment undertaken at Taranto was in a cement plant and a plant producing refractory material for smel-
ter crucible lining.[u]

In general, therefore, it appears that the 'technical interrela-
tedness' or technological external economies on which Tosco
and Isard both place such emphasis are an empty economic box,
and that governments assuming that the establishment of isolated complexes of interrelated industry will necessarily attract
further related industry to the area concerned in a self-
generating growth process are very ill-advised. A further factor
to be taken into account in the choice of complexes of the heavy
industry type, such as petroleum refineries and integrated steel
plant, is the very high capital–labour ratios involved. The initial
investment at Taranto cost some 350 mld lire but provided employment for only 5000 workers. That is, it cost three and a half
times as much as the estimated cost for the Tosco investment,

but employed only half as many workers. The psychological effect of locating so large a steel complex in the South is generally held to have been of great importance in the general strategy of the region's development, especially while northern management has to be persuaded rather than obliged to locate there. Also, the projected location of a FIAT motor vehicle plant, as well as that of Alfa-Romeo, in the South will mean that more of the Taranto steel can now be utilised in the region. In addition, some of the finance for the Taranto project was raised through market issues rather than directly through the Italian Treasury. To this extent, although the macro-economic effect in terms of saving would be the same either way, it did not draw on funds earmarked for regional development. None the less, the very high capital–labour ratios concerned in such integrated complexes clearly are a vital factor to be taken into account in any case in which their location excludes investment in more labour-intensive modern industry. The Taranto complex in fact was linked with more complementary industry by the early 1970s, but some fifteen years after its initial establishment. This was during a period in which the I.R.I. group had considerably diversified and extended its own holdings in other manufacturing sectors. The delay illustrates what could happen in other countries if governments attempt only isolated ventures rather than a comprehensive and balanced development package.

NOTES

[a] Perroux dismisses the external economies concept in passing as 'crude and opaque'. As the following argument suggests, this dismissal may not be necessary provided that a clearer definition of the use of 'technological' external economies is secured.
[b] If one re-examines Meade's 'bucolic' example of the bees and the orchard, one can see that it is in fact their proximate location which makes external economies possible.
[c] The use of this term in the following text is different from that of Isard's 'localization economies', which he contrasts with 'spatial juxtaposition' and 'urbanisation economies'.

^d Plant have been undertaken on this basis at Dunquerque and Taranto while a further integrated and shore-based steel plant is in course of completion in the Calabria region of the South of Italy.

^e The case for the concentration and dispersion of plant have been stated in the following two sections without a general evaluation. This follows in the subsequent section.

^f That is to say the loss to the donor area is to the benefit of the receiving area.

^g Benjamin Chinitz, *New York Metropolitan Region Study: Employment Projections for Parts of the Region* (1961). However, Chinitz qualifies this observation on *actual* concentration tendencies in an analysis of potential gains from dispersion in a study which he published the previous year with Raymond Vernon, which is considered in the following section of this chapter.

^h Both Davin and Pottier have argued that the transport 'axes' constituting such a transport network contribute to a spatial polarisation of activity. Davin points out that reciprocal trade flows between areas on a transport network do not mean equilibrated flows: Louis Davin, *Economie régionale et croissance* (1964) p.61. Pottier takes neo-classical location theorists to task, emphasising that 'transport lines only stretch in some, not all directions', and that 'transport axes have the effect of particularly concentrating profits within the agglomerations or poles which they connect, or in certain cases cross'. In fact, he is not content with this, and also maintains that 'the structural heterogeneity of a transport surface crossed by communications axes is the cause of the phenomenon of disymmetry and domination': Pottier, 'Les axes de développement', *Revue Economique* (January 1963) pp.67, 70 and 89.

ⁱ Interviews with plant managers at Alfa-Romeo, Arese, and Italsider, Taranto in July 1968.

^j Information from Dr Giuseppe Medusa, CENSIS, Rome (July 1969).

^k I am assured by Dr Brian Bayliss that unit transport costs can be markedly reduced under these conditions. I am indebted to Dr Bayliss for the figures on unit transport costs employed in Chapter 5 which summarises and applies the present argument.

^l A 1971 Italian study of size of company and locational factors showed that the importance of proximity to markets decreased with increasing size of company, corroborating the general argument. See further, Fig. 11, p.298.

^m It is interesting, if not definitive, to note that Arnold Weinstock chose to decentralise the G.E.C. giant's operations from central London to a country house.

ⁿ Cf. Table 10, p.286.

^o The Bergin and Eagan information is of particular interest granted that the firms concerned were not forced to relocate through government policy measures. Even government incentives played a very low role (ranked last).

cashire and West Cumberland. The Scottish Development Areas also included Dundee, Inverness and Dingwall.

^p North-west England included Merseyside, South Lancashire, North-east Lancashire and West Cumberland. The Scottish Development Areas also included Dundee, Inverness and Dingwall.

^q Possible locational advantages for industry in the South are estimated in the following section by applying British transport costs to differentials in effective

wage rates between the South and the North.
[r] This ranking, of course, is not explicitly of technological external economies, although suggestive of them.
[s] Interview with Dr Corrado Antonini, Finsider, Rome, April 1969.
[t] I.R.I. Research Department, 1969.
[u] Interview with Dr Antonini, Rome, April 1969.

CHAPTER 8

THEORY, PRACTICE AND
POLICY IMPERATIVES

The previous argument has illustrated the divorce between
theory and practice in most of what passes as regional economics. There are considerable differences between regional theory in Western Europe and North America. In Europe, mainly
under the influence of Myrdal and Perroux, most specialists in
regional economics give considerable weight to imbalance theory. They emphasise the extent to which the free working of the
market mechanism in capitalist economies can aggravate the
regional problem. In the United States the scale of the urban
crisis in a predominantly urbanised society has forced some reappraisal of the interrelation between urban and regional problems. This emerges in the previously cited submissions to
government commissions on rural poverty and urban crisis. But
with relatively few exceptions regional and location theory in the
United States is still hidebound by assumptions of self-balance
through the free working of the market. Such neo-classical theory still postulates conditions for harmonious adjustment between regions, and fails to help policy-makers precisely because
it is so unrelated to the structure and distribution of activity in
modern capitalist economies.

This chapter spells out some of the main conclusions which
can be drawn from the previous analysis. It parallels the
development of the argument in the main part of the text. Thus
it starts from the macro-economic background of interregional
trade, growth and migration. It follows this with an analysis of
the crucial role now played in regional distribution by the meso-
economic, multi-national firm, and the extent to which unequal
competition between meso- and micro-economic enterprises is a
major cause of contemporary regional and urban problems.
The chapter also draws policy implications from the role of
structure in regional growth and from the evidence on the case
for dispersion of industry into relatively minor areas which have
been backwashed by unequal regional development.

The Macro-Economic Framework

In themselves macro-economic models of regional growth and trade can only represent a term of reference for effective regional policy. Macro regional policy – like macro national policy – is substantially undermined by the power of meso-economic firms and multi-national capital. For instance, when big firms in the meso-economic leagues are not substantially influenced in their national policies by fiscal, monetary, or exchange-rate changes, it is not surprising that they should not be significantly influenced by a regionalisation of such policies.

Naturally, what is true for policies also is true of theory. The exposition of macro-economic models of cumulative regional imbalance in Chapter 3 assumed a competitive micro-economic structure and firms restricted to national markets rather than free to locate multi-nationally. Yet it is striking that, even on such assumptions, the free working of the market mechanism with higher capital than labour mobility prompted increased regional divergence. Such macro-economic models of cumulative interregional divergence therefore provide useful terms of reference for analysis which extends beyond macro theory to the meso- and micro-economic level.

For instance, it is frequently maintained that firms should locate where they choose, and that workers should be sufficiently mobile to search for the available employment. In terms of neo-classical theory, and in a two-region economy, this would be more subtly expressed on the lines that labour outflow from the L.D.R. should be encouraged to the point at which it reduces the population pressure within the region to a level comparable with that in the M.D.R., thereby permitting comparable regional levels of productivity. This case too blithely ignores the spatial inelasticity of labour. This may simply mean that insufficient people migrate from the region in response to higher income opportunities in the M.D.R. to offset the L.D.R.'s natural rate of increase in population. During the interim higher aggregate m.e.c. schedules in the faster growing M.D.R. will tend to mean that L.D.R. savings are reduced below the level which they would have achieved in other circumstances (e.g. rigid controls on capital outflow). The result can be a situation in which the L.D.R., in aggregate, 'gains' to the extent that, through labour

237

emigration, its total population is less than it otherwise would have been, but none the less will lose to the extent that savings outflow reduces the ratio between savings/investment and total regional population.

The net balance between these loss and gain factors will depend on actual rates of labour and capital outflow. However, unless government policies of capital transfer to the L.D.R. are undertaken, it is possible that the L.D.R. will be a net loser rather than a net gainer, and the more probable that this will be the case the longer the time period and the more perfect the institutions of the capital markets concerned which, in national economies with different regional branches of the same financial institutions, tend to be virtually perfect à la textbook. The interregional application of Keynesian trade cycle models indicates that the net loss for an L.D.R. may be unreversed over a long period of time. This would particularly be the case when the region's public expenditure was dependent on its own rather than national taxation, since this would result in a reduction in the longer-term public expenditure of the type hypothesised by Hicks's lower equilibrium line. Conversely, a short-term fall back in the upwards growth path of an M.D.R. drawing on both labour and capital from an L.D.R. would be less likely to result in an unchecked downwards spiral to the extent that the initially high growth path had permitted increased tax receipts and public expenditure. Expressed differently, while the regional economy of the M.D.R. might be checked momentarily in its upwards growth path by a fall off in the warranted growth rate, it would not be likely to 'hit the floor' in the same sense as it would in the L.D.R.

If labour migration were perfectly elastic, with much of the population of a capital-losing L.D.R. migrating through choice to higher-earning employment in the M.D.R., there would still be economic costs to the national economy in permitting such a run down of the L.D.R.'s labour force. These include the congestion costs registered in the areas of labour inflow, the costs of under-utilising S.O.C. in the areas of labour outflow, and inflationary pressures in the inflow areas. In general, the combination of such factors, reinforced by the marked spatial inelasticity of labour migration, supports the case for govern-

238

ment intervention to prevent a cumulative decline in investment and employment opportunities in the L.D.R.

For instance, the force of interregional differentials in rates of return on capital indicates that it is not sufficient for *some* profitable opportunities to be made available in the L.D.R. for a cumulative upwards growth spiral to be initiated in the region. If the development policy accepts the free working of the capital market in the allocation of savings, these opportunities must be *more* profitable than are obtainable in the national economy (and in the case of international freedom of portfolio flows, than in those parts of the international economy to which investors have access). The problem is neglected by many regional economists who in general admit the need for development incentives in favour of the L.D.R. For instance, Ingram has paraphrased Keynes in relation to the problem of under-development in North Carolina, writing that 'if Opportunity and Incentive are present, Thrift and Investible Funds will look after themselves'. The only problem, as he sees it, 'seems to lie in determining what will please the prospective investor'. But as the Whitman analysis suggests, what is likely to please a prospective investor is not a textiles company in Carolina but a Californian electronics firm. It is not *some* opportunity which is called for in the L.D.R. but *better* opportunities than in the M.D.R. Ingram writes that 'some put their faith in low taxes, cheap labour and free land or buildings, while others rely on good schools, abundant public services and skilled labour'. However, he adds that his own analysis 'furnishes no clues' on which policies should be adopted. He also appears unaware that a low-income region may not be able to mobilise internal resources for such public services if it is attempting to attract capital by low taxes.[1]

For a variety of reasons such opportunities are difficult to provide simply through the granting of interest-rate concessions, investment grants and other incentives in favour of investment in the L.D.R. This partly depends on the degree of backwardness of the region concerned. If the L.D.R. is identified as a 'problem' region shortly after some of the cumulative decline mechanisms of the Whitman type have occurred, then marginal concessions in interest rates or investment grants may prove effective. But the reason for their success would tend to be the initially comparable structure between the M.D.R. and L.D.R., as

239

assumed in the Whitman model for purposes of exposition. In practice there tends to be considerable delay in the recognition of a region as a problem area, and even longer delay before any major regional policy is undertaken. In the Italian case, for instance, the South had to wait ninety years from political unification before regional development policy got under way on any scale in 1951. By this time the region was not simply 'on the wrong foot' in the sense of being caught by an unfavourable import round from the L.D.R., but was flat on its back. Its firms and industries were of insufficient structure and scale to be in a position to take advantage of indirect government aids whose utilisation depended directly on the firms themselves. Even when investible funds and incentives were made available, the opportunity to grow was restricted by the superiority of northern firms in northern markets, the restricted income level and backward consumption pattern of the South, and the organisation and technology gap between southern and northern firms which could not be 'jumped' through the provision of improved infrastructure and government incentives.[2]

In addition, there is the problem that the more backward the region and the less developed its productive structure in relation to the M.D.R., the greater the problem of multiplier leakages from government development expenditure, with the perverse effect that initial expenditure undertaken in the L.D.R. either directly by the government, or indirectly by firms utilising government aid, mainly benefits the M.D.R. This was estimated to be a major factor explaining the disappointing results from the expenditure on infrastructure in the South of Italy by the Cassa per il Mezzogiorno in the 1950s, with a calculation that some 60 per cent of the multiplier effects of the expenditure concerned were registered in the more developed North. Taken in conjunction with the evidence that labour migration is insufficient in itself to improve the imbalance between capital and labour in a major under-developed region, these various arguments indicate that if a development policy is to prove effective for problem regions, it should be a continuous on-going dimension of national policy rather than a partial intervention unrelated to what happens elsewhere in the economy.

For instance, although an L.D.R. may be able to secure some form of comparative advantage through utilisation of more readily available and therefore probably cheaper labour than an M.D.R., this will be offset to the extent that the M.D.R. is able to secure immigrant labour from the L.D.R. at a cost comparable with those wages paid in competitive L.D.R. firms. The cumulative divergence models already outlined suggest that M.D.R. firms will be able to secure sufficient labour to restrain the rate of wage demands below what it would have been without interregional migration, while the 'capacity effects' of larger-scale investment of the kind likely under high growth conditions will tend to mean that M.D.R. firms can reduce unit costs through more capital per unit of labour than possible in the L.D.R. because of savings outflow. The margin of benefit in favour of the M.D.R. will depend on a variety of factors including the initial structure of the regions, the particular rate of labour inflow to the M.D.R. in relation to the demand for labour, and the net gains to M.D.R. firms from higher capital-intensity allowing for marginally higher wage rates. In practice, unionisation will very probably mean that leading L.D.R. firms have to pay the same (or nearly the same) wage rates as their leading M.D.R. competitors, and the actual competitive result may be determined in non-wage cost competition. In this case, the main benefit to the M.D.R. is in labour availability through immigration from the L.D.R., although this is likely to have a restraining effect on wage pressure in the region and sustain the region's warranted growth rate in the manner already described.

The policy implications which can be drawn from macro analysis are necessarily general. The problems are multidimensional and effective policies must interrelate the macro-, meso- and micro-economic dimensions. But at least three main conclusions are suggested at the macro level. First, that the investment opportunities in the L.D.R. will have to be greater than those in the M.D.R. if a re-entry of savings and a cumulative growth process are to be started by the free working of the market (a point which, however banal, is frequently overlooked). Secondly, that the later the development policy is undertaken and the greater the cumulative interregional divergence, the more difficult such a policy becomes. Thirdly, and importantly, there is no once-and-for-all element in a successful regional policy. For even if the productive structure and regional competitiveness of an L.D.R. is improved to the point at which it can be said

241

to be 'aligned' with the M.D.R., the free working of the market will initiate further cumulative imbalance unless monitored and offset by government policy.[a]

Labour Migration and Resource Use

There sometimes is a tendency to dismiss all migration as inherently undesirable, without distinguishing the degree of population pressure in an L.D.R., or admitting that in order for government development policies to prove effective in a foreseeable time period it may be necessary to permit continued high rates of emigration. On the other hand, there is a tendency in the U.S. literature to blame the incidence of social and private costs in migration on inadequate information to migrants about prospective job opportunities, and to argue that if migrants were better informed (for example on the lack of employment opportunities and the poor housing conditions in ghetto areas) they would migrate to lesser urban centres where the strain on provision of social infrastructure was less marked and where job opportunities (if not housing) were available.

Several conclusions can be drawn from the available evidence on migration and resource costs. The most important is the need for public intervention in the free working of the migrant labour market to ensure that job opportunities are fulfilled rather than frustrated without strain on resources in the areas of labour inflow, or inadequate structural change in employment opportunities in the areas of outflow. The patent failure of migration patterns in the United States to achieve this end has been well put by Kain and Persky, who write that

> we are struck by the contrast between the implications of migration from the rural South and the traditional view of mobility in the United States. The actual migration portends severe strain on both the metropolitan centres of the country and the individual migrants involved; the tradition invokes a vision of the workings of the free market place leading in the long run to an efficient distribution of economic activity. The long run may now have become too long, for it implies several more generations of ill-equipped rural–urban migrants, continued under-investment in education, and heavy strains on

242

the social institutions necessary to control and ameliorate these mistakes.[3]

The improved information and greater mobility argument is very weak. For instance, in the U.S. case it might result in fewer immigrants to the core areas of the main northern cities where there are declining employment opportunities, but will result also in an acceleration of migration to other urban areas (with populations greater than 250,000) in which marked scale diseconomies in the provision of S.O.C. occur, and which would not necessarily be able to adapt better to the increased inflow than the larger cities. The established social preference of immigrants for their own communities in areas of labour inflow would be likely to lead to an exchange of new ghetto problems for old, especially to the extent that the immigrants had a higher natural rate of increase than the previous resident population. Besides, white emigrants from the Appalachian states in the United States are already tending to locate in the lesser urban areas outside Appalachia, with black immigrants concentrating in the larger and longer established areas of labour inflow.[4] Racial discrimination would be likely to accentuate new ghetto problems for black migrants to urban centres with populations greater than 250,000 even if the problem was not initially as severe as in the larger metropolitan conurbations.

In the Italian case, the evidence already available indicates that ghetto-type problems are emerging in the central city areas, with strain on suburban infrastructure evident in the main cities of the North-West. To date the Italian situation differs from that in the United States inasmuch as there is no clear evidence of a decline in employment among those living in the central urban areas. This partly reflects the fact that, since the cities themselves are geographically smaller than the metropolitan centres in the United States, it is easier for immigrants to commute to employment on the city periphery. The bulk of immigrants certainly tend to locate in the suburban areas near their employment.[5] However, there are several direct and indirect costs from allowing a *laissez-faire* policy of migration between under-employed less-developed regions and pressured or over-developed regions. The direct costs of higher *per capita* expenditure on infrastructure in the areas of labour inflow have already been stressed. But they are only part of the picture. The indirect costs are less easy to quantify but much greater in their effect.

For instance, to the extent that higher S.O.C. costs in the labour inflow areas are paid by local residents and firms, they will tend to have an inflationary pressure on the cost of labour in the inflow area. This may be offset by the fact that the local authorities fail to provide sufficient S.O.C. infrastructure for the immigrants concerned, but in this case there is a net welfare loss in those cases in which S.O.C. facilities are lower in inflow areas than in areas of labour outflow. Inflationary pressure will certainly be exerted to the extent that the failure of construction and housing to respond to the accommodation needs of immigrants is reflected in high, and increasing, rents for accommodation in the inflow area. These pressures clearly are not the whole picture in inflationary cost-push pressures in areas of labour inflow, which will also depend on a variety of additional factors such as the rate of growth of real incomes, the degree of unionisation, and trade union militancy in securing wage increases for members. But to the extent that real wage increases are eroded by inflationary pressures in housing and accommodation costs, unions will understandably press wage demands which otherwise might not have been necessary for them and their members, and this may reduce the competitiveness of firms in the area of labour inflow.

In principle, such cost-push inflationary pressures should result in a spatial redistribution of direct investment in favour of the less-developed regions of the country concerned. But in practice such assumptions are unrealistic. In the first place the firms in which such trade union backed pressures are likely to prove successful are the larger multi-plant firms in the meso-economic sector which would find themselves as subject to such pressure for new plant located in an L.D.R. as in plant in the M.D.R.[b] Secondly, to the extent that the firms had not accumulated sufficient self-finance to be able to ride out the wage increases without cutting back on investment at given price levels for output, they would be likely to pass on a substantial part of the wage demands in price increases. This was the case in Italy following the concession of union wage demands in the early 1960s, when the price increases concerned resulted in a rapid

244

deterioration of the national trade balance, a deflationary package combined with a disguised devaluation, and a recession in investment.[6] In other words, when the M.D.R. economy runs into cost-push pressures, these may tend to reduce the capacity of its management to launch new initiatives in an L.D.R. or undertake productivity-gaining investment in the M.D.R. itself. Indivisibilities play an important part in this process, since the location of a new initiative in an L.D.R. necessitates an entirely new plant, rather than the new assembly line which might be introduced to secure productivity gains in an existing M.D.R. plant.

However, one of the clearest indirect losses to an L.D.R. from the incidence of cost-push inflation in an M.D.R. is the fact that such inflation may well occur before the M.D.R. has depleted the 'labour pool' of the L.D.R. The cost-push pressures in the M.D.R. may well be a combination of rising costs of accommodation and relative labour shortage in the M.D.R. during a period in which demand for labour outstrips the current rate of immigration. Such a lagged response in immigration to employment opportunities reflects the less than wholly 'economic' nature of the migration process already outlined, in which the hope of economic gain plus social links with the M.D.R. are more important than the chance of some employment. But the result for the L.D.R is a situation in which the inflationary pressures in the M.D.R. may aggravate its own problems by undermining government-promoted investment inflow from the M.D.R. To the extent that the recession in the M.D.R. is reflected in reduced demand for L.D.R. exports, it will also tend to further 'backwash' those L.D.R. firms whose growth has been based on the assumption of continued M.D.R. imports. This is the more likely the longer the period in which the labour migration to the M.D.R. has sustained both warranted and natural growth rates. Where L.D.R. firms are less strongly unionised than those in the M.D.R., and paying lower effective wage rates (as tends to be the case in their smaller establishments), they may be able to partly offset their relative loss through increased interregional competitiveness during the period in which the larger M.D.R. firms are meeting cost inflationary wage demands. But lower wage costs will not sustain them through a major recession in demand.

The higher S.O.C. costs in the main areas of labour inflow in

245

an M.D.R. have indicated that an 'improved' mobility policy of more out-migration from the L.D.R. is undesirable because of its demand on more resources for the same services than in smaller urban areas. But a further reason for not basing regional policy on acceleration of labour outflow from an L.D.R. is the evidence on the spatial inelasticity of L.D.R. labour in the sense of its unresponsiveness to potential income gains through migration. 'Congestion' costs in high rents for housing in the labour inflow areas, as well as short-term losses incurred through migration show that the irrationality in such resistance to migration lies in the spatial-elasticity assumptions of some migration models rather than with those who refuse to move. The fact that substantial migration over long time-periods in the United States and Italy has not managed to do more than equal the natural increase in resident population in their southern regions shows that out-migration would have to be substantially higher than that already achieved during periods of relatively high M.D.R. growth of demand for labour to reduce population pressure in under-employed agricultural and urban areas in such L.D.Rs. The high re-entry proportion of migrants from the U.S. South indicates that the policy would be likely to prove only partly successful. In the meantime an even greater demand would be imposed on S.O.C. provision in the areas of labour inflow and employment opportunity in the higher cost M.D.R. In addition the urban unemployed (if not the rural under-employed) will be drawing unemployment income in those states which provide it. In general, this is disadvantageous to the L.D.R. compared with the alternative of job provision, since it will mean lower *per capita* income in the region than industrial or service employment could assure, and in the absence of local industrial employment opportunities will tend to increase demand from the M.D.R. In the U.S. case such unemployment relief not only will tend to increase demand for industrial goods from outside the region but also reduce the resources available for infrastructural expenditure or industrial incentives where it is the state and not the federal government which is responsible for such welfare provision.

The net costs of S.O.C. provision in M.D.R. inflow areas plus the spatial inelasticity of L.D.R. labour give at least two terms of reference for the case of bringing M.D.R. work to L.D.R. workers, rather than vice versa. Of the two factors the spatial immobility of labour is the more important, since if L.D.R. labour were prepared to migrate on a greater scale, the S.O.C. and other congestion costs in the M.D.R. might be reduced by a conscious distribution of employment policy within the M.D.R. For instance, while pressure on urban land use in the Italian northwestern cities such as Genoa, Turin and Milan is very marked, only Genoa faces severe geographical constraints on urban expansion. It is the uncontrolled nature of surburban sprawl in the other main urban areas of the North, and the failure to plan for infrastructural provision in line with new housing which has been substantially responsible for the S.O.C. crises in these areas. A 'new towns' policy, providing satellite urban areas for the main centres of labour inflow, with industrial estates and advance factory building, could do much to reduce their congestion pressures. But such policies are only one side of the picture. So long as labour outflow from the L.D.R. does not accelerate, and, given that it does, unless this acceleration is accompanied by an increase in the location of directly productive activity in the L.D.R., the L.D.R. will tend to remain under-employed, with the macro-economic disequilibrium process tending to promote a dual-economy structure. This has important implications for the long-run development of the national economy in the sense that the L.D.R.'s growth will be restrained in favour of M.D.R. growth. In other words, while continued emigration from an L.D.R. may assist it through the early stages of a government-promoted development policy, emigration without such development will increasingly aggravate the L.D.R.'s economic and social problems. Moreover, while the intermittent incidence of cost-push inflationary pressures may restrain the M.D.R. growth rate (and that of the national economy), the cost in the first instance will tend to be carried by the migrant population from the L.D.R., and be expressed in both a fall in actual immigration and an acceleration of re-entry of emigrant labour to the L.D.R.[7] Yet with reflation in the M.D.R. the long-term cumulative process will re-engage in its favour rather than that of the L.D.R.[c]

To focus on these aspects of labour migration and national resource use, it is evident that it would pay to provide employment opportunities in urban areas with populations below 250,000, the level at which significant net S.O.C. costs occur, subject to

247

the assumption that there are no net costs to firms (at least in the long run) from the location of plant in such areas. But under conditions in which M.D.R. demand for labour is mainly provided through L.D.R. labour outflow, it will, to a great extent, be the *same* labour which is employed by the firms expanding in the M.D.R. as would be employed by them if they located in the main areas of labour outflow in the L.D.R.

Evidence on the comparability of M.D.R. and L.D.R. labour is available from an Italian enquiry conducted at firm level by SVI-MEZ and FORMEZ in the early 1960s.[8] For instance, before its merger with Montecatini, the independent Edison company reported that 'southern labour presents the same intellectual capacity as northern labour'. The food processing and distribution company, Motta, reported that the relative productivity of labour employed in its southern plant was satisfactory, and Vedeme Manifatture reported that 'the number of intelligent and willing workers is *higher* in the South than in the North'. As could be expected with the low level of industrialisation in the South in the early 1960s, incoming firms found that skilled labour was virtually non-existent. The La Centrale company found that it was necessary to import skilled workers and foremen from the North since 'the southern worker is absolutely untrained'. On the other hand, it also found that these originally unskilled workers were 'intelligent and responsive to specialist training'. Of the 2300 unskilled workers which it recruited locally for its Brindisi plant, Montecatini found that only 12 per cent left the company in the period immediately after initial employment, and in general commented that 'when it is made plain to the worker that he has a chance of a career in the firm he will leave it only unwillingly'.[d] The evidence from such firms corroborates the claim of Compagna that 'if Sicilian and Calabrian labour can learn skills in Oldensaal, they certainly can do so in the South'.[9]

Any regional policy which is concerned to make a quantified approach to resolving such imbalance should be guided by a systematic, if flexible, cost–benefit framework. So far too little has been pioneered in this area. The Regional Science school in the United States includes some of the most accomplished mathematicians to have escaped the NASA space programme. But since they mainly have been concerned to give algebraic elegance to equilibrium models which assume-away regional imbalance in the first place, their talents have not resulted in major advances in cost–benefit models. Otherwise such cost–benefit as has been attempted has been limited to project analysis of the water resource or electrification type: that is to say a restricted consideration of a once-off micro-economic project, rather than a continuing interregional macro-economic problem.[10]

A notable recent exception to this lacuna in regional theory has been the effort of Barry Moore and John Rhodes to estimate the costs and benefits of British regional policy. This has included an assessment of the jobs created up to 1970 by the Labour Government's regional wage subsidy (Regional Employment Premium), and of the overall budget costs of regional expenditure in relation to claw-backs from raised regional tax receipts and the like. Moore and Rhodes's estimates of the benefits from the Regional Employment Premium are open to qualification granted the assumptions which have to be made in calculating what would have been the regional distribution of jobs without the R.E.P. But their estimates of the claw-backs from government regional expenditure are more directly plausible and highly impressive.[11] The trouble with macro-economic cost–benefit analysis is that the further the estimates depart from specific projects, the greater the number of external effects and interactions which have to be taken into account, and the greater the number of unknowns. This means that in many respects its quantification can only be numerate guessing. In addition, the scale of the information which should be encompassed is so vast that no individual can attempt more than a minor part of it for a national economy as a whole. Even a major research team occupied with little else would be hard put to crack the main dimensions of the problem in less than several years granted the amount of basic information which is lacking through government concentration of data collation in other macro-economic areas.

None the less, the previous text has shown that in cases where the national governments have been faced with a major regional problem, funds have been channelled successfully to the measurement of some of the main costs of imbalance in regional resource use. This so far mainly concerned estimates of increased cost of infrastructure with increased urban size. In both

249

the United States and the European Community the problem of imbalanced use of regional resources is assuming greater importance through the patent urban crisis in the United States and through political pressures in the E.E.C. (where Britain joined Italy in demanding more decisive action on regional policy).

If future regional cost–benefit analysis is to be of real use as a policy guideline it must attempt to quantify the main macro dimensions of the regional problem. The data secured will necessarily be incomplete and partial. Central or federal governments cannot afford to monitor the social costs of every infrastructure project or every pocket of unemployment. Such a macro-regional framework therefore would lack the completeness of some of the water resource, Tennessee Valley Authority type models developed in the United States for micro projects. But governments must rapidly adopt some standards for macro-regional data collection to complement meso- and micro-regional cost–benefit. At present they are working almost entirely in the dark when considerable new light is both desirable and possible.

Figures 13 and 14 (pp. 299–300) indicate some of the main features of the costs of imbalanced use of regional resources which could be sketched in by government departments or work sponsored to regional research institutes. They are simply indications of areas for further work rather than quantified frameworks. But they do have the limited merit of showing the interrelated nature of costs from the imbalanced use of resources in different regions: that is costs from pressure and congestion in more-developed regions, and costs from under-utilisation in less-developed regions. In practical terms they would have to represent existing administrative regions if used as the basis for more systematic regional cost–benefit accounting. Thus while macro-economic for regions as a whole, they would be less than macro-economic for the national economy. They would constitute a halfway house in national accounting. But for that reason they could be used to estimate the scale of both local or intra-regional resource costs, and national and international resource use. The indications of M.D.R. congestion pressures on the cost of living and wages could be traced through leading firms in the framework of the Planning Agreements or Programme Contracts system in operation in Belgium, France and Italy, and proposed by the Labour Party in Britain.[12 e] This would give an indication of the foreign-trade costs of internal regional imbalance. Similarly, the quantification by main categories of urban size within major regions could give a clearer indication of the different cost of infrastructure through dispersion of industry. The framework would also permit a more effective use of the already available data on training costs and labour utilisation through national employment exchanges (which so far have not been coherently integrated into regional planning in Western Europe).

Harnessing Meso-Economic Power

To the extent that meso-economic big-league firms tend to concentrate plant expansion in M.D.R.s the mechanism of unequal competition under the free working of the market will tend to disadvantage small-league firms in L.D.R.s. In general, smaller-scale L.D.R. firms will tend to survive either because they operate in relatively low quality and low profit markets in which meso-economic leaders are uninterested, or in markets which they have not yet got round to 'mopping up'. There is no necessary constraint on the continued expansion of meso-economic leaders other than management inefficiency or government anti-trust or competition policy. Size can actually bring gains in efficiency through specialist division of responsibility of the kind now widely accepted and taught in business management schools. For its part, vigorous State competition policy may result mainly in a stimulus to multi-national rather than multi-regional location by big-league firms. In other words, if rigidly applied, a national competition policy may prevent a cumulative increase in the market share of a dominant company, but encourage its expansion abroad rather than in a less-developed region.

Besides, while such a policy might give a formal breathing space to L.D.R. companies, it does not give them a guarantee that meso-economic leaders will not be able to employ a variety of market tactics which continue to restrict the potential growth of small-league firms in L.D.R.s. For instance, under inflationary conditions 'no-entry' market tactics are difficult to identify from outside the boardroom of the company concerned. The maintenance of prices in a manner which could deter entry for a small-league L.D.R. firm into a national market would pass as public virtue rather than private vice. The same is even more true of price reduction of the kind which the big-league M.D.R. firm might have to employ in an elimination price tactic.

Also, there is the problem that the L.D.R. firm which is successfully managed up to a given stage may find its problems increased by meso-economic power the more successful it becomes. In other words, the more the small-league L.D.R. firm encroaches upon the national markets of big-league M.D.R. firms the more likely it will find itself subject to oligopolistic price tactics of a kind which the M.D.R. firms did not previously bother to apply. The development of an L.D.R. market in more sophisticated and higher priced goods will tend to attract the attention of big-league M.D.R. firms the further it is developed, with the new L.D.R. demand frequently supplied from M.D.R. plant. This is in addition to the fact that, while L.D.R. firms in early stages of development may benefit from the control of operations by an enterprising single individual, their expansion at a rate which would permit them to challenge M.D.R. sector-leaders in national markets may well coincide with the critical time at which they have to devolve decision-making and adapt to new management techniques, with temporary efficiency losses at the time when they most need continued growth and strength.

If unchecked by government policies the result of such tendencies may be a situation in which interregional dualism in the sense of effectively separate regional economies with different growth rates will be matched and reinforced by an intra-sectoral dualism, in which the different regional markets are composed of meso-and micro-economic firms which are effectively different in structure, actual growth, and growth potential. The low overall growth rate in the L.D.R. will affect the manner of investment decision-making as well as the level of investment in relation to regional income, with defensive investment patterns contributing to a defeatist investment psychology. This combination of factors operating within and between firms will limit the effectiveness of government policy designed to promote L.D.R. investment and expansion through development incentives such as investment loans and grants, company and personal tax concessions, regional employment premiums and similar indirect measures.

For instance, a low warranted growth rate will reduce a firm's preparedness to borrow, since if the rate of growth of demand for its products has been low for long, its management may simply remain unconvinced that the increased investment concerned is justified by prospective future demand. An investment-grants policy also would be limited by this demand-constraint factor, even if it constituted a very high proportion of the investment concerned. In an extreme case in which the grants totalled the value of the investment to be undertaken there could well be a change in investment psychology independent of the estimated market prospects, since the direct risk to the firm concerned would be reduced. On the other hand, for a variety of reasons it would not be eliminated. For one thing the firm would have to employ additional labour if the investment involved significant expansion, and would not readily enter into a situation in which it could face union pressure to maintain this labour force in the event of running into sales problems, particularly if this affected production for existing capacity. For another, it could appreciate that it would face increasing problems of interregional competition from big-league firms if it undertook a major expansion which encroached significantly on their share of national markets. A labour premium could assist in the problem of maintaining an under-employed labour force, but again would not cover the total 'lost' wages bill under all circumstances. Also, as already mentioned, competition policies which are unable to distinguish no-entry and elimination pricing tactics from virtuous price reductions would not safeguard the expanding L.D.R. firms against oligopolistic price tactics from M.D.R. competitors.

It is such factors which underline the futility of assuming that indirect incentives alone will ensure the growth of small and micro-economic firms into medium meso-economic firms in less-developed regions. The previous analysis also has cited evidence showing that present regional policies are least effective for those meso-economic firms most needed in problem regions and areas. Multi-national companies not only have shown that they can organise the division of the same production process in different plant around the world but have also shown, by their survival and growth, that they tend to be the companies whose market position is most assured over the long run. Their access

253

to low-cost foreign labour reduces the effect of regional labour subsidies such as the R.E.P. Their capacity to charge themselves high import prices in high-tax countries from subsidiaries in tax havens or low-tax countries abroad both reduces the effect of regional capital incentives, and damages the national balance of payments (especially since such companies do not take full advantage of increased price competitiveness through devaluation in those cases where this would mean more competition with their own products abroad). Their capacity to site a projected plant in at least three of the four quarters of the globe can drive a government department to relax the intended location control of I.D.C.s. At the same time the rigorous application of I.D.C. policy to small, nationally based companies can seriously compromise their profit and survival position.

In terms of value for public money in the private sector, the continued distribution of general assistance to all companies locating or expanding in problem regions should be challenged on several grounds. First, there is the evidence to the Commons Expenditure Committee that such assistance frequently was seen as a bonus rather than as an important factor in the location decision. In practice, in the case of multi-national companies, regional aid can mean massive hand-outs to some of the wealthiest companies in the world, which at the same time are avoiding tax through the transfer pricing of profits abroad. Secondly, replacement investment alone accounts for a major proportion of the capital expansion of leading companies in Development Areas (for example I.C.I.'s evidence on its Scottish plant and Courtaulds' expansion at Spennymoor). One of the main reasons why firms expand in Development Areas rather than attempt to secure premises outside them – on their own evidence – is labour availability. They are not staying in the regions because of government assistance.

For these reasons it is recommended that new selectivity should be introduced in regional policy for leading meso-economic and multi-national firms. These firms have already been conveniently scheduled under the Category 1 teminology by the government in the British case, that is to say those enterprises whose sales in the domestic market have a value of £50 million per annum at current prices. The range might be limited relative to the Category 1 definition, which includes not only manufacturing concerns, but also mining, public utilities, transport, postal services and telecommunications. Only manufacturing enterprise and head-office services are effectively mobile among these activities, since the rest are bound to particular localities.

The leading manufacturing firms falling in the Category 1 range could be brought within a new system of regional policy already developed in France, Belgium and Italy since 1968. This is the Planning Agreements or Programme Contracts system.[13] As the system at present works, especially in Italy where the government is compelled to give major priority to regional development, leading firms are supposed to submit their major investment and job programmes to the Ministry of the Budget and Economic Planning, where they are assessed for regional implications. The location of new plant should then be negotiated between the firms and the Ministry. This differs in principle from I.D.C. practice, since the government assesses a flow of information from leading firms well before their location of new plant is decided, rather than location in isolation once the firm's decision is imminent.

In the Italian case the firms secure the available regional incentives by right if they locate in one of the Development Areas. But Italian companies are not so extensively multi-national as British companies, nor is Italy the host to so many foreign multi-national companies as Britain. In the British case there would be a strong argument in favour of making regional assistance conditional on the fulfilment of strategic requirements of government policy. For instance, at present, leading firms may be informally pressured by government departments to locate in particular areas. But by and large they are left free in their location in those regions where general regional assistance is available.

The Labour Party's Planning Agreements system could be used to improve on this situation by (1) giving an advance framework for harnessing the location of leading firms to specific locations; (2) permitting better forward planning of linkages between incoming leaders and local firms, thereby ensuring more 'led' firms and fewer 'laggards'; and (3) making possible an improved scrutiny of the possible location costs to individual companies.

However, no such system will work simply by legislation. Leading multi-national companies will seek to evade Planning

Agreements much as they manage to evade location controls of the British I.D.C. type unless some form of sanction or penalty can be invoked to constrain them. The Italian State Holdings have already shown that public enterprise can be used in a highly selective manner, tailored to the needs of particular areas in problem regions. It thereby constitutes a direct instrument for the development of such regions. But such holdings also have shown an interesting indirect result in regional policy. They have provided a selective public-enterprise reinforcement to the general Planning Agreements or Programme Contracts system.

For instance, pressure had been brought on the leading domestic Italian vehicle producer – FIAT – since the late 1950s to locate a new construction plant in the under-employed South. The company was strong enough to stalemate this pressure with counter proposals for expansion in other less-labour-intensive production in the South, plus a car assembly unit, but meanwhile did little about either. The government then asked I.R.I. to diversify the Alfa-Romeo company from its specialised high-performance vehicles and challenge FIAT in the production of medium-range vehicles, locating the new Alfa-Sud venture near Naples. The direct result has been the Alfa-Sud factory now nearing completion at Pozzuoli. This can produce up to one-third of a million vehicles a year and provide direct employment for some 15,000 people, with indirect employment for up to 35,000. I.R.I. alone was too small, and controlled an insufficient proportion of total national engineering to be able to close the gap between North and South Italy in terms of engineering value-added and employment single handed.[f] Yet the announcement of official approval for the Alfa-Sud project was followed within two years by a government Planning Agreement with FIAT to locate its next major plant in the South. This was followed by a Planning Agreement with Pirelli, which undertook to locate its expansion for the following five years in the region. In other words, FIAT followed the Alfa-Romeo initiative when it would not take such an initiative itself. The result will be a major stimulus to not only direct employment in engineering in the South, but also to indirect employment through provision of inputs for the new plant by local firms which either are already in a position to supply them, or are being built up to a position from which to do so through the S.M.E. investment bank of the I.R.I. group.

The Alfa-Romeo case does not constitute a politically neutral formula for harnessing a leading firm's growth to the needs of a problem region, and thereby ensuring a follow-the-leader effect from other companies. One of the reasons for FIAT and Pirelli deciding to enter into Planning Agreements after the autumn of 1968 was the three-month engineering strike which hit them at that time. The engineering unions knew better than anyone that the additional employment needs of the big northern companies were supplied by that time almost wholly from southern labour. They had to find accommodation for them and smooth their adjustment to northern urban life where management found that it could neither supply labour with local housing nor provide sufficient social facilities. It was union pressure on the government to make FIAT and Pirelli locate their future expansion in the South which triggered off a chain reaction in which both FIAT and Pirelli came to fear that, unless they entered Planning Agreements for southern locations, the government conceivably might nationalise them to break the continuing union deadlock and avert a national crisis. This is a lesson which has to be learned from the unwillingness of private enterprise leaders to co-operate with government planners. Unless additional social and political pressures are mobilised, State enterprise itself may only substitute for what private enterprise fails to do.

On the other hand, if employed in such a politicised context, public enterprise not only can countervail leading private enterprise, but can also constrain the flight of multi-national companies to countries in the Third World whose governments have banned or prevented the rise of unionised labour. The main constraint in this sense would be nationalisation of the physical assets which the government could prevent the multi-national from exporting abroad. The classic deadlock so far in such a situation has been the lack of credibility that a government could incorporate the physical plant and equipment into an efficient on-going operation. But the availability of a major multi-sectoral State Holding Company such as I.R.I., or the proposed National Enterprise Board in Britain, could give credibility to the success of such a nationalisation. The State Holding could provide management skills sufficient to ensure that the company continued to operate successfully at a national and international level, particularly if the new public enterprise secured union backing of the kind which normally could be expected. The result might be that the sanction of taking over a foreign-controlled multinational need only be invoked in exceptional circumstances. But such indirect pressures on private enterprise companies, as well as location controls over both private and new public enterprise in the meso-economic sector, could make possible the direction of most expansion in new plant to less-developed regions rather than abroad.

Priorities for Regional Structure

Several recommendations for structural planning have already been made explicit. Basically, the larger the region and the more backward its initial industrial structure, the stronger the case for adopting an industrialisation strategy rather than attempting to promote its development through either agricultural specialisation or concentration of development effort in the promotion of services such as tourism. The policy should aim to 'unbalance' investment allocation in favour of particular sectors within industry, employing international and national evidence on the recent rate of growth of product and employment by industrial sectors, rather than through estimating input–output linkages which give rise to anomalous results. The wide error margins in Chenery's studies indicate that achieving target *rates* of growth for even broad sectors is difficult to achieve with precision for a variety of reasons including the difficulty of predicting variations in national and international demand patterns. Moreover, even if such particular target rates for the L.D.R. are met, they will be inadequate to significantly reduce interregional productivity and income disparities in the event of higher rates being achieved by the rest of the national economy. For these reasons targets should be set for given *proportions* of national investment in priority sectors within the L.D.R. This would mean that variations in demand which could not be foreseen at the beginning of the period of the development policies would be translated into an investment distribution in favour of the L.D.R. It also would mean that endogenously promoted growth, in the sense of new products creating new demand as a result of indig-

258

enous or imported technical progress and innovation, would not exclusively benefit the M.D.R. In practice, inasmuch as they requ-ired investment in entirely new plant, they would tend to bene-fit the L.D.R. to the extent that locational controls were em-ployed to fulfil the particular sectoral investment targets.

In a case of major structural backwardness the government should employ a development policy which harnesses the mech-anism of growth in the leading or spearhead industrial sectors in the region's favour. In other words, it should not simply employ an across-the-board locational controls policy such is at present employed in the United Kingdom through Industrial Develop-ment Certificates, but should specifically unbalance the sectoral composition of industrial investment in problem regions in fav-our of those manufacturing sectors with records of higher than average rates of growth of product and employment. The sec-tors registering the highest product and employment growth rates are engineering and chemical products. These sectors have the additional advantage that they are below, and in some cases well below, the average for manufacturing as a whole in terms of capital cost per employee. In the case of a major problem re-gion, these should not be the only sectors employed in a development policy of sectoral unbalance, but should be sup-ported by complementary target proportions for the location of investment in what has been identified as 'modern' manufactur-ing within the region, with lower proportions for manufacturing in general. The precise percentage proportions of these targets would be of less importance than that they should be significant-ly unbalanced in the problem region's favour. In the Italian case guidelines are available from the low proportion of national value-added and employment which they have represented over nearly a twenty-year period in the South – in the case of en-gineering and chemicals and chemical products only about one-third of the region's share of national population. The small im-provement in the South's share of national value-added in both engineering, chemicals, and chemical products, plus the regi-stered decline in the region's share of national engineering em-ployment from 1950 to 1967 indicate that only a major degree of unbalance in the region's favour in these sectors is likely to lead to significant improvement in its industrial structure. If the targets were over-attained during the development period, they could be scaled down with less difficulty than could the reverse process of up-scaling.

The setting of such target proportions for engineering and chemical products, 'modern' manufacturing and manufacturing as a whole does not mean to say that no estimates should be made within a national and regional planning framework for either national or regional rates of growth by industrial sub-sector. But such forecasting of sectoral growth rates should not simply project past trends at a highly aggregated sectoral level, but should require meso-economic firms to submit their investment programmes for a specified period through a Planning Agreements framework. If such firms are informed of the rate of growth which the government considers feasible as a policy objective for the national economy over this period, and if this is also accompanied by a projection, by main sectors, reflecting both past trends and government targets, such leading firms should be able to take account of the government's major objectives in determining their own investment programmes in a Planning Agreements or Programme Contracts system. Information could be categorised to give details on their anticipated rate of growth of investment, productivity, prices, exports and imports, jobs, and purchases and sales to other leading firms in the same planning system. It would be more effective the greater the degree of monopoly concentration in individual sectors. In 1960 the largest single company in Italy controlled, on average, nearly 50 per cent of the output of the leading seventeen industrial sectors, and this concentration has since increased.[14] In 1970 the leading hundred companies in Britain controlled some 50 per cent of manufacturing output, and are set fair to control 66 per cent around 1980. In such countries a Planning Agreements system operating on a few dozen leading companies would therefore give advance information on the coming changes in sectoral structure which would make possible new advances in input–output analysis, based on information which included expected change in technical coefficients where they count most – in the meso-economic firms which set the pace for the rest of industry. The leaders account for so large a proportion of the individual boxes of any input–output table that in policy-resource terms they give the most results for the least data collection. Since they also act as leaders for the rest of the sectors

260

in which they operate, policy-makers would risk little by operating mainly through them rather than the thousands of smaller firms crowding into the rest of industry.

However, as previously shown, there is no guarantee that a Planning Agreements system will work unless the State is able to exercise constraints on the leading private enterprises. In essence it must do so through either indirect or direct controls. Indirect incentives which make concessionary finance available may be effective in limited cases, and the French planners have considerable expertise in this area. On the other hand, meso-economic market power increases the proportion of funds which can be secured by self-financing, while the improved integration of international capital markets means that creditworthy meso-economic firms do not have to go 'cap in hand' to governments for external finance. They can largely get it either through horizontal integration – running their own investment and finance houses – or though the Eurobond and Euro-dollar issues made available by consortia of leading investment banks. For such reasons any State with major regional imbalance should use new public enterprise to ensure both a direct instrument for regional policy, and an indirect lever on the co-operation of leading private enterprise. In other words, the questions of intra-industry and inter-industry structure cannot be divorced in either national or regional planning. There is a crucial link between the role of the modern capitalist firm, the new public enterprises now being introduced in most Western European economies, and the feasibility of any improved procedure for structural planning in regional policy.

Micro-Economic Planning and Job Dispersion

It has been seen that the priority accorded to labour and site costs for expanding firms indicates that they can benefit considerably from lower production costs in less-developed areas and regions. The low importance attached to transport costs, particularly when a modern transport network is available, indicates that firms locating plant in such lower cost areas can distribute products and, conversely, can secure inputs from an entire national market. Although Luttrell's evidence indicates that larger firms find it easier to decentralise all operations or locate

261

new plant in such areas, benefiting from internalisation of services, labour training and management divisibility, the Società Autostrade evidence demonstrates that very small plant can locate successfully outside main urban centres provided that sufficient labour and E.O.C. are available, with access to a good transport network, and that production is in modern industry with relatively routinised production. Neither the Bergin and Eagan nor the Società Autostrade evidence included a minimum standard of pre-existing S.O.C. (as opposed to E.O.C.) or a Marshallian skilled-labour market as essential conditions for successful plant location. They also gave a unanimously low ranking to the proximity of technically related industry, while the benefits from such proximity anyway were not specified to be of the 'external technological economies' type, but were rather viewed in such terms as ease of communication, and so on.

Moreover, both the Luttrell and the Società Autostrade evidence demonstrated that the firms relocating or locating new plant in less-developed areas included not only traditional industries such as textiles, clothing, footwear, food, drink and tobacco, and also light modern industry such as vehicles and their components, electrical goods and equipment, machine tools, precision instruments, and plastics, but also heavy modern industry such as metallurgy, oil refining and chemicals. That is to say that these types of production not only could operate successfully in dispersed locations rather than integrated production complexes in or near urban areas, but also include the broad range of production found in those modern chemicals, metal and metal-processing sectors identified by Kuznets and Kuklinski as having the fastest rates of growth of product and employment. This evidence of the breadth of modern industry suited to dispersed location in less-developed areas demonstrates that sophisticated techniques of analysis employed to identify suitable interrelated complexes for a narrower ranve of industry may understate the growth potential of the areas concerned. Such techniques also entail analytical and administrative difficulties which seriously compromise their usefulness in practice.

In general therefore, it appears that the case for the development of backward regions and areas through the concentration of industry in certain 'growth poles' has been exaggerated. This might appear to simplify government locational policy considerably, with the extension of the range of industrial sectors and locations suggesting that a government need only grant general incentives, provide an up-to-date motorway system and wait for the automatic development of the region to occur. In practice, of course, the situation is more complicated. One of the principal factors which locational policy must confront is the fact that up to 80 per cent of industrial investment in the economies considered by Kuklinski was found to be in the expansion of existing plant rather than in plant in new locations.[15] To this extent, if firms were left to decide whether or not to locate new plant (or relocate operations) in less-developed areas, only 20 per cent of all new investment might be available. Further, not even all of this 20 per cent would necessarily be located in such areas, in preference to lower cost sites in the immediate vicinity of the original location.

On this basis it might be maintained that such suburban location should be permitted on the basis that management is best fitted to estimate its relative advantage as against location in a more backward area designated as needing development. But there are several arguments against this. First, management may not make any comprehensive evaluation of the relative costs and benefits to the firm from a suburban location or location in a backward area. Many micro-economic firms are not completely informed even of the available investment grants and concessions available in such areas, far less being able to estimate the comparative labour, site and transport savings in such locations.[16] Secondly, where any estimation is undertaken, there is an understandable tendency to justify a nearer rather than a farther location. As Hirschman has suggested, 'investors spend a long time mopping up all the opportunities around some "growth pole" and neglect those that may have arisen or could be made to arise elsewhere'.[17] This tendency occurs not so much because management in some way 'cooks the books' on the cost–benefit account, but because the unknowns in any such estimation of cost or benefit may persuade them that location in a backward area is too great a risk. Alain Bienaymé has neatly summarised the role of such unknowns as '*la peur de manquer*'.[18] The regional development agencies may have a low reputation for efficiency, so that the firm may with some reason fear that it will lack the vital E.O.C. in a given location.[g] Not least, any collective decision to locate in a less-developed area will have to be initiated by someone at some time, who will become identified with its success or its failure over a given period. This may in fact be too short to produce the full benefits of location, or the venture may fail for other reasons. Nevertheless, whoever is first identified with the proposal to undertake such a venture may rightly fear that one of the things he will lack is continued membership of the board.

Further, of course, there is the higher S.O.C. cost and the inflationary higher rents, rates, wages and costs spiral which follows the unchecked expansion of large industrial centres. Yet, as Kuklinski expresses it, 'the industrial managers who overestimate the role of external economies in the development of a plant have in quite a number of cases greater bargaining power than the urban and regional planners who correctly indicate the cumulative consequences of the expansion of industrial plants, in growing social costs.'[19] In addition to this, firms which do decide to locate new plant in a less-developed region may continue to over-estimate the benefits from urban concentration in the L.D.R., choosing sites in the suburbs of large urban centres whose social infrastructure is approaching or is already at a 'critical' stage, requiring massive additional investment in 'ring roads', access routes, and so on to avoid congestion. In Italy this already is the case with Naples, where the local authorities have proved unable to cope with the new S.O.C. investment and urban planning required to support labour inflow from elsewhere in the South, and where I.R.I. has undertaken a major congestion-reducing programme at considerable cost.[h] Meanwhile, other areas of labour outflow in the South have underutilised S.O.C., in many cases of up-to-date quality.

These arguments, in addition to those forwarded in the previous sections on intra-and inter-sectoral structure, further support the case for some kind of control over the location of industry. But without legislation both government and that management open to the potential advantages from location in less-developed areas are critically handicapped in recommending particular locations. Just as a member of a management board opens himself to some risk from recommending a move which is legally avoidable, so even a major Minister – particularly in a party reliant generally on the support of management – may find his career jeopardised by pressure on a leading firm to locate a particular new initiative. It has already been shown in analysis of multi-national versus multi-regional companies that formal powers over location are not a sufficient condition for control of meso-economic location. It will be necessary to supplement them with meso-economic public enterprise. Such selective controls and new public enterprise must range through the meso-economic sector if small-scale planning of location is to be effective at the micro-economic level.[i]

One principle which might usefully be taken into account in locational planning would be the degree of maturity and standardisation of the product in the plant concerned. For instance, it has already been seen that there is considerable evidence that it is the smaller micro-economic firms which most need to be in a position to secure external economies from location near other firms which can provide them with the different inputs for their changing products both relatively quickly and at low unit cost. Cost and time tend to be more important when the firms concerned are small, and in markets with frequently changing tastes they tend to be small both because they cannot secure very large-scale production runs and because the lack of such runs limits the scope for long-term brand attachment of a kind which could permit 'imperfect' pricing. The New York garment industry is the classic case in point.

On the other hand, it also has to be admitted that even relatively large firms in the meso-economic sector face time and cost problems in the initial stages of introducing a new product. This first phase of the product cycle is well known to involve considerable trial and error with an unstandardised product which is subject to considerable changes in components, design and production. The market for the good is relatively unstable; the 'learning curve' for the product is shallow, with high supervision costs through the necessity to employ specialist supervisory personnel; production itself will tend to employ a higher proportion of skilled workers, and overall management co-ordination of purchases for changing inputs, sales of a possibly modified or 'snagged' product, relations with late R and D breakthroughs, new union contracts for bulk production, and keeping a lead on competitors will tend to mean a disproportionate allocation of management in relation to the product's proportion of company output. It appears to be clearly in this phase of a product's life cycle that communication and the ability to quickly command new inputs from other firms already enjoying bulk-production internal-scale economies can be as important for the large meso-economic firm as for a virtually handicraft operation in a New York downtown loft.

During the second main phase of the product cycle – the 'growth' phase – the product, by definition, has been standardised. An established market permits both internal-scale economies and pecuniary external economies for inputs, with the latter likely to be reinforced to the extent that oligopsonistic bargaining power is exercised by the management of the company concerned. On the production side both the skilled labour and specialist supervisory needs are likely to fall, while the learning curve rises. Company management is likely to turn its attention more to export outlets and the possibility of establishing multi-national subsidiary operations than to be preoccupied with ironing out snags in the production process. itself. This reduced involvement with what happens in the production is likely to continue through the third or 'mature' phase of the cycle, when the rate of growth of domestic market demand tends to fall, with a stable demand pattern established which increases partly by extension and partly by replacement demand. During this phase further innovations tend either to be relatively simple process innovations or 'cosmetic' product innovations with which central management can easily cope while concerning itself more closely with diversification into other products either in or approaching the 'new' first phase of the cycle.

Vernon's application of the product cycle to multi-*national* location patterns is well known, and has played an important role as a departure point for the theory of behaviour of multi-national corporations in general.[20] However, later analysis has shown that such a. product-cycle model is over-simplified. Not all production conforms to the convenient three-stage cycle of the kind outlined. In the food-processing and manufacturing industries, for example, U.S. firms went multi-national in the second phase of the cycle, rather than in the third stage suggested by Vernon's model. . Therefore, generalised application of the model should only be taken as a point of departure, complemented by further analysis and empirical research. On the other hand, provided that it is employed in this context, and is used as a term of reference in conjunction with other guidelines for locational policy, it may prove useful as at least one parameter in the concentration versus dispersion issue. For instance, product-cycle analysis would suggest that the management of even large firms with relatively established national markets may be justified in claiming that they need to introduce a major innovation from a 'central' location in which they both have face-to-face contact between themselves, and with their R and D staff, their marketing team, senior union representatives, and so on. If there is any case for continued central location by meso-economic firms it is this first phase of the new-product cycle. On the other hand, the case for a central or M.D.R. location is reduced the further the product moves in its life cycle, for the already expressed reasons of reduced necessity to secure new inputs at short notice, the reduced demands on central company management time, the reduction in specialist supervision and services required and so on. Taken in conjunction with other location criteria such as the need to reduce large-scale unemployment in major urban areas within an L.D.R. the second or 'growth' phase of the product therefore might well be considered that most suitable to an L.D.R. 'growth centre' location. On the same basis the third or 'mature' product phase could be considered most appropriate for a more dispersed L.D.R. location. This would partly be through the further reduction of central company management involvement in the production and marketing process. But it could also be considered justified on two other bases. First, the later the phase of the cycle the less the dependence of the firm on a fast-expanding labour force for the production concerned. Secondly, the 'mature' stage of the cycle is one in which wage pressure in either M.D.R. or L.D.R. growth-centre locations is likely to be already marked or may become increasingly cost-push inflationary. The more dispersed the L.D.R. location the more likely the securing of wage rates which at least are marginally lower than in the growth-centre locations.

These arguments are summarised briefly in Figure 10 (p.297). As already stressed, they are not suggested as substitutes for other criteria in location policy either between or within regions, but are essentially complementary and might be employed in conjunction with them. Apart from anything else, it is not suggested that the phase of its life cycle is conveniently branded on the delivered product, nor that the phases themselves are of equal length in the product's life. In automobiles, for example, the product itself has been mature in the sense of incorporating few major innovations for more than half a century. A company innovating a rotary piston engine therefore might have a strong case for maintaining that it can either innovate or undertake an L.D.R. location, but not both. But most companies (including those now producing rotary engines under licence) should be hard put to it to justify their continued expansion within M.D.R. central locations on the basis that they were still innovating. Similarly, as already suggested, the volume of labour necessary for a major automobile plant would be such that it would, by definition, be unlikely or impossible for it to undertake a major new initiative in a minor L.D.R. dispersed location, even if it could be constrained with some justification to locate a plant in such an area if this was providing one of its own inputs on a small labour volume scale. Like any other useful guideline, the regional-location implications of the product cycle are relative.

None the less, two implications appear quite clear. First, if meso-economic companies can go multi-national at different stages of the product cycle, they can also go multi-regional. Secondly, more advantage can be taken of the product cycle as a policy guideline if the government is prepared to employ locational controls which at least distinguish between three main categories of location (M.D.R., L.D.R. growth centre and L.D.R. dispersed). Specific locational controls which obliged an M.D.R. firm to place a new plant in a particular area within the L.D.R. would also have the additional advantage of facilitating the provision of E.O.C. where it was wanted, thereby increasing the extent to which utilisation of S.O.C. investment can be guaranteed. Further, with regard to indivisibilities, it has already been suggested that not every community of 30,000 people needs a technical college or an airport. Especially for essentials such as health and education, a co-ordinated policy of investment could ensure that minimal scale requirements for hospitals and higher education centres were served by their location within relevant population 'catchment areas'. This has already been undertaken successfully in regions with lower population density than the South of Italy, such as the Highlands of Scotland.

In general, therefore, precise control of industrial location offers advantages not only in the provision of employment and income where it is most needed in the problem region, but also in the estimation of the relative costs and benefits of the provision of the appropriate infrastructure. To offset resistance to the location of plant by firms from outside the region, for example through the submission of under-optimistic expansion estimates, and to overcome short-term financial needs in the establishment of new plant, for which self-financing may not be sufficient, there would be a strong case for the granting of development aids to the firms concerned. However, if backed by sufficient public pressure, including new public enterprise, the aids concerned could if necessary be reduced to a level estimated to be equivalent to the short-term location costs above the costs of expansion in the home area. Since one of the basic aims of policies in favour of a major less-developed region is to improve the region's competitive structure through the location of more new plant, any reduction per firm might not lead to a reduction in total expenditure on aids as a whole. But it would mean more plant (or more total employment) for a given allocation of funds for such aids. Further, the utilisation of precise locational controls on this basis would mean the abandonment of any quantitative distinction between aids for location in growth poles or centres, and location elsewhere, in contrast with French and Italian policy. For, even if main urban centres were the principal areas for controlled location in the early stages of a policy, simply on the basis that absolute unemployment was greater there than elsewhere, the controls framework could allow determination of whether a plant of a given scale in a given type of production should be located there rather than in a more isolated location.

Finally, granted the emphasis given to locational controls, some evaluation should be given to their effectiveness in those Western European economies in which they have been attempted. Limited controls on the construction of plant and offices have been attempted within a 100-kilometre radius of the Commune of Paris. More extensive controls have been operated in Britain through the use of Industrial Development Certificates (I.D.C.s). These were first introduced in the Town and

Country Planning Act of 1947 which specified that permission for such a certificate must be obtained from the Board of Trade (now from the Department of Industry) by any manufacturing company wishing to extend its premises or build new premises above a given number of square feet. The Local Employment Act of 1960 covered an important loophole in this legislation, whereby warehousing premises were constructed (which were not covered by the Act) and later used for manufacturing plant. Another expedient adopted to evade controls has been the construction of buildings of less than the permitted area adjacent to existing accommodation, and later removing the partitions between the two.[21]

Cameron and Clark admit that opinion varies as to the extent of such evasion of I.D.C. controls in Britain, but claim that 'there is no doubt that thorough enforcement would require a large number of government inspectors and lengthy litigation in order to punish offenders'. They also maintain that 'the government must allow for the possibility that refusal to grant an I.D.C. may result in the company cancelling an export programme and a reduction of the rate of growth of exports.'[22] Sarah Orr has made a similar claim in the context of the government trying to oblige companies to locate within specific areas in the Development Areas, rather than anywhere they choose, and for which they can secure local authority approval: 'the industrialist, faced with the choice of expanding in a location which he regards as unsuited to his industry or not expanding at all, may well choose the latter course'.[23] Holmans has found that 70 per cent of the employment created in manufacturing industry in London and South-east England between 1952 and 1961 did not come within the scope of the I.D.C. legislation, involving either premise extensions of less than 5000 square feet, or moves to existing premises vacated by other companies, or expansion of employment without the construction of new premises.[24] Cameron and Clark have estimated that the government's movement of industry policy from 1958–63, effected mainly through I.D.C.s, created less new employment in the Development Areas than was lost from the decline of traditional declining industries in the areas during that period.[25] In addition, with regard to enforcement of controls, French evidence indicates that companies in the Paris area prefer to expand there and pay the fines for evading restrictions rather than relocate elsewhere.[j]

However, Holmans and Hammond are of the view that I.D.C. evasion could be effectively tightened up in Britain without a large inspection team and lengthy litigation.[26] Similarly, the scope of I.D.C. legislation could be tightened to include moves into premises vacated by other firms.[k] As far as the French case of evasion is concerned, it appears that the fines incurred by companies are nominal, and therefore are insufficient deterrents. The reasons for the French not raising the fines are not wholly clear, but in part appear to amount to a ranking of their regional problem below that of restructuring French industry in the face of E.E.C. competition.[l] In Britain the determination of the government in granting or refusing I.D.C.s has varied to some extent in relation to the priority given to regional development by the government of the time, with relatively stricter evaluation of I.D.C. claims and a stricter control over the illegal erection of buildings since the late 1950s.[27] Otherwise, the fears that firms may not expand production if they are refused I.D.C.s have not been supported by comprehensive evidence. In practice, it is not difficult to see that a firm which has not even estimated the private benefits of relocation in a less-developed area and does not support the social costs of expanding where it is should threaten that refusal to grant a certificate would damage the nation's balance of payments or rate of growth of production. On the other hand, if the firm is convinced that it has sound long-term growth prospects in either national or international markets, and if the government shows by example that it will, if necessary, bring it into public ownership either partly or outright, it seems unlikely that it will remain indefinitely oblivious of the advantages from expansion in the Development Area.

In general, it is clear that the effectiveness of locational controls depends not only on their intrinsic scope and the extent to which they are enforced, but also on wider considerations such as the rate of growth of the economy and the public-enterprise component in national and regional planning. If the rate of growth of the economy is low or negative, there will be either little or no expansion, and therefore few or no firms applying for development certificates. To the extent that a government has

271

deflated national growth, there will be little demand for additional labour, while the possible check to the rise in wage rates may reduce the incentive to locate in less-developed regions to take advantage of lower money-wage rates. To this extent it would not be surprising if the record of employment creation in Britain since 1966 through I.D.C.s were to prove to be poorer than even the 1958–63 period analysed by Cameron and Clark. On the other hand, the Italian economy until the late 1960s showed a high and largely sustained growth rate, with a massive expansion of output in manufacturing, which could have been expected to lead to substantial location in the South if locational controls had been employed and administered effectively. The Italians had a wide-ranging public sector through State Holdings in profitable manufacturing, but lacked complementary powers of locational control over leading private enterprise. The British had formal controls, but lacked the competitive public enterprise which could have made them more effective. But if both components of policy are purposively used over a wide range of meso-economic companies the easier it should be for management to appreciate: (1) that they are not likely to lose ground *vis-à-vis* other firms by taking an isolated action with some element of risk; (2) that both more of their suppliers and more of their markets (if these are intermediate) will also be moving to the area with them, reducing the possibility of costs from unanticipated stock shortages or losing contact with purchasers; and (3) that the rate of growth of final demand in the region should increase in a dynamic manner sufficient to justify location there in the medium rather than the long term.[m]

It has been observed that locational controls will be relatively ineffective in promoting an increase in investment in an L.D.R. if there is insufficient national growth to promote that investment in the first place. I.D.C.-type policies can only work at all when growth is relatively high. When growth is low most governments are faced with the macro-economic problem of promoting it in the first place, rather than simply making decisions as to its location. On the other hand, as already suggested in a previous chapter, this is in itself no reason why it should not use the same kind of instrument for national and regional growth promotion under low 'warranted' and 'natural' growth conditions – in particular investment through publicly owned or controlled firms in the growth-initiating manufacturing sector. There is no necessary reason why M.D.R. recovery should be pursued at the cost of continuing policies for L.D.R. development, even if it is probable that macro reflationary policies should principally benefit the M.D.R. Generally, there is a clear case for planning a reflationary policy which includes the L.D.R.s as well as the M.D.R.s, and for ensuring that any medium-term reflation for the national economy focuses investment in entirely new plant in the L.D.Rs rather than in the M.D.Rs. In terms of the argument for harnessing meso-economic power towards regional development, the public enterprise pace-setters within manufacturing sectors might well be the sector leaders in L.D.R. location of subsidiary plant, with their location specifically controlled through the relevant policy-making body. But the decision whether or not they should locate plant in L.D.R. dispersed areas rather than L.D.R. growth centres should in principle be undertaken on the same criteria as for those expanding private enterprise companies subject to locational controls.

Strategy, Tactics and Techniques

This analysis already indicates the need for new dimensions in regional policy-harnessing big-league meso-economic power through new public enterprise, backed by powers of specific locational controls.

It has been stressed in the previous argument that the macro, meso and micro factors must constitute a consistent and continuing dimension of regional economic policies. In short – yes – regional policy forever.[n] How they are actually implemented must vary in different national and political circumstances. The range of criteria available from the macro, meso and micro evidence is considerable, but can only provide a frame of reference for particular decisions based on specific information. Economists can point out the false hope of general policies such as assuming that infrastructural expenditure and aids to small and medium L.D.R. firms will in due course promote a self-sustaining growth process in the region. But the more specific their policy recommendations become, the more they must be taken into account in conjunction with specific information on actual circumstances. For example, the previous

273

chapters have indicated that there is no point in encouraging the regional policy-maker to believe that there may be universal location criteria awaiting the pilgrim prepared to spend a lifetime in the undergrowth of input–output or linear programming analysis. They also suggested that for economists to expect that politicians will wait for a generation while they sophisticate their analytical techniques is both unrealistic and a reversal of the priorities on which regional and location policy actually should be based.[28] At the practical level at which regional policies must actually be implemented, those responsible for that implementation need guidelines to assist their judgement rather than a body of largely Panglossian rules.

The general ability of some of the more metaphysical techniques of locational analysis to survive their own authors' qualifications suggests an 'objectivity illusion' which policy-makers will not be able to challenge unless aided by not only economists but also social geographers, demographers, urban planners and others. The widespread failure of regional economists in Western Europe and the United States to put their techniques into a social and political context partly lies in the suggestion that to oppose their dominance in regional analysis is at best opposition to the queen of the social sciences, and at worst admission of economic illiteracy. It also must be admitted that in the rare cases where the decision to base policy on such techniques actually lies with politicians rather than officials they have the additional advantage of not challenging the prevailing economic and social relations of society itself. The approval by governments of further in-depth studies into the usefulness of techniques alone has the additional convenience of postponing politically sensitive decisions under the alibi of taking action. They do not involve the subjective evaluation of particular projects by either politicians themselves or by those civil servants nominally responsible to them, which itself reduces the extent to which politicians in either their own or other parties who are not professional economists can challenge either the project or the manner in which it is being carried out.

In other words, one of the main obstacles to the development of effective regional and locational strategy may well be the regional economist. This does not mean to say that there is no intermediate ground between the completely generalised *a pri-*

274

ori model and *ad hoc a posteriori* muddling. For instance, in the present study a variety of policy implications have been drawn from both theoretical analysis and from empirical data. Both processes are important. Facts do not speak for themselves. They have to be interpreted. Also, facts are not 'pure' and therefore do not suggest unqualified policy implications. Few governments are so rash as to employ no regional development policy at all, and therefore there is little direct evidence on what the results of a free working of the market in regional resource allocation actually would be. Few techniques of analysis at present are sufficiently related to policy needs to determine the precise extent to which different techniques can successfully be interrelated in regional policy-making. But there clearly is a need for analysis of actual trends in regional location, and the employment of policy techniques related to actual as well as hypothetical policy options. A regional plan does not have to be perfect to be operational any more than perfection is demanded of effective policy makers. In particular, as Streeten has stressed in another context, a plan should be understood, not deduced.[29] It should be seen as an evolving process relating a variety of tactical instruments to broadly conceived strategic ends. It certainly is not likely to prove effective if the deductive techniques necessary to understand it are available only to a self-elected élite of academic specialists. The result of such a situation would be a continuation of the rule-of-thumb methods and groping in the dark which frequently substitute for effective regional policy.

NOTES

[a] Clearly the point at which governments might identify a declining region as a problem area will depend on political as well as economic parameters, while the nature of the economic criteria for intervention will depend on the theoretical assumptions concerning the national resource costs from particular degrees of under-development.

[b] This has proved the case with the new plant located in the South in the later 1960s by the State-owned Alfa-Romeo company and by FIAT (under government pressure).

[c] In terms of Fig. 4, p. 291, the recessions in the M.D.R. would be expressed by a staggering of the upward M.D.R. growth line A^1–C^1, with a downward staggering of the L.D.R. line A^2–C^5.

^d For evidence on the short time period necessary for the training of previously illiterate labour in routinised tasks cf. further, Chapter 5.

^e One of the benefits of the forward information from leading companies which a Planning Agreements system would secure is the increased degree of certainty in estimating the benefits for the national and regional economy from location of new plant in less-developed regions.

^f As elaborated in Chapter 5, the I.R.I. Group like other State Holding companies in Italy has been obliged since 1957 to locate 40 per cent of its total investment and 60 per cent of its investment in new plant in the South – with a raising of the obligation to 60 per cent of total investment and 100 per cent of investment in new plant in the South and certain areas of the Centre-North in the later 1960s.

^g This certainly has been the case with large companies in Italy, such as Motta at Bari.

^h I.R.I. has formed a new company (INFRASUD) to cope with the problem. One of its principal tasks is the creation of a new four-lane ring road around Naples.

ⁱ The submission of a given investment programme would be less liable to unforeseeable error than a programme including detailed information on an input–output basis (especially the quantity and composition of imports and exports).

^j Interview with M. Risse-Raud of the Délégation à l'Aménagement du Territoire et l'Action Régionale, Paris, November 1969.

^k The lowering of the limit within which expansion may be undertaken without reference to the authority responsible for locational controls would clearly involve greater administration. But, allowing that permission can be given to expand in the existing location, it could permit a distinction between small firms which would be incapable of the organisational implications of relocation (and, even with assistance, could not locate a plant of minimally efficient modern size in a development region) from those which could.

^l Risse-Raud, Interview.

^m This would be independent of any aids offered by government to firms.

ⁿ Graham Hallett et al., Regional Policy Forever? (London: Institute of Economic Affairs, 1973).

TABLES

TABLE I(A)

AVERAGE COST OF S.O.C. INVESTMENT PER NEW INHABITANT

Type of social overhead capital	Cost per inhabitant (in lire)		
	Up to 30,000	From 30,000 to 200,000	Over 200,000
Public services	102,000	143,000	274,000
Public utilities	21,000	51,000	83,000
Total	123,000	194,000	357,000

Source: SVIMEZ (1957).

TABLE 1(B)

SELECTED INVESTMENT COSTS FOR KEY PUBLIC SERVICES

	Cost per inhabitant (in lire)						
Type of service	Up to 5,000	5,000 to 20,000	20,000 to 50,000	50,000 to 100,000	100 000 to 250,000	250,000 to 600,000	Over 600,000
Park	6,000	6,000	13,200	15,600	18,000	20,400	22,800
Local government offices	4,800	5,400	6,000	6,600	7,200	8,400	9,600
Police	600	700	900	1,100	1,300	1,600	1,900
Sewage and cleansing	1,300	1,400	1,500	1,600	1,800	2,000	2,200
Other			10,000	15,000	20,000	25,000	30,000
Total	12,700	13,500	31,600	39,900	48,300	57,400	66,500

Source: SVIMEZ (1967).

TABLE 2

Type of social overhead capital	Maximum no. of persons served by one unit	Cost per inhabitant (in lire)			
		Up to 5,000	5,000 to 20,000	20,000 to 50,000	Over 50,000
Public library	6,000	7,300	3,800	3,100	2,900
Children's nursery	3,300	12,700	8,800	7,900	7,600
Playschool	2,700	21,600	16,500	14,900	14,400
Elementary school	3,300	37,600	29,200	26,100	25,100
Intermediate school	9,300	58,000	32,500	26,200	23,100
High School	21,000	51,500	51,500	51,500	51,500
Park	–	6,400	6,400	6,400	6,400
3–6-year-olds' playground	2,700	1,200	900	800	800
6–11-year-olds' playground	3,300	3,400	2,700	2,400	2,300
11–14-year-olds' playground	9,300	19,000	8,000	6,400	5,700
Over 14-year-olds' sportsground	10,500	86,900	41,300	29,600	26,000
Clinic	–	8,300	8,300	8,300	8,300
General hospital	80,000	18,000	18,000	18,000	18,000
Specialised hospital	120,000	3,000	3,000	3,000	3,000
Neuropsychiatric hospital	160,000	9,000	9,000	9,000	9,000
Cemetery	–	3,500	3,500	3,500	3,500
Post office	5,000	2,700	1,900	1,600	1,500
Prison	–	1,400	1,400	1,400	1,400
Law court	–	700	700	700	700
Fire brigade	30,000	1,500	1,500	1,500	1,500
Police station	7,000	7,000	7,000	7,000	7,000
Total	–	300,700	255,900	229,300	219,700

Source: TEKNE (1964).

TABLE 3

AVERAGE PER CAPITA EXPENDITURE OF MUNICIPAL GOVERNMENTS IN THE UNITED STATES, 1962, BY POPULATION SIZE

Population size class	Capital outlay	Other	Total
	$	$	$
Less than 2500	9.43	32.48	41.91
2500 to 4999	10.05	42.24	52.28
5000 to 9999	13.63	47.09	60.72
10,000 to 24,999	17.26	55.17	72.43
25,000 to 49,999	20.66	75.41	96.08
50,000 to 99,999	23.79	87.66	111.46
100,000 to 299,999	30.36	93.76	124.12
300,000 to 499,999	32.48	91.56	124.04
500,000 to 999,999	41.27	125.23	166.51
1,000,000 and more	46.80	172.31	219.12

Source: Hansen, in *Rural Poverty and the Urban Crisis*, p. 17.

TABLE 4

A: Resident Population, October 1961

Rome	2,188,000	Palermo	588,000
Milan	1,583,000	Bologna	445,000
Naples	1,183,000	Florence	437,000
Turin	1,026,000	Catania	364,000
Genoa	784,000	Venice	347,000

B: Annual Rate of Natural Increase in Population (per cent)

	1951–61	1961–9		1951–61	1961–9
Turin	0·31	0·63	Bologna	0·13	0·32
Genoa	−0·03	0·13	Florence	0·13	0·26
Milan	0·46	0·52	Rome	1·00	1·22
Venice	0·60	0·84	Naples	1·53	1·52

C: Net Immigration as a proportion of total increase in Resident Population (per cent)

	1951–61	1961–9		1951–61	1961–9
Turin	92	61	Bologna	95	71
Genoa	102	85	Florence	92	57
Milan	80	40	Rome	65	55
Venice	46	–	Naples	4	–

Source: Mainardi, *Le Grande Città Italiane*, pp. 67, 76–7.

TABLE 5

A: Registered Unemployment by Main Region (per cent)

	South	North
1951	11·3	9·1
1961	11·5	6·4
1967	8·8	4·0

B: Net Imports and Fixed Investment in South Italy (per cent)

	Net imports*	Fixed investment*
1951	17·5	13·6
1961	18·8	20·3
1962	21·2	21·3
1963	21·5	22·2
1967	15·8	19·5
1968	15·1	19·5

Source: Sylos-Labini, in SVIMEZ, *Scritti in Memoria di Alessandro Molinari*, pp. 345–6.
* As percentage of total resources.

TABLE 6

ᴌᴀɢᴇ Dᴇɢʀᴇᴇ ᴏғ Iɴᴛᴇʀᴅᴇᴘᴇɴᴅᴇɴᴄᴇ ᴏғ Eᴄᴏɴᴏᴍɪᴄ Sᴇᴄᴛᴏʀs ɪɴ Iᴛᴀʟʏ, Jᴀᴘᴀɴ, ᴀɴᴅ ᴛʜᴇ Uɴɪᴛᴇᴅ Sᴛᴀᴛᴇs

	Interdependence through purchases from other sectors* (Backward linkage)	Interdependence through Sales to Other sectors† (Forward linkage)
1. 'Intermediate Manufacture' (backward and forward linkage both high)		
Iron and steel	66	78
Non-ferrous metals	61	81
Paper and products	57	78
Petroleum products	65	68
Coal products	63	67
Chemicals	60	69
Textiles	67	57
Rubber products	51	48
Printing and publishing	49	46
2. 'Final Manufacture' (backward linkage high, forward linkage low)		
Grain-mill products	89	42
Leather and products	66	37
Lumber and wood products	61	38
Apparel	69	12
Transport equipment	60	20
Machinery	51	28
Non-metallic mineral products	47	30
Processed foods	61	15
Shipbuilding	58	14
Miscellaneous industries	43	20
3. 'Intermediate Primary Production' (forward linkage high, backward linkage low)		
Metal mining	21	93
Petroleum and natural gas	15	97
Coal mining	23	87
Agriculture and forestry	31	72
Electric power	27	59
Non-metallic minerals	17	52
4. 'Final Primary Production' (backward and forward linkage both low)		
Fishing	24	36
Transport	31	26
Services	19	34
Trade	16	17

Source: Hirschman, *Strategy of Economic Development*, pp. 106–7.
* Ratio of inter-industry purchases to total production (per cent).
† Ratio of inter-industry sales to total demand (per cent).

282

TABLE 7(A)

PRODUCT AND EMPLOYMENT INCREASES IN 'MODERN'
MANUFACTURING, 1950–62*

	Basic metals	Metal products	Chemical products	Paper
Employment				
U.S.S.R. and Eastern Europe	–	5·7	–	1·6
United States and Canada	−0·4	2·3	1·7	1·9
Industrialised Western Europe	2·0	3·6	2·7	2·5
Southern Europe	3·9	6·7	9·0	6·2
Product				
U.S.S.R. and Eastern Europe	–	15·3	–	8·6
United States and Canada	0·6	3·5	6·0	4·0
Industrialised Western Europe	5·9	5·6	7·4	5·6
Southern Europe	11·6	9·2	11·0	9·5

Source: Derived from Kuklinski, *Location of Industrial Plant.*
* Annual average rates of increase. Data for U.S.S.R. and Eastern Europe
excludes Albania and refers to the years 1951–61 only. Industrialised Western
Europe includes the E.E.C. and EFTA economies plus Finland and Ireland.
Southern Europe includes Greece, Turkey and Yugoslavia.
† Including coal-mining and crude petroleum.

TABLE 7(B)

PRODUCT AND EMPLOYMENT INCREASES IN 'MODERN' MANUFACTURING, 1962–69

	Basic metals	Metal products	Chemical products	Paper
Employment				
U.S.S.R. and Eastern Europe	5·4	8·0	8·0	5·9
United States and Canada	2·3	4·5	3·6	2·6
Industrialised Western Europe	−0·6	1·1	1·7	0·7
Product				
U.S.S.R. and Eastern Europe	2·9	4·6	6·1	2·7
United States and Canada	6·2	7·8	10·1	6·1
Industrialised Western Europe	6·4	6·5	13·8	7·1

Source: Derived from U.N. Statistical Yearbooks 1968 and 1970, tables 9 and 10.

Table 8(a)

Product and Employment Increases in 'Traditional' Manufacturing, 1950–62*

	Textiles, clothing	Food, drink, tobacco	Wood	Non-metallic† minerals
Employment				
U.S.S.R. and Eastern Europe	4·7	3·3	2·6	6·6
United States and Canada	−0·1	−0·1	−1·4	0·6
Industrialised Western Europe	2·2	2·2	1·1	1·7
Southern Europe	6·5	6·5	4·8	9·3
Product				
U.S.S.R. and Eastern Europe	9·3	8·6	12·8	15·3
United States and Canada	2·1	2·6	2·0	3·5
Industrialised Western Europe	2·5	4·4	4·4	5·6
Southern Europe	4·6	5·8	5·5	9·2

Source: Derived from Kuklinski, *Location of Industrial Plant.*
* Annual average rates of increase. Some data qualifications as for Table 7(a).
† Including non-metallic mineral products.

Table 8(b)

Product and Employment Increases in 'traditional' Manufacturing, 1962–9

	Textiles, clothing	Food, drink, tobacco	Wood	Non-metallic minerals
Employment				
U.S.S.R. and Eastern Europe	3·4	2·5	5·6	7·0
United States and Canada	1·4	0·3	2·0	1·6
Industrialised Western Europe	0·1	0·4	0·6	−0·1
Product				
U.S.S.R. and Eastern Europe	2·9	3·9	1·3	2·6
United States and Canada	4·0	3·2	3·9	5·6
Industrialised Western Europe	2·7	4·6	5·2	6·2

Source: Derived from U.S. Statistical Yearbooks 1968 and 1970, tables 9 and 10.

TABLE 9

CAPITAL COST OF INVESTMENT PER EMPLOYEE IN NEW
MANUFACTURING IN SOUTHERN ITALY 1967–9*

1	Rubber	280
2	Primary chemicals	165
3	Primary chemical derivatives	54
4	Cement and related products	50
5	Petroleum derivatives	36
6	Steel	25
7	Aircraft	21
8	Automobiles	20
9	Textiles	19
10	Pharmaceuticals	19
11	Plastic manufactures	13
12	Paper and paper products	12
13	Printing	12
14	Woodwork and furniture	10
15	Non-electrical machinery	10
16	Office machinery and equipment	10
17	Glass	8
18	Electronics	8
19	Precision engineering and instruments	8
20	Electrical products	6
21	Shoes	4
22	Clothing	3
23	Other manufacturing	4
	Total manufacturing	24

Source: ISRIL – Comitato dei Ministri per il Mezzogiorno,
cited in Cacace, *Quaderni ISRIL*, no. 2, 1970.
* Manufacturing in new plant; million lire; three-year average
1967–9.

TABLE 10

Rank	Reasons for plant location	No. of Times Ranked as No.						
		Total	1	2	3	4	5	Other
1	Availability of labour	559	93	147	96	75	63	85
2	Convenience to markets	457	143	97	65	54	43	55
3	Availability of buildings or other property	394	96	84	57	65	41	51
4	Lower labour costs	343	38	53	79	69	55	49
5	Availability of raw materials	327	89	59	53	32	39	55
6	Less unionisation	299	31	53	50	57	65	43
7	Local co-operativeness	294	20	28	55	71	89	31
8	Home of management	246	81	41	25	27	32	40
9	Climate	239	48	37	33	29	42	50
10	Transportation costs	230	22	48	42	52	37	29
11	Adequate power	229	18	30	49	41	45	46
12	Centre of particular industry	221	69	30	29	27	33	33
13	Transportation facilities	174	11	24	37	38	35	29
14	Decentralisation of operation	151	25	27	31	27	25	16
15	Favourable tax structure	127	16	8	17	34	30	22
16	Financial aid	101	18	21	16	14	22	10

Source: International Information Centre for Local Credit, *Government Measures for the Promotion of Regional Economic Development* (1964) p. 22.

TABLE 11

Industry group	Labour	Premises	Other	Total
Shoe	15	–	–	15
Hosiery	24	–	–	24
Clothing	5	–	–	5
Textiles	7	1	1	9
Engineering	5	2	–	7
Electrical goods	8	1	–	9
Metal goods	6	3	3	12
Miscellaneous	4	3	5	12
Total	74	10	9	93

Source: W. F. Luttrell. *Factory Location and Industrial Movement* (1962) p. 48.

TABLE 12

REASONS FOR LOCATION OF PLANT ON THE AUTOSTRADA DEL SOLE

1	Proximity of access to the motorway
2	Fiscal incentives
3	Labour availability
4	Reasonable cost of land for plant construction
5	Good transport infrastructure
6	Financial and credit facilities
7	Supply facilities
8	Other infrastructure (light, water, etc.)
9	Primary materials and natural resources
10	Personal reasons of management
11	Geographical nature of the area
12	Existence of other complementary industries
13	Socio-economic environment of the Commune
14	Availability of power supplies

Source: I.R.I. Società Autostrade, *Primi Effetti Economici dell' Autostrada del Sole* (1965).

FIGURES

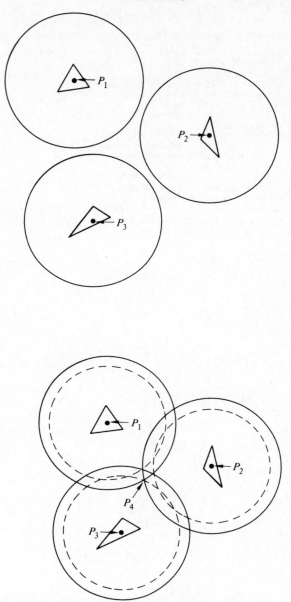

Fig. 1. (a) Non-intersecting isodapanes: no agglomeration of production points P_1 to P_3. (b) Intersecting isodapanes and agglomeration at P_4.

288

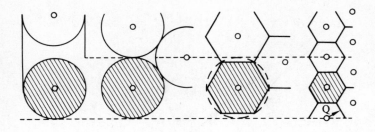

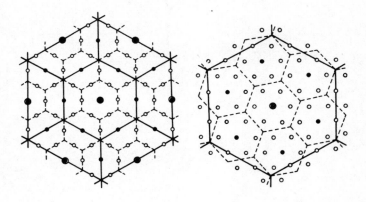

Fig. 2. (a) Development of Lösch market areas from circles to hexagons. (b) Löschian 'regions' of equal structure. Central point (larger circle) 'towns' dominate lower rank towns.

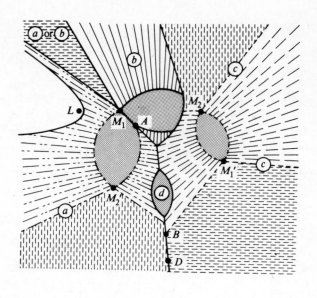

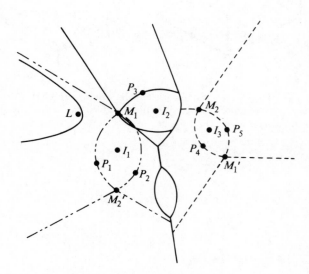

Fig. 3. (*a*) Isardian location: two sources of two raw materials and one labour site. (*b*) Isardian location: introduction of 'scale' economies.

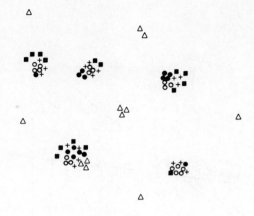

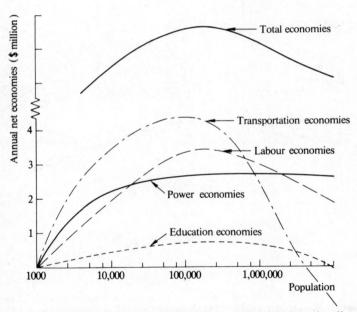

Fig. 4. (a) Isardian location: introduction of urbanisation, localisation and scale economies. (b) Isard's hypothetical scale economies with increased urban size.

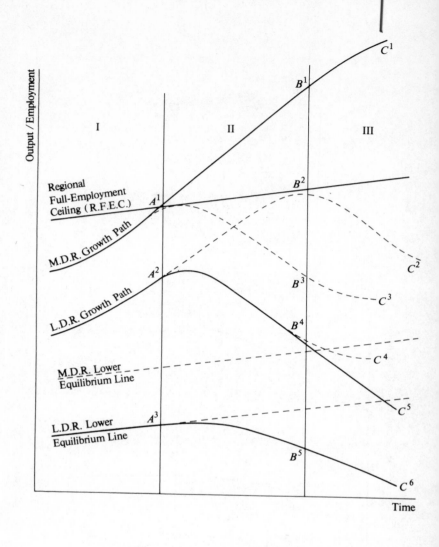

Fig. 5. Brief key: Dotted lines A^1–C^3 and A^2–C^2 hypothetical M.D.R. and L.D.R. growth paths without interregional factor migration. Solid lines A^1–C^1 and A^2–C^5 actual M.D.R. and L.D.R. growth paths with interregional factor migration. Solid line A^3–C^6 actual L.D.R. downturn without M.D.R. financed long-term expenditure.

NORTH	SOUTH
Factor earnings equal to South: some unemployment and/ or under-employment	Factor earnings equal to North: substantial unemployment and under-employment
Autonomous increase in rate of investment: approach to full-employment ceiling	Induced investment at same rate as previously
Multiplier effect: rise in factor earnings over South	Multiplier effect: fall in factor earnings below North Migration of factors of production to North, but proportionately more capital than labour (granted greater 'spatial elasticity')
Rise in warranted rate of growth (accelerator effect) in reaction to higher m.e.c. schedule than previously and availability of labour from South PLUS Rise in natural rate of growth from capital and labour imports from South, raising full-employment ceiling	Decline in both warranted and natural growth rates (fall off in level of investible funds, lowering both potential investment and capital–labour ratio)
Increase in rate of investment from higher 'domestic' savings PLUS additional increase from savings imported from South	First decline in intra-regional rate of investment from lowered domestic savings
Increased productivity from higher capital–labour ratio (both from increase in domestic savings and from import of proportionately more capital than labour from South) PLUS greater technical progress than South from more capital-intensive investment	Decreased productivity from lowered capital–labour ratio; either reduction of rate of technical progress or possibly negative technical progress from more labour-intensive investment
Increased multiplier effect and further rise in factor earnings, inducing further factor inflow from South Further rise in warranted and natural rates of growth, etc.	Decreased multiplier effect and possible absolute decline in factor earnings: intensified factor outflow to North Further fall in warranted and natural rates of growth, etc.

Fig. 6.

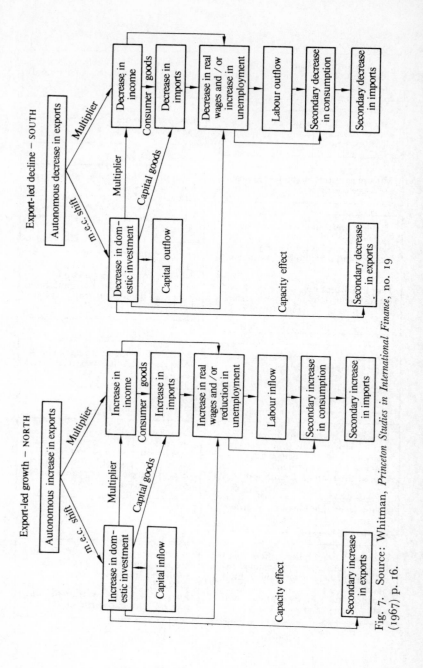

Fig. 7. Source: Whitman, *Princeton Studies in International Finance*, no. 19 (1967) p. 16.

Export-led growth – NORTH

Autonomous increase in exports

Multiplier → Increase in income → Consumer goods → Increase in imports → Increase in real wages and / or reduction in unemployment → Labour inflow → Secondary increase in consumption → Secondary increase in imports

m.e.c. shift → Increase in domestic investment → Capital inflow

Multiplier / Capital goods

Capacity effect → Secondary increase in exports

Export-led decline – SOUTH

Autonomous decrease in exports

Multiplier → Decrease in income → Consumer goods → Decrease in imports → Decrease in real wages and / or increase in unemployment → Labour outflow → Secondary decrease in consumption → Secondary decrease in imports

m.e.c. shift → Decrease in domestic investment → Capital outflow

Multiplier / Capital goods

Capacity effect → Secondary decrease in exports

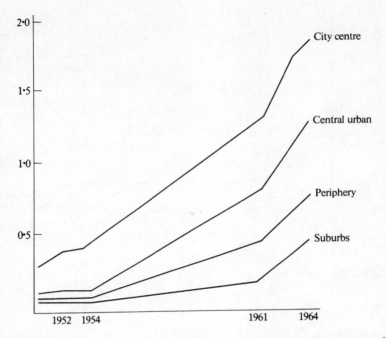

Fig. 8. Building costs in Milan city centre, central urban area, peripheral urban area, and suburbs (million lire). Source: ILSES, in *L'Immigrazione nel Triangolo Industriale*, ed. Pellicciari.

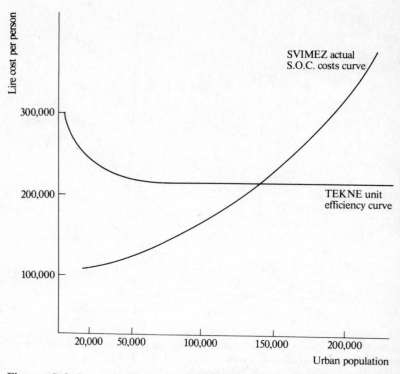

Fig. 9. S.O.C. costs and unit efficiency. Source: SVIMEZ (1957) TEKNE (1964).

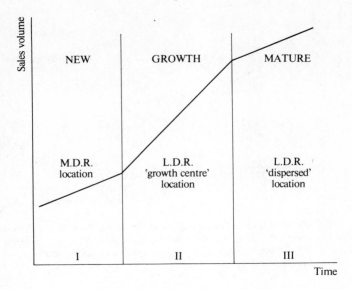

Fig. 10. Regional policy implications of the product cycle. Brief key: Phase I (New product) – unstandardised product; input, design and other changes; relatively insecure market; high proportional specialist labour and management co-ordination. Phase II (Growth product) – standardised product in more established market; reduction of specialist labour and management co-ordination to supervisory function. Phase III (Mature product) – stable market; scale economies of firm's organisation and distribution, and capital inputs; possible wage pressure and market saturation main growth constraints.

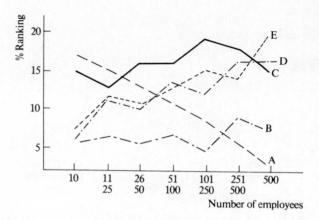

Fig. 11. Size of enterprise and change in locational factors. A: Proximity to final market. B: Personal motives of management. C: Proximity to motorway. D: Labour availability. E: Government aids. Source: *Notizie I.R.I.*, no. 141 (June 1971).

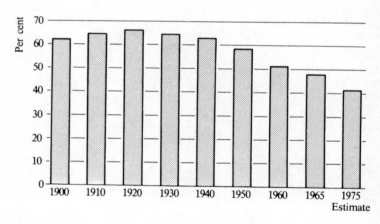

Fig. 12. Declining percentage of population in U.S. central cities, 1900–75 (standard metropolitan statistical areas). Source: U.S. Advisory Commission on Intergovernmental Relations, *Urban and Rural America – Policies for Future Growth* (April 1968).

298

More-Developed Region	Less-Developed Region
Higher pressure on S.O.C. necessitating faster provision than in L.D.R.	Lower S.O.C. pressure and under-utilisation of existing S.O.C.
Provision of S.O.C. for immigrant labour.	Reduced S.O.C. utilisation from emigrant labour.
Higher S.O.C. cost per head in centres over 200,000 persons.	Lower S.O.C. cost per head in smaller urban centres.
Higher rents.	Lower rents.
Higher rates offset in real value by higher S.O.C. provision costs.	Lower rates and reduced local S.O.C. renewal potential.
Higher prices in local services from S.O.C. congestion costs.	Lower prices in local services from lack of congestion.
Higher effective wages to offset higher rents, rates and local prices.	Lower effective wages through lower rents, rates and local prices.
Cost-push price inflation through leading firms offsetting higher cost of living.	Lower inflation through less price leadership, in lagging firms and lower cost of living.
Reduced export competitiveness of leader firms from cost-push inflation.	Higher export potential not realised through lagging firms structure.
Lower quality of life through pressured infrastructure-environment in inner urban areas.	Lower S.O.C. environment pressures not matched by regeneration of inner urban areas.
Training costs for immigrant labour from less-developed countries.	Training costs for labour not locally employed.

Fig. 13.   Macro-regional costs through imbalanced resource use (simplified two-regional economy).

More-Developed Region	Less-Developed Region
Employment of immigrant labour raised and educated in L.D.R.	Education and pre-work costs of raising emigrants to M.D.R.
Benefit from inflow of already skilled and adapted immigrants.	Loss of more skilled and better adapted labour to M.D.R.
Labour supply adapted to needs during sustained long-term expansion.	Excess of labour supply over local employment opportunities.
Raised full-employment ceiling preventing earlier business cycle downturn.	Loss of capital to M.D.R. preventing sustained initial growth and promoting downturn.
Re-emigration of excess labour from region in event of business cycle downturn.	Aggravation of surplus unemployed by re-immigration of M.D.R. labour in event of downturn.
Higher proportion of remaining skilled and adapted labour in unemployed during recessions.	Higher proportion of unskilled and unadapted labour in regional reserve of unemployed over long run.
Marginal transport cost savings to main national markets for medium and small firms.	Marginal transport cost disadvantages to main national market in M.D.R.
More rapid local communications for small and medium firms to other suppliers.	Less rapid communications to suppliers in M.D.R. for some small and medium firms.
Greater social facilities for retention or attraction of middle management in leading firms.	Fewer social facilities for middle management in leading firms, partly offset in some cases by less congested environment.

Fig. 14. Macro-regional cost and benefits from imbalanced resource use (simplified two-region economy).

REFERENCES

Chapter 1

[1] Alfred Weber, *Uber den Standort der Industrien* (1909) (translated by C. J. Friedrich under the title *Alfred Weber's Theory of the Location of Industries*, University of Chicago Press (1928). Page references in this text refer to Friedrich's translation).

[2] J. H. von Thünen, in *Der Isolierte Staat in Beziehung auf Landwirtschaft und Nationalökonomie* (1826) had broken new ground in location theory some eighty years earlier than Weber but mainly in terms of agriculture rather than industry, with a less direct influence on later location theory.

[3] Weber, *Location of Industries*.

[4] Ibid. pp. 20–1.

[5] Ibid. pp. 60–1.

[6] Weber himself foresaw this impact on transport costs and thus location patterns. See ibid. p. 168.

[7] Ibid. p. 167.

[8] Cf. the ranking of location criteria in Tables 10–12, pp. 286–7.

[9] Alfred Marshall, *Principles of Economics* (first published 1890; 8th edn, 1920).

[10] Weber, *Location of Industries*, pp. 128–31.

[11] Ibid. pp. 102–4, 122, 144ff., and Appendix. Cf. Figure 1(*a*) and (*b*), p. 288.

[12] Ibid. pp. 153–4 (our underlining).

[13] Ibid. p. 187.

[14] Ibid. pp. 192–3.

[15] Ibid. p. 102.

[16] Ibid. p. 225.

[17] Ibid. p. 213.

[18] Isard claims that it is only through use of the Weberian approach that he has found it meaningful to undertake location analysis. Cf. Walter Isard, *Location and the Space Economy* (Massachusetts Institute of Technology Press, 1956) p. 37. For further admission of Weber's influence on location theory, cf. Melvin Greenhut, *Plant Location in Theory and Practice* (University of North Carolina Press, 1956) p. 256.

[19] August Lösch, *Die Raümliche Ordnung der Wirtschaft* (1944) translated by W. H. Woglom and W. F. Stolper under the title *The Economics of Location* (Yale University Press, 1952). Page references in this text to the English translation.

[20] Ibid. pp. 28–31.

[21] Ibid. pp. 36–67.

[22] Cf. Figure 2(*a*) and (*b*), p. 289.

[23] Walter Christaller, *Die Zentralen Orte in Suddeutschland* (1933) translated by C.

301

W. Baskin as *Central Places in Southern Germany* (University of North Carolina Press, 1966).

[24] Lösch, *Economics of Location*, p. 94.

[25] Ibid.

[26] Wolfgang Stolper, Introduction to Lösch, *Economics of Location*.

[27] Isard, *Location and the Space Economy*, p. 49.

[28] Claude Ponsard, *Economie et Espace* (1955) p. 34.

[29] Uosch, *Economics of Location*, p. 363 (his exclamation marks).

[30] Ibid. p. 4 (his exclamation marks).

[31] Ibid. p. 363.

[32] Ibid. p. 215.

[33] Ibid. pp. 255–6.

[34] Bertil Ohlin, *Interregional and International Trade*, first published in English, 1933. References in this text to the revised edition (Harvard University Press, 1967).

[35] Ibid. especially pp. 1–2, 35–6 and 119.

[36] Ibid. p. 12.

[37] Ibid. p. 6.

[38] Ibid. p. 36.

[39] Ibid. p. 7.

[40] Ibid. p. 116.

[41] Ibid. p. 118.

[42] Ibid.

[43] Ibid. pp. 118–19.

[44] François Lucien Brocard, *Principes d'économie nationale et internationale*, 3 vols (1929–31). Cf. vol. 1, p. 11, and later in this text.

[45] Joan Robinson, *The Economics of Imperfect Competition* (London: Macmillan, 1933); Edward Chamberlin, *The Theory of Monopolistic Competition* (Harvard University Press, 1933).

[46] C. P. Kindleberger, *Foreign Trade and the National Economy* (Yale University Press, 1962) p. 77.

[47] Gardner Ackley and Luigi Spaventa, 'Emigration and Industrialisation in Southern Italy', *Banco Nazionale del Lavoro Quarterly Review* (June 1962).

[48] Cf. A. Kuklinski, *Criteria for the Location of Industrial Plant*, Economic Commission for Europe (1966).

[49] Cf. the employment of an Ohlin type 'imperfect competition' analysis by Mrs Vera Lutz in *Italy: a Study in Economic Development* (Oxford University Press, 1962) criticised later this text (Chapter 5).

[50] Cf. further, Chapter 3 this text and Bela Balassa, *The Theory of Economic Integration (1962) p. 191ff.*, Paul Streeten, *Economic Integration*, 2nd edn (Leiden: Sythoff, 1964), pp. 57–66, and Gavin McCrone, *Regional Policy in Britain* (London: Allen & Unwin, 1969) p. 79.

[51] Cf. Isard, *Location and the Space Economy*, Isard (ed.), *Methods of Regional Analysis: An Introduction to Regional Science* (Massachusetts Institute of Technology Press, 1960) and Isard (in association with Tony E. Smith *et al.*), *General Theory: Social, Political, Economic, and Regional* (Massachusetts Institute of Technology Press, 1969).

[52] Weber, *Location of Industries*.

REFERENCES

[53] Isard, *Location and the Space Economy*, p. 37.

[54] Ibid. p. 271.

[55] Ibid. pp. 252–3.

[56] Ibid. pp. 262–5.

[57] Ibid. pp. 264–5.

[58] Ibid. p. 266 (cf. also pp. 176–9).

[59] Harold Hotelling, 'Stability in Competition', *Economic Journal* (1929).

[60] Isard, *Location and the Space Economy*, pp. 268–9.

[61] Ibid. ch. 8.

[62] Ibid. chs 3 and 9. His U.S. data is based almost exclusively on railroad shipments, which partly reflect the fractionalised rate structure of U.S. regional rail companies.

[63] Ibid. p. 219.

[64] Ibid. pp. 282–6.

[65] Isard, *General Theory: Social, Political, Economic and Regional*, p. vii.

[66] Isard, ibid. The work in question is his *Methods of Regional Analysis*.

[67] Cf. Isard, *Methods of Regional Analysis*, chs 2–6.

[68] Ibid. chs.8, 10.

[69] Ibid. pp. 338–40.

[70] Ibid. p. 341. The one technique extensively described by Isard (in conjunction with Eugene Schooler) which has not been considered so far – industrial complex analysis – is evaluated in some detail in Chapter 7 in the context of 'growth-pole' theory.

[71] Cf. Isard, *General Theory*, p. vii.

[72] Ibid. pp. vii–viii.

[73] For the utility-maximisation assumption cf. ibid. p. 19.

[74] For political leadership as 'mechanistic maximising' cf. ibid. pp. 22 and 820. For social behaviour explicitly concerned with economic maximising cf. ibid. p. 506. Isard neglects that even radical politicians may prove loss-minimisers when in power, and that social maximisation for the manager's wife may mean threatening divorce if he plans an L.D.R. location which would maximise locational benefits.

[75] Ibid. pp. 119, 150, 603–4 and 825–7.

[76] Ibid. ch. 16.

[77] Louis Lefeber, *Allocation in Space* (Amsterdam: North-Holland, 1958) pp. 3–5, 11 and 130.

[78] Edwin von Böventer, *Theorie des räumlichen Gleichgewichts* (1962) pp. 4ff., 163 and 192; 'Die Struktur der Landschaft' in *Schriften des Vereins für Sozialpolitik*, Neue Folge, Bd. 27 (1962) pp. 132ff.

[79] J. Tinbergen, 'The Spatial Dispersion of Production', in *Schweizerische Zeitschrift f Volkswirtschaft und Statistik*, no. 4 (1961); 'Sur un modèle de la dispersion géographique de l'activité économique', in *Revue d'Economie Politique* (January–February 1964).

[80] Tinbergen, in *Revue d'Economie Politique* (January–February 1964) pp. 30–1.

[81] H. C. Bos, *Spatial Dispersion of Economic Activity* (New York: Gordon, 1965) pp. 21, 33–5, 67–77, 80–1 and 99–100.

[82] Cf. M. B. Teitz, 'Regional Theory and Regional Models', *Papers and Proceedings of the Regional Science Association*, IX (1962) pp. 35–50; Kevin Lynch, 'The

Pattern of the Metropolis', *Daedalus* (Winter 1961) pp. 79–98; B. J. L. Berry and W. L. Garrison, 'Recent Developments of Central Place Theory', *Papers and Proceedings of the Regional Science Association,* IV (1958) pp. 107–20.

[83] Leslie Curry, 'Central Places in the Random Spatial Economy', *Journal of Regional Science* (1967) pp. 217–38.

[84] Cf. Gunnar Olsson, 'Central Place Systems, Spatial Interaction and Stochastic Processes', *Papers and Proceedings of the Regional Science Association* (1966) pp. 13–45.

Chapter 2

[1] Karl Marx, *Capital,* vol. I, 3rd edn (Moscow: Foreign Languages Publishing House, 1961) p. 657.

[2] Ibid. pp. 368 and 322. (Cereal manufacture). Capitalist production for Marx also, of course, is intrinsically linked with the alienation of the surplus value of the worker over and above his socially necessary subsistence value. But, as he says himself (*Capital,* vol. I, p. 235) capital has not invented surplus value, which previously was alienated from workers (e.g. under feudal service) in a different form.

[3] Ibid. p. 380.

[4] Ibid. pp. 380–6.

[5] Ibid. pp. 395, 443–5. However, Marx comments in addition that 'the place occupied by these (entirely new) branches of production is, even in the most-developed countries, far from important', p. 445.

[6] Ibid. pp. 635–8 and 642.

[7] Ibid. p. 352.

[8] Ibid. p. 353. As examples he gives the specialisation of fine cloths in Somerset, coarse in Yorkshire, long ells at Exeter, silks at Sudbury, crapes at Norwich, linseys at Kendal, blankets at Whitney, and so on.

[9] Ibid. p. 352. The relevance of such an internal-economy approach to planned industrial growth complexes is developed in the criticism of the Isardian industrial complex analysis in Chapter 7.

[10] Ibid. pp. 352–3. In *Grundrisse* Marx gives an extensive analysis of the mechanism of improved transport communications in relation to the need to reduce time and costs in the distribution of commodities – mainly in international trade. Cf. Marx, *Grundrisse der Kritik der Politischen Okonomie* (Dietz Verlag, 1953) pp. 419–35.

[11] Ibid. p. 430 (own italics).

[12] Ibid. p. 678.

[13] Ibid. pp. 638, 682.

[14] 'Ireland, having during the last twenty years reduced its population by nearly one half, is at this moment undergoing the process of still further reducing the number of its inhabitants, so as exactly to suit the requirements of its landlords and of the English woollen manufacturers.' Ibid. p. 444. Cf. also pp. 687–712.

[15] Cf. in particular the analysis of Mrs Vera Lutz in *inter alia, Italy: a Study in Economic Development,* criticised in Chapter 5.

[16] Marx, *Capital,* vol I, pp. 673–98.

[17] Ibid. p. 638. This amounts to a 'cobweb' effect of the kind to which Brown refers in the post-war British context. Cf. A. J. Brown, *The Framework of Regional Economics in the United Kingdom* (Cambridge University Press, 1972) p. 234.

[18] Ibid. p. 639. The concept of wage restraint through high availability of labour during periods of exceptional expansion therefore clearly antedates both Phillips and Kindleberger. Cf. further, Chapter 4.

[19] Ibid. p. 642. This dependence of labour under modern industrial conditions on the location of manufacturing is contrasted by Marx with the handicraft-manufacturing period in which manufactures 'change(d) their locality from one country to another with the emigrating or immigrating worker'. Ibid. p. 368.

[20] Ibid. p. 642.

[21] Ibid. p. 643.

[22] Ibid. pp. 643–4.

[23] Ibid. pp. 663ff.

[24] Ibid. pp. 658–9.

[25] Ibid. p. 657.

[26] Ibid. pp. 657–8.

[27] Ibid. p. 659.

[28] Ibid. p. 622.

[29] Ibid. p. 644.

[30] South-East Joint Planning Team, 'Strategic Plan for a South-East Framework', *Regional Studies*, vol. II (1971). It is of some interest that the team working on this project frequently referred to the lack of an overall theoretical framework capable of explaining the persistence of the inner London problem. Ibid. pp. 18, 35 and 41.

[31] Gunnar Myrdal, *Economic Theory and Underdeveloped Regions*, (London: Duckworth, 1957) and *An American Dilemma* (New York: Harper & Row, 1944).

[32] Myrdal, *Economic Theory and Underdeveloped Regions*, pp. 26–27.

[33] Ibid. pp. 17 and 26.

[34] Ragnar Nurkse, 'Some International Aspects of the Problem of Economic Development', *American Economic Review* (May 1952).

[35] François Perroux, 'La Notion de Pôle de croissance', *Economie Appliquée*, nos 1–2 (1955); 'Les points de développement et les Foyers de Progrés, *Cahiers de l'I.S.E.A.*, 94 (November 1959); 'La Firme Motrice et la Région Motrice', *Actes du colloque international de l'Institut de Science Economique de l'Université Libre de Liège* (Brussels, 1961) and other essays reprinted in Perroux, *L'Economie du XXe siècle*, (Presses Universitaires de France, 1964).

[36] J. Milhau, 'Théorie de la Croissance et l'Expansion Régionale', *Economie Appliquée*, (1956) p. 361.

[37] Albert Hirschman, 'Investment Policies', *American Economic Review* (September 1957) pp. 554–5, and *The Strategy of Economic Development* (Yale University Press, 1958) p. 183.

[38] Cf. Francesco Parillo, *Teoria della politica Economica e Pianificazione Regionale* (1963) p. 67.

[39] Cf. J.-R. Boudeville, *Problems of Regional Planning* (Edinburgh University Press, 1966).

[40] Cf. Stuart Holland, 'Regional Under-Development in a Developed Economy: the Italian Case', *Regional Studies*, vol. 5, no. 2 (1971).

[41] J. Paelinck, 'La Théorie du Développement régional polarisé', *Cahiers de l'I.S.E.A.*, no. 15 (March 1965) p. 47.

[42] Niles Hansen, 'Development Pole Theory in a Regional Context', *Kyklos*, vol. XX, fasc. 3 (1967) p. 725.

[43] Cf. A. Kuklinski, *Criteria for Location of Industrial Plant*, Economic Commission for Europe (1966).

[44] In the U.S. case, Hansen has recommended concentrating on expanding cities, in particular in the 250,000 to one-million range. Cf. Niles Hansen, *Rural Poverty and the Urban Crisis* (Indiana University Press, 1970) p. 252.

[45] For more on the chronic nature of downtown 'core' areas in the United States, cf. Chapter 3.

[46] J. R. Meyer, 'Regional Economics: A Survey', in *Surveys of Economic Theory*, vol. 2 (London: Macmillan, 1965) p. 266.

[47] J. G. Williamson, 'Regional Inequality and the Process of National Development', *Economic Development and Cultural Change*, vol. 13 (1963).

Chapter 3

[1] H. W. Richardson, *Regional Economics* (London: Weidenfeld & Nicolson, 1969) pp. 281–6.

[2] Ibid. pp. 324–5.

[3] Richardson, *Regional Economics*, pp. 330.

[4] Ibid. p. 329.

[5] Brown, *Framework of Regional Economics in the United Kingdom*.

[6] Ibid. pp. 251–2.

[7] Ibid. p. 268.

[8] Ibid. p. 187.

[9] Ibid. pp. 190–1.

[10] Cf. Economic Consultants Ltd, *Study for an Industrial Complex in Central Lancashire*, (1969).

[11] Brown, *Framework of Regional Economics in the United Kingdom*, p. 180. Brown admits that considerably higher values for the input multiplier ranging from $1 \cdot 1$ to $2 \cdot 5$ for exports from a variety of industries were obtained for the Utah study of F. T. Moore and J. W. Peterson, 'Regional Analysis: An Inter-industry Model of Utah', *Review of Economics and Statistics* (November 1955).

[12] Cf. Ibid. pp. 21, 198–9. Brown admits that the outcome of his capital-stock-adjustment analysis very much depends on the size of region, though does not in this context take account of differences of regional structure and major initial disparities. See Ibid. p. 194.

[13] Ibid. pp. 192–8.

[14] R. F. Harrod, 'An Essay in Dynamic Theory', *Economic Journal* (March 1939) pp. 14–33; and *Towards a Dynamic Economics* (London: Macmillan, 1948).

[15] Harrod, *An Essay*.

[16] Ibid.

[17] Ibid.

[18] J. R. Hicks, 'Mr Harrod's Dynamic Theory', *Economica* (1949) pp. 106–21.

[19] See A. W. Phillips, 'The Relationship between unemployment, and the rate of

change of money wage rates in the United Kingdom 1861–1957', *Economica* (1958) pp. 283–99.

[20] James Ingram, 'State and Regional Payments Mechanisms', *Quarterly Journal of Economics* (November 1959) pp. 619–32.

[21] Cf. 'Regional Under-Development in a Developed Economy: the Italian Case', *Regional Studies*, no. 2 (1971).

[22] Ibid.

[23] C. P. Kindleberger, *Europe's Postwar Growth: the Role of Labour Supply* (Harvard University Press, 1967).

[24] A more persuasive account of the variety of factors, including government policies, is given by Michael Postan, *An Economic History of Western Europe* (London: Methuen, 1967) and Andrew Shonfield, *Modern Capitalism* (Oxford University Press, 1965).

[25] Cf. W. Arthur Lewis, 'Development with Unlimited Supplies of Labour', *The Manchester School* (May 1954) pp. 139–91; John C. H. Fei and Gustav Ranis, *Development of the Labour Surplus Economy: Theory and Policy* (New York: Irwin, 1964); and 'A Theory of Economic Development', *American Economic Review* (September 1961) pp. 533–65. Cf. further, Chapter 3.

[26] Marina von Neumann Whitman, 'International and Interregional Payments Adjustment: a Synthetic View', *Princeton Studies in International Finance*, no. 19 (1967).

[27] Ibid. pp. 15–18.

[28] Ibid. p. 20.

[29] G. H. Borts and J. L. Stein, 'Regional Growth and Maturity in the United States: A Study of Regional Structural Change', *Schweizerische Zeitschrift für Volkswirtschaft und Statistik*, vol. 98 (1962). Page references in this text are to the reprint, L. Needleman (ed.), *Regional Analysis* (Harmondsworth: Penguin, 1968).

[30] Ibid. pp. 183–6.

[31] Cf. Richard Andrews, 'The Mechanics of the Urban Economic Base', *Land Economics*, no. 3 (1953) and George Hildebrand and Arthur Mace Jr, 'The Employment Multiplier in an Expanding Industrial Market: Los Angeles County 1940–47', *Review of Economics and Statistics* (August 1950) pp. 241–9.

[32] Douglass North, 'Location Theory and Regional Economic Growth', *Journal of Political Economy* (June 1955).

[33] Edgar Hoover and Joseph Fisher, 'Research in Regional Economic Growth', in *Problems in the Study of Economic Growth* (July 1949) Universities National Bureau Committee on Economic Research, mimeographed.

[34] Ibid. p. 184. In other words, the authors' stages-of-growth case is non-Rostowian, and stresses the difficulty of progression to increasingly higher income stages.

[35] Ibid. pp. 184–6.

[36] Shonfield, *Modern Capitalism*, ch. 13, pp. 301ff. on 'The Tradition of Public Enterprise'. Also G. S. Callander, 'The Early Transportation and Banking Enterprises of the States in Relation to the Growth of Corporations'. *Quarterly Journal of Economics*, vol. 17 (1902) pp. 111ff; and Stuart Bruchey, *The Roots of American Economic Growth 1607-1861* (Hutchinson University Library 1965) chs 5 and 6.

f. among others, Arthur Schlesinger, *The Age of Roosevelt* (New York: ghton Mifflin, 1959).

⌐Data from Richard Easterlin, *Personal Income of the United States* (1958) and the Department of Commerce indicates that the share of the Plains farming states fell from 97 per cent to 82 per cent of the national average from 1900 to 1930, and that of lhe South–East from 56 per cent to 50 per cent from 1920 to 1930, recovering to some 57 per cent by 1940. For the South-east, which includes the main Appalachian and 'Deep South' states the federal expenditure programme might well be thought of in terms of a Hicksian lower equilibrium path promoting an upturn in regional income, as opposed to the cumulative downturn which otherwise might have been expected to continue.

[39] Werner Hochwald, 'Interregional Income Flows and the South', in *Essays in Southern Economic Development*, ed. Melvin Greenhut and W. Tate Whitman (University of North Carolina Press, 1964) ch. 9.

[40] Cf. U.S. Department of Commerce, 'Total and *Per Capita* Personal Income by Regions and States', *Survey of Current Business* (August 1969). (The South-East region states increased their *per capita* personal income level from 1948 to 1968 from 59·9 per cent to 60·9 per cent of the average for the Mid-East (New York, New Jersey, Pennsylvania, etc.). For an analysis of the regional contribution of defence expenditure since the war cf. Roger Bolton, *Defense Purchases and Regional Growth*, (Washington D.C.: The Brookings Institution, 1966) especially ch. 6.

[41] North, 'Location Theory and Regional Economic Growth'. The quotation is from the last sentence of North's article, and is perhaps the more significant in terms of its implicit long-run equilibrium assumptions for its throw-away character.

[42] Perloff, Dunn, Lampard and Muth point out that much of the inflowing capital on which the development of U.S. agriculture, forestry and mining in the West and South-East was based came not from the urban capitals of the Eastern seaboard, but from the urban–industrial economies of Western Europe. Cf. Harvey Perloff, Edgar Dunn, Eric Lampard and Richard Muth, *Regions, Resources and Economic Growth* (1960) p. 287.

[43] Charles Tiebout, 'Exports and Regional Economic Growth', *Journal of Political Economy*, vol. 64 (April 1956).

[44] 6·8 million southerners migrated from the region between 1876 and 1930, and 6,050,000 of them abroad. Cf. SVIMEZ, *Un Secolo di Statistiche Italiane, Nord e Sud 1861–1961* (1961).

[45] Pasquale Saraceno, 'La Mancata Unificazione Italiana a Cento Anni dall' Unificazione Politica', reprinted in Saraceno, *L'Italia Verso la Piena Occupazione* (1963) p. 26. Cf. also among post-war analyses of the post-1861 effects of integration of the South with the rest of Italy: Alberto Benzoni, 'Il Mezzogiorno nello Stato Italiano', in *Mezzogiorno e politica di piano*, ed. Achille Parisi and Goffredo Zappa (1964); Paolo Sylos-Labini, 'Osservazioni sull'Evoluzione Economica del Mezzogiorno', in *Scritti in Memoria di Alessandro Molinari*, SVIMEZ (1963); Luigi del Pane, 'Les transformations des structures économiques de l'Italie unifiée, *Revue Economique* (May–September 1965).

[46] Cf. Paolo Sylos-Labini (ed.), untitled contribution to Club Turati and Fondazi-

one Adriano Olivetti, *Nord-Sud: i nuovi termini di un problema nazionale* (1970) p. 345.

[47] Cf. Roberto Mainardi, 'Caratteristiche Demografiche ed Economiche delle Grandi Città Italiane', Appendice statistica, in *Le Grandi Città Italiane*, ed. Mainardi, Franco Angeli (1970). It should be noted that the foreign-trade proportions of the cities and their provinces understates the total foreign trade of the regions concerned since it excludes the other regional provinces.

[48] Cf. R. I. McKinnon, 'Optimum World Monetary Arrangements and the Dual Currency System', *Banca Nazionale del Lavoro Quarterly Review* (December 1963) p. 19.

[49] Cf. R. A. Mundell, 'A Theory of Optimum Currency Areas', *American Economic Review* (November 1961) pp. 509–17.

Chapter 4

[1] Cf. R. S. Eckhaus, 'The North–South Differential in Italian Economic Development', *Journal of Economic History* (September 1961); Vera Lutz, 'The Growth Process in a Dual Economic System', *Banco Nazionale del Lavoro Quarterly Review* (September 1958); 'Italy as a Study in Development', *Lloyd's Bank Review* (October 1960); 'Some Structural Aspects of the Southern Problem: the Complementarity of Emigration and Industrialisation', *Banco Nazionale del Lavoro Quarterly Review* (December 1961); *Italy: A Study in Economic Development.*

[2] Cf. Vera Lutz, ibid. Mrs Lutz's argument is closely linked with the zero marginal productivity literature and debate, but can be both expressed and evaluated without venturing into the metaphysics of that questionably useful maze.

[3] Eckhaus, 'The North–South Differential', p. 317.

[4] For the U.S. South cf. Dale Hathaway, 'Migration from Agriculture: the Historical Record and its Meaning', *American Economic Review* (1960) pp. 379–91. Cf. also Clarence Danhof, 'Four Decades of Thought on the South's Economic Problem', in *Essays on Southern Economic Development*, ed. Melvin Greenhut and W. Tate Whitman (University of North Carolina Press, 1964) p. 16: 'the population resident in the South has grown almost at the national rate, and out-migration has served only as a mild alleviation of the region's economic problems'. For the South of Italy from 1950 to 1967 cf. Chapter 6.

[5] Gardner Ackley and Luigi Spaventa, 'Emigration and Industrialisation in Southern Italy', *Banca Nazionale del Lavoro Quarterly Review* (June 1962).

[6] U.S. Department of Commerce, Bureau of the Census, *Current Population Reports*, Series P-20 (April 1968).

[7] Dale Hathaway and Brian Perkins, 'Occupational Mobility and Migration from Agriculture', in *Rural Poverty in the United States*, p. 198. Italian data for 1960–66 shows that some three-fifths of migration for the South was to other parts of the region rather than from the region, and that nearly a half of total movement was within rather than from the same province in the South. Cf. *Informazioni SVIMEZ*, no. 7 Appendice Statistica (1968) p. 309.

[8] Cf. *Informazioni SVIMEZ*, 50–2 (1965) and F. Lechi, *La Produttività in Agricoltura* (1964).

[9] *Relazione General sulla Situazione Economica del Paese* (1962).

309

[10] Lechi, *La Produttività in Agricoltura.*

[11] The number of tractors employed rose by 139 per cent in the South against 152 per cent in the North-West and 161 per cent in the Centre–North. The value of chemical fertilisers in the South in 1962 was 3·1 per cent that of gross saleable product against 3·8 per cent in the North. Cf. *Informazioni SVIMEZ*, 18–19 (1964).

[12] M. Rossi-Doria, *Dieci Anni di Politica Agraria nel Mezzogiorno* (1964).

[13] Censis–Formez, *Le Zone Agricole in Espansione*, cyclo-styled paper (1964).

[14] Ibid., *Le Zone Agricole in Espansione* (1964). In France, Paul Marie de la Gorce similarly found that the peasant farmers in the areas of highest labour emigration (Massif Central, Pyrenees, and major areas of Brittany, Lorraine, Champagne and Franche–Comté) were those least able to generate any kind of income surplus to undertake capital-intensive improvements, and that this was reflected in the low demand for Government financial assistance for agricultural improvements. Cf. Paul Marie de la Gorce. *La France Pauvre* (1965) ch. 3 ('Détresse Paysanne').

[15] Censis-Formez, *Le Zone Agricole in Espansione* (1964).

[16] Malfatti and Graziani found that the average age of emigrants from southern agriculture between 1951 and 1961 was 20 to 30 years. E. Malfatti and F. Graziani, *Le Forze di Lavoro*, Svimez–Formez, cyclo-styled paper (1963).

[17] *Informazioni SVIMEZ*, Appendice Statistica, 18–19 (1964).

[18] Cf. Giuseppe Galasso, *Problemi Demografici e Questione Meridionale* (1959).

[19] Francesco Compagna found that some nominally 'emigrant' labour from agriculture in the South had not in fact broken its links with the land, and returned at peak labour-demand periods such as harvesting, reducing the pressure for introduction of labour-substituting techniques. Cf. Francesco Compagna, 'Problemi Inerenti Alle Zone di Fuga', in *Gli Squilibri Regionali*, Centro Nazionale de Prevenzione e Difosa Sociale (1967).

[20] Umberto Casinis, *Il Mercato di Lavoro*, Censis (1964) p. 60.

[21] Bruno Pagani, *Mondo Economico*, no. 15 (1960).

[22] Wilson Gee, 'The Drag of Talent out of the South', *Social Forces*, no. 15 (March 1937) pp. 343–6.

[23] John Van Sickle, *Planning for the South* (1943) p. 99; Clarence Danhof, in *Essays on Southern Economic Development.*

[24] Danhof, ibid. and Dorothy Thomas, 'Selective Migration', *Millbank Memorial Fund Quarterly* (October 1948) pp. 403–7. In support of the inconclusiveness of general hypotheses on migration selectivity and the need for attention to particular circumstances cf. also Paul Johnson, 'Effects of Off-Farm Migration of Managers on Managerial Resources in Agriculture', *Journal of Farm Economics* (1962) p. 1463.

[25] J. F. Gravier, *Décentralisation et Progrès Technique* (1954) p. 135.

[26] SVIMEZ, *La Localizzazione Industriale ed i Costi Sociali dell'Insediamenta di Nuove Unità Lavorative* (1957). This study was undertaken jointly with the Massachusetts Institute of Technology.

[27] SVIMEZ, *Ricerca sui Costi di Insediamento, Previsioni di Fabbisogno di Capitale Fisso e Sociale-Urbano al 1981* (1967).

[28] TEKNE, *Ricerca sui Costi di Insediamento, Urbani ed Industriali, in Varie Citta*

REFERENCES

d'Italia (1963). Both the SVIMEZ and TEKNE Studies employed comparative international data as a parameter in their estimates.

[29] ILSES, 'Indagine sul Valore delle Agree Fabbricabili in Milano e nel suo Territorio metropolitano dal 1956 al 1963, 1964, in *L'Immigrazione nel Triangolo Industriale,* ed. Giovanni Pellicciari (Franco Angeli, 1970) p. 219. For reference to high rent costs in downtown metropolitan New York in the 1950s cf. E. M. Hoover and R. Vernon, *Anatomy of a Metropolis* (New York: Doubleday Anchor, 1962) p. 31.

[30] U.S. Bureau of the Census, *Finances of Municipalities and Townships* (1964) cited in Niles Hansen, *French Regional Planning,* (Edinburgh University Press, 1968) p. 17.

[31] Advisory Commission on Intergovernmental Relations, *Urban and Rural America: Policies for Future Growth* (April 1968).

[32] W. Z. Hirsch, *Expenditure Implications of Metropolitan Growth and Consolidation, Review of Economics and Statistics* (1959).

[33] Cf. J. T. Hughes and J. Kozlowski, 'Threshold Analysis: An Economic Tool for Town and Regional Planning', *Urban Studies* (1968).

[34] A totally sea-locked city such as Venice presents even greater problems, quite apart from its gradual settlement below flood levels. Cf. Leonardo Benevolo, 'Venezia non è condannata a morte', in *Le Grande Città Italiane,* ed. Roberto Mainardi (1971).

[35] Lack of urban planning, of course, can permit major congestion problems. Cf. later this section and Giuseppe Dematteis, 'Torino dai borghi alla cintura', and Umberto Melotti, 'Il problema sociale delle periferie urbane a Milano', in *Le Grande e Citta Italiane.*

[36] Hansen claims that scale diseconomies in public expenditure in cities of more than 250,000 persons 'will probably be outweighed by external economies in the private sector'. Cf. Niles Hansen, *Rural Poverty and the Urban Crisis,* p. 251.

[37] Robert Weaver, *The Urban Complex: Human Values in Urban Life* (New York: Doubleday-Anchor, 1966) p. 192. Cf. also Donald Schon, 'Assimilation of Migrants into Urban Areas', in *Rural Poverty in the United States.*

[38] John Kain and Joseph Persky. 'The North's Stake in Southern Rural Poverty', in *Rural Poverty in the United States,* p. 294.

[39] Kain and Persky, ibid. are a notable exception, as also is Hansen in *Rural Poverty and the Urban Crisis.*

[40] In 1969 there were 360 bidonville communities in the Paris region alone ('bidonville' named after the beaten-out petrol cans from which the primitive housing is made). Their immigrant population totalled 38,000, mostly from Algeria, Morocco, Tunisia, Portugal, Spain and Turkey. Only about half the dwellings have electricity or some kind of primitive sanitation. Cf. *Agenor,* no. 15 (January–February 1970) p. 40.

[41] Giacomo Ghirardo, 'La "Congestione" di Turino e l'Esodo dal Sud', *Il Mattino* (14 September 1969) reprinted in *Informazioni SVIMEZ,* no. 18 (1969).

[42] Renato Calamida, Mariaemma Cioni Mori, and Fabrizio Schiaffonati, 'Contributo al Problema dei Rapporti tra Migratoria e Modificazioni Spaziali Indotte', in *L'Immigrazione nel Triangolo Industriale,* ed. Giovanni Pellicciari (1970).

[43] Cf. Wilbur R. Thompson, *A Preface to Urban Economics* (Baltimore: Johns Hopkins Press, 1968) p. 18.

311

[44] Calamida, Mori and Schiaffonati, 'Contributo al Problema', p. 228.

[45] Commissione per il Coordinamento dei Servizi e dei Lavori Publicci in Periferia, *Il Rapporto al Consiglio Communale* (1964) p. 25.

[46] Melotti, in *Le Grande Città Italiane*, p. 187.

[47] Kain and Persky, in *Rural Poverty in the United States*.

[48] During the mid-1960s recession Rome became the main such limbo area. Cf. *Informazioni SVIMEZ*, no. 7, nota statistica (1968) p. 295.

[49] Jonathan Lindley, 'Paper to the National Planning Association', reprinted in *Congressional Record* (19 May 1967) pp. 7164–7.

[50] C. E. Bishop, 'The Need for Improved Mobility Policy', in *Manpower Problems and Policies: Full Employment and Opportunity for All*, ed. John Delehanty (New York: International Textbook, 1969).

[51] Robert Marsh, 'Geographic Labour Mobility in the United States', *Social Security Bulletin* (March 1967), cited in Bishop.

[52] E. D. Smith, 'Non-farm Employment Opportunities for Rural People', *Journal of Farm Economics* (1956) cited in Bishop.

[53] Ibid. and Cafiero, *Le Migrazioni Meridionale*, SVIMEZ, 7 (1964) p. 21.

[54] L. A. Sjaastad, 'The Costs and Returns of Human Migration', *Journal of Political Economy*, vol. 70, Supplement (1962) pp. 80–93.

[55] Hathaway and Perkins, 'Occupational Mobility and Migration from Agriculture', in *Rural Poverty in the United States*, pp. 203–7.

[56] Paul Johnson, 'Labour Mobility: Some Costs and Returns', in *Rural Poverty in the United States*, p. 247.

[57] Dale Hathaway and Brian Perkins, 'Movement of Labour Between Farm and Non-Farm Jobs', *Michigan Agricultural Statistical Research Bulletin*, no. 13 (1966).

Chapter 5

[1] Joan Robinson, *The Economics of Imperfect Competition*, and E. H. Chamberlin, *The Theory of Monopolistic Competition*.

[2] Otto Engländer, Three articles in *Zeitschrift für Volkswirtschaft und Sozialpolitik* (1926).

[3] Tord Palandar, *Beiträge zur Standortstheorie* (1935).

[4] Harold Hotelling, 'Stability in Competition', *Economic Journal* (1929).

[5] Piero Sraffa, 'The Laws of Returns under Competitive Conditions', *Economic Journal* (1926).

[6] Paolo Sylos-Labini, *Oligopoly and Technical Progress* (Harvard University Press, 1962). The following page references are to this edition. (The original Italian edition appeared in 1957 under the same title, *Oligopolio e Progresso technico*).

[8] Ibid. pp. 75–6.

[9] Ibid. pp. 63–4, 145–9. Sylos-Labini later argues that large firms will use their powers of control over major innovations with a view to minimising business losses from premature obsolescence.

[10] Ibid. p. 40. Sylos-Labini distinguishes 'concentrated' and 'differentiated' oligopoly, meaning by the former oligopolistic concentration without product differentiation, and by the latter concentration with differentiation. The distinction does not affect the main features of his analysis.

[11] Ibid. pp. 40, 62, 65, 150–51.

[12] See Marx, *Capital*, vol. I, p. 626: 'The battle of competition is fought by the cheapening of commodities. The cheapness of commodities depend, *ceteris paribus*, on the productiveness of labour, and this again on the scale of production. Therefore the larger capitals beat the smaller. It will further be remembered that, with the development of the capitalist mode of production, there is an increase in the minimum amount of individual capital necessary to carry on a business under its normal conditions. The smaller capitals, therefore, crowd into spheres of production which Modern Industry has only sporadically or incompletely got hold of.'

[13] Sylos-Labini, *Oligopoly and Technical Progress*, pp. 50–2. The 'no entry' elements in the Sylos-Labini analysis have of course been paralleled in the United States by Bain. Cf. J. S. Bain, *Barriers to New Competition* (Harvard University Press, 1962) pp. 15–16; 'A Note on Pricing in Monopoly and Oligopoly', *American Economic Review* (March 1949); 'Conditions of Entry and Emergence of Monopoly', in *Monopoly and Competition and their Regulation*, ed. E. H. Chamberlin (Harvard University Press, 1954). Sylos-Labini refers to both the earlier Bain works in his own.

[14] Sylos-Labini, ibid. pp. 41ff.

[15] Cf. J. M. Clark, *Competition as a Dynamic Process* (Washington D.C., The Brookings Institution, 1961) especially chs 3 and 19.

[16] On this basis, Bain found that only one of nineteen Italian industries in the 1950–9 period was significantly less concentrated than in the United States (flour), while fourteen were significantly more concentrated. Cf. J. S. Bain, *International Differences in Industrial Structure* (Yale University Press, 1966) pp. 96–8.

[17] Jack Downie, *The Competitive Process* (London: Duckworth, 1958) pp. 60, 69 and 99.

[18] Ibid. pp. 84–8 and 90–1.

[19] H. R. Edwards, *Competition and Monopoly in the British Soap Industry* (Oxford University Press, 1962) pp. 112–13.

[20] Edith Penrose, *The Theory of the Growth of the Firm* (Oxford: Blackwell, 1959) p. 150. Cf. also the similar argument of Robin Marris, *The Economic Theory of 'Managerial' Capitalism* (New York: Basic Books, 1964).

[21] Raymond Vernon, 'International Investment and International Trade in the Product Cycle', *Quarterly Journal of Economics* (May 1966).

[22] P. Sargent Florence, *The Logic of British and American Industry* (London: Routledge & Kegan Paul, 1953) p. 64.

[23] For the 'speeding-up' (or shorter time period) for major innovations cf. Andrew Shonfield, *Modern Capitalism*, ch. 3 and M. M. Postan, *An Economic History of Western Europe 1945–64*, ch. 6.

[24] *National Institute of Economic and Social Research* (February 1973).

[25] Cf. further, Monopolies Commission, *A Survey of Mergers* (1970); U.S. Department of Commerce, *Statistical Abstract of the United States* (1973) tables 779 and 780; Jörg Huffschmid, *Die Politik des Kapitals, Konzentration und Wirtschaftspolitik in der Bundesrepublik* (Suhrkamp, 1973) ch. 2; Michel de Vroey, *Propriété et Pouvoir dans les Grandes Entreprises*, Centre de Recherche et d'Information Socio-Politiques (Brussels, 1973) and André-Paul Weber, 'L'Economie industrielle de

313

1950 a 1970: Concentration des entreprises et politique économique', *Revue d'Economie Politique* (September–October 1970).

[26] Cf. William J. Baumol, 'On the Theory of Expansion of the Firm', *American Economic Review* (December 1962) pp. 1078–87.

[27] The terminology is Streeten's; cf. *Economic Integration.*

[28] Cf. Penrose, *The Theory of the Growth of the Firm*, p. 150. An additional reason for such a regional 'price umbrella' could be that toleration of high prices in higher cost and lower profit margin firms in the L.D.R. keeps profits high for lower-cost M.D.R. firms.

[29] In contrast with the management indivisibility constraint hypothesis Averitt bluntly claims that 'the greatest strength of centre firms comes from their independence of one man'. Cf. Robert T. Averitt, *The Dual Economy: the Dynamics of American Industry Structure* (New York: Norton, 1968) p. 108.

[30] Ibid. especially chs 1, 5 and 6.

[31] Galbraith has volunteered that he considered using an identical title to Averitt's for his better known and earlier published *The New Industrial State* (London: André Deutsch, 1967).

[32] In an exceptional but perhaps unnecessarily charitable lapse from his criticism of the perfect competition model Galbraith described the American farmer in the early 1950s as 'the producer who most closely approaches the competitor of the model'. Cf. *American Capitalism* (Harmondsworth: Penguin, 1956) p. 104.

[33] S. H. Franklin, *The European Peasantry* (London: Methuen, 1969) p. 129.

[34] Cf. Renzo Stefanelli, *Agricoltura e Sviluppo Economico* (1968) pp. 58–68.

[35] Cf. Frederick W. Bell and Neil B. Murphy, *Economies of Scale in Commercial Banking* (Federal Reserve Bank of Boston, 1967).

[36] Lamfalussy, *Investment and Growth in Mature Economies.*

[37] Ibid. pp. 87ff.

[38] Ibid. especially pp. 78–9.

[39] This section on multi-national versus multi-regional companies is based on my memorandum, *Multi-national Companies and a Selective Regional Policy*, Expenditure Committee (Trade and Industry Sub-Committee) Session 1972–3, *Regional Development Incentives* (H.M.S.O. 1973) vol. II, minutes of evidence. Unless specified, all cited evidence is from this source.

[40] See Robin Murray, 'Underdevelopment, International Firms and the International Division of Labour', in *Towards a New World Economy*, Society for International Development, Introduction by Jan Tinbergen (Rotterdam University Press, 1972).

[41] See Wayland Kennet, Larry Whitty and Stuart Holland, *Sovereignty and Multinational Companies*, Fabian Tract 409, The Fabian Society (1971).

Chapter 6

[1] Cf. Hoover and Fisher, and North. Chapter 2 of this work cites their studies.
[2] Simon Kuznets, *Modern Economic Growth: Rate, Structure and Spread* (Yale University Press, 1966).
[3] Ibid. pp. 96–7 and table 3.1, pp. 88–91.
[4] Ibid. pp. 105ff. Cf. also Seymour Broadbridge, *Industrial Dualism in Japan: A Problem of Economic Growth and Structural Change* (London: Frank Cass, 1966).
[5] Nicholas Kaldor, *Causes of the Slow Rate of Economic Growth of the United Kingdom* (Cambridge University Press, 1966).
[6] R. Nurkse, *The Conflict between 'Balanced Growth' and International Specialisation*, Lectures on Economic Development, Istanbul (1958).
[7] Streeten, *Economic Integration*, pp. 114ff. With regard to anabolism, Streeten adds that perhaps 'metabolism' including the destructive process (katabolism) is a better metaphor, since the shift in demand towards new items may be at the expense of industries from which the demand is diverted. However, he points out that 'since income grows, this need not be so, and even where there is an absolute decline in demand for a particular good or service there will be a net stimulus to investment, because disinvestment is limited to not replacing whereas net investment can be larger.'
[8] Ibid. pp. 147–9.
[9] Hirschman, *The Strategy of Economic Development*, pp. 66–70; H. G. Barnett, *Innovation: the Basis of Cultural Change* (New York: McGraw-Hill, 1953) p. 148 (cited in Hirschman): 'The fulfilment of one need establishes conditions out of which others emerge.... In most cases it is impossible for people to foresee [these emergent wants] even if they try ... entrained wants are a consistent feature of motivational stresses for cultural change.'
[10] Perroux, *La Firme motrice*, reprinted in *L'Economie du XXe Siécle* (Presses Universitaires de France, 1964) p. 257. Also, *Les Techniques quantitatives de la planification* (Presses Universitaires de France, 1965) p. 49.
[11] Perroux, *Les Techniques*, pp. 118–19 and 35ff. As Posner and Woolf have pointed out in their introduction to *Italian Public Enterprise* (London: Duckworth, 1967); Perroux's analysis is disappointing in terms of the quantitative techniques which it considers to measure such effects. However, in *qualitative* terms his approach is both useful and instructive.
[12] H. B. Chenery and T. Watanabe, 'International Comparisons of the Structure of Production', paper presented at the Cleveland Meeting of the Econometric Society (December 1956).
[13] Hirschman, *Strategy of Economic Development*, pp. 99, 100.
[14] Ibid. pp. 107–9.
[15] Kuznets, *Modern Economic Growth*; Bain, 'International Industrialisation and

Per Capita Income', in *Studies in Income and Wealth*, vol. 8 (1946); Chenery, 'Patterns of Industrial Growth', *American Economic Review*, no. 4 (1960).

[16] Kuznets, *Modern Economic Growth*, unnumbered table p. 128.

[17] Ibid. p. 141, and tables 3.6 and 3.7.

[18] A. Kuklinski, *Criteria for Location of Industrial Plant: Changes and Problems*, cyclo-styled provisional draft (E.C.E., 1966).

[19] Kuznets, *Modern Economic Growth*, p. 155.

[20] Postan, *Economic History*, pp. 128–30.

[21] Nicola Cacace, 'Una Strategia Progressiva per il Mezzogiorno: le Technologie Intermedie', *Quaderni ISRII* no. 2 (1970), reprinted in *Informazioni SVIMEZ*, nos 23–4 (1970).

[22] Cf. Streeten, *Economic Integration*, pp. 114ff.

[23] Cf. Holland, in *Regional Studies*, vol. 5, no. 2.

[24] Cf. further Kevin Allen, 'Regional Intervention', in *The State as Entrepreneur*, ed. Stuart Holland (London: Weidenfeld & Nicolson, 1972).

[25] Paul Rosenstein-Rodan, 'Reflections on Regional Development', in *Scritti in Memoria di Alessandro Molinari*, pp. 527–30.

[26] Walter Isard and Eugene Smolensky, 'Application of Input–Output Techniques to Regional Science', in *Structural Interdependence and Economic Development*, ed. Tibor Barna (New York: St Martin's Press, 1963) p. 109.

[27] Edith Thorne, 'Regional Input–Output Analysis', in *Regional and Urban Studies: A Social Science Approach*, ed. S. C. Orr and J. B. Cullingworth (London: Allen & Unwin, 1969) pp. 114–15.

[28] Vera Cao-Pinna, 'Problems of Establishing and Using Regional Input–Output Accounting', in *Regional Economic Planning* (O.E.C.D., 1961) pp. 311–12.

[29] Isard and Smolensky, in *Structural Interdependence and Economic Development*, p. 107 (my emphasis).

[30] L. H. Klaassen, *Methods of Selecting Industries for Depressed Areas* (O.E.C.D., 1967).

[31] L. H. Klaassen, *Area Economic and Social Redevelopment* (O.E.C.D., 1965) p. 36.

[32] Ibid. p. 38.

[33] Ibid. pp. 38–9 and 50. In other words, the Klaassen method is even less sophisticated than that recommended in the previous section.

[34] H. B. Chenery, P. G. Clark and V. Cao-Pinna, *The Structure and Growth of the Italian Economy* (New York: Greenwood, 1953).

[35] H. B. Chenery and P. G. Clark, *Inter-Industry Economics* (London: Wiley, 1965) pp. 251–2.

[36] Ibid. pp. 252–5.

[37] Ibid. pp. 257–67.

[38] H. B. Chenery, *Politiche di Sviluppo per l'Italia Meridionale* (1962) pp. 44–6.

[39] Ibid. pp. 22, 26–7 and 46–7.

[40] Cf. *Informazioni SVIMEZ*, no. 8 (1971) p. 307.

[41] Cf. *Informazioni SVIMEZ*, no. 2, Nota statistica (1970).

[42] Cf. *Informazioni SVIMEZ*, no. 6, Nota statistica (1971).

[43] H. B. Chenery, 'Development Policies for Southern Italy', *Quarterly Journal of Economics* (1962).

[44] Chenery and Clark, *Inter-Industry Economics*, p. 296.

[45] Chenery, *Politiche di Sviluppo per l'Italia Meridionale*, p. 20.

REFERENCES

Chapter 7

[1] Cf. Myrdal, *Economic Theory and Underdeveloped Regions.*

[2] Cf. Perroux, *Economique Appliqée,* nos 1–2 (1955).

[3] Cf. Francois Perroux, *Les Techniques quantitatives de la planification* (1965) p. 49.

[4] Tibor Scitovsky, 'Two Concepts of External Economies', *Journal of Political Economy* (April 1954).

[5] J. E. Meade, 'External Economies and Diseconomies in a Competitive Situation', *Economic Journal,* vol. LXII (1952).

[6] Jacob Viner, 'Cost Curves and Supply Curves', *Zeitschrift für Nazionalökonomie,* III (1931).

[7] Scitovsky, *Journal of Political Economy* (April 1954).

[8] Alfred Marshall, *Principles of Economics,* 8th edn (London: Macmillan, 1962) p. 221.

[9] Ibid.

[10] Ibid. pp. 225–7. In his introduction Marshall acknowledges a debt to von Thünen, but cannily avoids constructing a general theory of location on perfect competition assumptions such as von Thünen undertook at the cost of losing reality.

[11] Cf. Eugene Schooler, 'Industrial Complex Analysis', in *Methods of Regional Analysis,* ed. Walter Isard (1960) pp. 375–412.

[12] Cf. Jozsef Csillaghy, *Intégration économique internationale et differentiation régionale* (1966) p. 98.

[13] E. M. Hoover, *The Location of Economic Activity* (New York: McGraw-Hill, 1948) p. 113.

[14] Marshall, *Principles of Economics,* p. 226.

[15] Ibid. p. 225.

[16] M. Parodi. Submission to the E.C.E. Study undertaken by Kuklinski, *Location of Industrial Plant,* p. 5.

[17] Hoover, *Location of Economic Activity,* p. 36.

[18] Ibid. p. 30.

[19] Marshall, *Principles of Economics,* p. 225.

[20] Raymond Vernon, 'International Investment and International Trade in the Product Cycle', *Quarterly Journal of Economics* (May 1966) pp. 190, 195.

[21] Cf. Edgar Hoover and Raymond Vernon, *Anatomy of a Metropolis* (New York: Doubleday-Anchor, 1962) pp. 58–63.

[22] Melvin L. Greenhut, *Plant Location in Theory and Practice* (University of North Carolina Press, 1956) p. 164.

[23] Philippe Aydalot, 'Note sur les Economies Externes et quelques notions connexes', *Revue Economique* (November 1965) p. 960.

[24] Siro Lombardini, *Informazioni SVIMEZ,* no.1 (1968) p. 24.

[25] Hirschman, *Strategy of Economic Development,* p. 84.

[26] Lombardini, *Informazioni SVIMEZ,* no. 1, p. 24.

[27] McCrone, *Regional Policy in Britain,* p. 214. Cf. Also the conclusion of R. Grieve and D. J. Robertson that 'a population of more than 100,000 is likely to offer the best chance of success', in 'The City and the Region', *University of Glasgow Social and Economic Studies, Occasional Paper,* no.2 (1964).

[28] G. C. Cameron and B. D. Clark, in an enquiry concerning seventy-nine companies which had located in U.K. development areas between 1958 and 1963, found that 'some areas are rejected on social criteria and particularly because of the poor physical and social environment which they are said to possess.... In particular, companies transferring their plants were often greatly influenced by the views of key staff who were not keen to settle away from the Southern countries.' Cf. Cameron and Clark, 'Industrial Movement and the Regional Problem', *University of Glasgow Social and Economic Studies, Occasional Paper*, no. 5 (1966) pp. 156–7.

[29] With regard to the Scottish designated growth areas in the 1958–63 period G. C. Cameron and G. L. Reid commented that 'they are small in size, competition for labour will probably be severe, and if similar companies competed for scarce skills, their labour turnover might be high'. Cameron and Reid, 'Scottish Economic Planning and the Attraction of Industry', *University of Glasgow Social and Economic Studies, Occasional Paper*, no. 6 (1966) pp. 65–6.

[30] Cf. Ackley and Spaventa, in *Banco Nazionale del Lavoro Quarterly Review* (June 1962).

[31] Cf. Società Autostrade, *Primi Effetti Economici dell'Autostrada del Sole* (I.R.I., 1965).

[32] François Coront-Ducluzeau, *La Formation de l'éspace économique National* (1964) p. 57.

[33] Hoover, *Location of Economic Activity*, p. 174.

[34] Parodi [in Kuklinski, *Location of Industrial Plant*] does not envisage the possibility of training of technical personnel in order to countervail polarisation of activity on Paris.

[35] W. F. Luttrell, *Factory Location and Industrial Movement* (Cambridge University Press, 1962) vol. I, p. 42.

[36] Florence, *Logic of British and American Industry*, pp. 72–3. There is now considerable uniformity of opinion on the relative insignificance of transport costs in location. Cf. Philippe Leurquin, *Marché Commun et Localisations* (1962) p. 266; Sylvain Wickham, *L'Espace industriel européen* (1969) p. 114; and *The Report on the Scottish Economy*, Toothill Report, Scottish Council Development and Industry (1962) p. 85.

[37] Pottier, *Revue Economique* (January 1963).

[38] Kuklinski, *Location of Industrial Plant*, p. 47. Kuklinski's evidence indicates that from 60–80 per cent of industrial investment in the economies he considered is allocated to the expansion of existing plant rather than to the establishment of new ones.

[39] This, of course, is the conclusion reached by Hotelling in his model of location under duopoly. Cf. Harold Hotelling, 'Stability in Competition', *Economic Journal* (1929) pp. 52ff.

[40] Vernon and Hoover allow this point with regard to the distribution of bakery products in the New York region. As they put it, 'with a location outside the nub [centre], plants avoid the need to start each delivery trip from the place of worst congestion'. Cf. Edgar Hoover and Raymond Vernon, *Anatomy of a Metropolis*, p. 38.

[41] Benjamin Chinitz and Raymond Vernon, 'Changing Forces in Industrial Location', *Harvard Business Review* (January–February 1960) pp. 130–2.

318

[42] Cf. also Luttrell, *Factory Location and Industrial Movement*, vol. I, p. 335. With regard to management efficiency in dispersed locations where plant of the same company were separated, Luttrell concluded that 'too great a distance from the point of control (or from another factory with an interlocking programme) was a disadvantage, but that *this chiefly affected the smaller subsidiary branches*'. Overall, he concluded that 'the difficulties caused directly by the locations that had been chosen were generally marginal, and they were *normally outweighed by differences of operating efficiency*'. (My emphasis.)

[43] Aydalot, *Revue Economique* (November 1965).

[44] Hoover and Vernon, *Anatomy of a Metropolis*, pp. 50–1.

[45] Hirschman, *Strategy of Economic Development*, p. 83.

[46] Hansen, *French Regional Planning*, pp. 9–10.

[47] Jeanneney has drawn attention to the extent of unpaid-for costs in the location of a new firm – housing for workers, extension of schools, hospitals and transport – in 'A la recherche des principes pour une politique de développement des économies régionales', *Revue Economique*, no. 6 (1956) p. 867.

[48] Luttrell, *Factory Location and Industrial Movement*. Cameron and Clark found that this factor was the 'originating pressure' for a new location for fifty-five of sixty-eight companies replying to this part of their questionnaire, *University of Glasgow Social and Economic Studies, Occasional Paper*, no.5 (1966) pp. 71–3. Cf. also P. M. Townroe, 'Locational Choice and the Individual Firm', *Regional Studies* (April 1969) p. 19.

[49] Cf. Streeten, *Economic Integration*.

[50] T. P. Bergin and W. F. Eagan, in *Government Measures for the Promotion of Regional Economic Development* (1964) pp. 22ff. ☐ ✳

[51] Luttrell, *Factory Location and Industrial Movement*.

[52] Ibid. vol. 7, pp. 40–8, 340–1. Cf. Table 11, p. 286. Of eighty-five firms studied by Luttrell 41 per cent located in Development Areas, 26 per cent in 'intermediate regions' and 33 per cent in 'prosperous regions'. Seventy-three of the original locations had been in prosperous regions and nineteen in intermediate. Cf. ibid. vol. I, p. 363.

[53] Ibid. vol. I, pp. 340–1.

[54] Ibid. vol. I, pp. 176, 322. Cameron and Clark, *University of Glasgow, Occasional Paper*, no. 5 (1966), p. 201, also found that 'some of the largest companies, particularly in the engineering and electrical goods sector, established units up to 400 miles from parent plants'.

[55] Luttrell, ibid. vol. I, p. 343.

[56] Ibid. vol. I, pp. 114–15, 169, 298–9.

[57] Ibid. vol. I, p. 40.

[58] Ibid. vol. I, pp. 341–2.

[59] Società Autostrade, *Primi Effetti Economici dell'Autostrada del Sole* (1965).

[60] Ibid. p. 56.

[61] Ibid. pp. 74–6. Cf. Table 12, p. 287.

[62] Ibid. p. 68.

[63] Ibid. p. 80: 'It would seem possible to conclude that the type of growth promoted by the Autostrada del Sole represents a new solution: a solution which contains the advantages of a wide spatial distribution and a rapid rate of growth.'

[64] Italconsult, *Studio per la Creazione di un Polo Industriale di Sviluppo in Italia Meridionale*, Rome (1965).

[65] Ibid. pp. 19–22.

[66] Ibid. pp. 12–15 (my emphasis).

[67] Hunter, 'Planning and the Labour Market', in *Regional and Urban Studies*, ed. Orr and Cullingworth p. 76.

[68] Walter Isard and Eugene Schooler, 'Industrial Complex Analysis', in *Methods of Regional Analysis*, ed. Isard, pp. 375–6.

[69] Ibid. pp. 375–8.

[70] Ibid. p. 378.

[71] Ibid. pp. 378–404.

Chapter 8

[1] J. C. Ingram, 'State and Regional Payments Mechanisms', *Quarterly Journal of Economics* (1959) pp. 619–32.

[2] Paolo Sylos-Labini, 'Reflections on the Process of Growth of Southern Italy', in *Essays on Planning and Economic Development* (Centre of Research on Underdeveloped Countries, Warsaw 1965) pp. 9–37.

[3] Kain and Persky, in *Rural Poverty in the United States*, p. 303.

[4] Ibid.

[5] Cf. Pierre Gabert, 'La localizzazione della Popolazione Industriale nella Città di Torino e i Problemi dei Transporti Urban', section 4 (La Tendenza dei lavoratori a raggruparsi nel dintorni delle aziende), in *Le Grande Città Italiane*, ed. Roberto Mainairdi, pp. 104ff.

[6] Cf. Francesco Forte, *La Congiuntura in Italia 1961–1965* (Einaudi, 1966).

[7] Cf. *Informazioni SVIMEZ*, Nota statistica, 'Le Migrazione Interne: Causa la Congiuntura Sfavorevole si Attenua il Processo di Meridionalizzazione nel Nord', no. 6–8 (1967).

[8] SVIMEZ–FORMEZ, *L'Azienda e il Processo Economico-Sociale*, cyclo-styled (1963) pp. 15–27.

[9] Francesco Compagna, 'L'Emigrazione Interna Italiana e il Mercato Europeo del Lavoro', in SVIMEZ–FORMEZ, *Le Migrazione Interne* (1964) p. 33.

[10] See *inter alia* S. A. Marglin, 'Objectives of Water Resource Development', in *Design of Water Resource System*, ed. A. Maas *et al.* (1962).

[11] B. Moore and J. Rhodes 'Evaluating the Effects of British Regional Economic Policy', *Economic Journal* (March 1973); and 'Economic and Exchequer Implications of Regional Policy', *Memorandum to the Trade and Industry Sub-Committee of the Commons Expenditure Committee* (H.M.S.O., May 1973).

[12] See further, Stuart Holland (ed.), *The State as Enterpreneur* (London: Weidenfeld & Nicolson, 1972) and *The Socialist Challenge* (London: Quartet Books, 1975). For Labour policy see *Labour's Programme 1973*, The Labour Party (London, 1973) and Department of Industry, *The Regeneration of British Industry*, Cmnd. 5710 (H.M.S.O., August 1974).

[13] See further, Stuart Holland, *European Para-Governmental Agencies*, in Expenditure Committee (Trade and Industry Sub-Committee) Session 1971–2, *Public Money in the Private Sector*.

REFERENCES

[14] Bain, *International Differences in Industrial Structure*, p. 97.

[15] Kuklinski, *Location of Industrial Plant*, p. 47.

[16] Cameron and Clark found that more than 25 per cent of the companies which they investigated undertook some form of locational-cost analysis, but added that 'it is not possible for us to state explicitly that these comparative cost surveys were fully comprehensive or analytically correct.... We have not discovered any companies which evaluated all cost and non-cost factors in a way which gave particular weights to each item.' Cameron and Clark, *University of Glasgow, Occasional Paper*, no. 5 (1966) p. 118. It could be added that these were companies which were obliged to relocate through government refusal to grant I.D.C.s for expansion outside Development Areas.

[17] Hirschman, *Strategy of Economic Development*, pp. 184–5.

[18] Alain Bienaymé, *Politique de l'innovation et distribution des revenus* (1966) p. 159.

[19] Kuklinski, *Location of Industrial Plant*, p. 44.

[20] Vernon, *Quarterly Journal of Economics* (May 1966).

[21] Cameron and Clark, *University of Glasgow, Occasional Paper*, no. 5 (1966) p. 31.

[22] Ibid. pp. 30–1.

[23] Sarah Orr, 'Regional Economic Planning and the Location of Industry', in *Regional and Urban Studies – A Social Science Approach*, ed. Orr and Cullingworth (1969).

[24] A. E. Holmans, 'Restriction of Industrial Expansion in South-East England: A Reappraisal', *Oxford Economic Papers* (July 1964).

[25] Cameron and Clark, *University of Glasgow, Occasional Paper*, no. 5 (1966) p. 68. *Town and Country Planning* (March 1964) p. 140.

[26] A. E. Holmans, *Urban Studies* (November 1964) pp. 143–4; E. Hammond, *Town and Country Planning* (March 1964) p. 140.

[27] Cameron and Clark, *University of Glasgow, Occasional Paper*, no. 5 (1966) p. 68.

[28] Cf. Franco Simoncini's observation that 'in theory these problems require a long preliminary work of research and elaboration. In practice the problems of disequilibrium, of polarisation, of concentrated growth do not wait.' In 'Economia Regionale e Programmazione', *Scritti in Memoria di Alessandro Molinari* (SVIMEZ, 1963) p. 624.

[29] Cf. Paul Streeten, 'Unbalanced Growth – Programmes and Prognoses and the Ideal Plant', *Banco Nazionale del Lavoro Quarterly Review* (June 1964).

INDEX

Capital Mkts field

Ⓐ Weber, Alfred. _Theory of Location of Industries_
Univ. Chicago, 1928.
① historical prospective to capital mkts reading list
② interface w/ read. Chicago School readings

Ⓑ Isard, Walter _Location and the Space Economy_.
M.I.T. Press, 1956

Ⓒ Myrdal, Gunner _Economic Theory + Underdeveloped Regions_. London, Duckworth, 1957
An American Dilemma N.Y, Harper + Row '44

Ⓓ Baran, Paul + _____ Sweezy. _Monopoly Capital_

Ⓔ Shonfield, Andrew _Modern Capitalism_ Oxford Univ, 1965
** Q.13 "The Traction of Public Enterprise"

*Ⓕ Holland, Stuart _The Regional Problem_ London: MacMillan, 1976 Q.6 ⇐ critique of Borts + Stein

*Ⓖ Borts, G.H. and J.L. Stein "Regional Growth + Maturity in the U.S.: A Study of Regional Structural Change" in _Needleman, L., ed._ _Regional Analysis_ Harmondsworth, Penguin, 1968.

Ⓗ _____. _Economic Growth_ . . . . .

** Ⓘ Callander, G.S. "The Early Transportation + Banking Enterprises of the States in Relation to the Growth of Corporations" _Quarterly Journal of Economics_ vol. 17 (1902) 111 ff.

* Ⓙ Bruchey, Stuart _The Roots of American Economic Growth_ Hutchinson Univ. Lib, 1965 Q's 5 + 6. uz. public investment

*Ⓚ Averitt, Robt T. _The Dual Economy: The Dynamics of American Industry Structure_. N.Y Norton 1968
└ use in gen. Lit. section

LOCATION THEORY - comp. w/ WHEATON'S READING LIST

Ⓛ Hoover, E.M. The Location of Economic Activity
N.Y. McGraw Hill, 1948

Ⓜ Marshall, Alfred Principles of Economics

Ⓝ Bergin, T.P. and W.F. Eagon. Gov't Measures for the
Promotion of Regional Economic Development, 1964
Louney results 180 firms (p.217)

Ⓞ Kulclinski, _____. Location of Industrial
Plant. ___